D1106094

JUSTUS JONAS
LOYAL REFORMER

JUSTUS JONAS
LOYAL REFORMER

by

Martin Lehmann

AUGSBURG PUBLISHING HOUSE
Minneapolis, Minnesota

JUSTUS JONAS, LOYAL REFORMER

MANUFACTURED IN THE UNITED STATES OF AMERICA

Preface

The age of the Reformation possesses cardinal importance and a unique fascination for the student of church history. And it is natural that a study of this age revolves chiefly around its best-known leaders, Luther, Zwingli, and Calvin. However, there is a distinct advantage in getting better acquainted with persons who collaborated with the great Reformers in their work. For thus one gains a deeper insight into and a better understanding of the nature and influence of the reform movement. One comes to realize that men of subordinate rank were truly important in extending the influence and effectiveness of the Reformation in various parts of Europe.

Justus Jonas, a close friend of Martin Luther and a staunch defender of Reformation principles, deserves to be better known. He helped mightily in the establishment and consolidation of the Lutheran Church in Germany. He, more than anyone else, was responsible for winning the city of Halle for the evangelical cause. If Halle had not been secured for the Reformation, the fate and future of the Lutheran Church here in North America might have been quite different. Approximately two centuries after that German city had embraced the evangelical faith, it sent Henry Melchior Muhlenberg to the United States. As a loyal son of his church Muhlenberg became the patriarch of American Lutheranism.

This biographical study of Justus Jonas is based on a doctoral dissertation which was completed at Princeton Seminary. The material has been thoroughly revised and rewritten in order to make it an interesting biography. It is also hoped that this volume on Jonas will meet a definite need by presenting some significant and supplementary aspects of the German Reformation.

The writer wishes to acknowledge most gratefully the suggestions, help, and counsel given him by the editorial staff of Augsburg Publishing House. Dr. Norman V. Hope and Dr. Lefferts A. Loetscher of the church history department at Princeton Seminary, and Dr. Kenneth S. Gapp, librarian of Princeton Seminary, helped and encouraged the author in the initial work on Justus Jonas. The author is responsible for the translations from the German and Latin into English when these are quoted from German and Latin sources. Acknowledgments made here would be incomplete without mentioning with a deep sense of gratitude and appreciation the valuable and patient assistance of my wife in this intriguing and rewarding undertaking.

MARTIN LEHMANN

v

Contents

vii

Introduction

In the spring of 1519 a twenty-six-year-old Humanist scholar, a doctor of both civil and canon law, was preparing to leave, for a short while, the University of Erfurt at which he was then lecturing. His tall frame and pleasant countenance invested him with a striking appearance. Accompanied by a like-minded friend named Caspar Schalbe, this young man was about to undertake an adventurous journey to the Netherlands to meet the celebrated Humanist and man of letters, Erasmus of Rotterdam. Although he had been recently appointed canon in one of Erfurt's churches, the practice of canon law was losing its appeal for him. As a respected member of the Humanist circle in the city he was beginning to display more and more interest in the study of theology. He was Justus Jonas of Nordhausen.

The contemplated journey of Justus Jonas and his companion was an official mission carried out at the behest of the Elector of Saxony, Frederick the Wise. Jonas was acting as the confidant of the Elector, who had entrusted him with letters of his own and also of Luther. These letters were to be delivered into the hands of Erasmus. Jonas was also expected to relay detailed information on the forthcoming debate between Luther and Eck at Leipzig. In this way, it was hoped, mutual understanding and close collaboration could be effected between two important men in Europe, Martin Luther, the zealous monk and professor at Wittenberg University, and Desiderius Erasmus, the influential Humanist.

1

Jonas met Erasmus in Antwerp. The great Humanist readily responded to the overtures contained in the letters which Jonas brought with him. Erasmus gave his immediate answer in the form of a writing intended for publication to the Electoral escort who departed at once. Jonas and his friend, however, were permitted to enjoy a stay of several weeks with Erasmus. On his return Jonas stopped at Frankfurt on the Main to report to the Elector of Saxony. For Frederick the Wise was staying in the Franciscan Cloister of that city during the session of the diet gathered there for the purpose of electing an emperor. Simultaneously, Jonas delivered a letter for Luther from Erasmus which outlined the future plans of action in their common struggle to revive evangelical Christianity within the church.[1]

In a letter of June 24, addressed to his Nordhausen friend, Melchior von Aachen, Jonas gave vent to his enthusiastic admiration of and loyal adherence to Erasmus and also alluded briefly to the secret character of his journey. "Why do you marvel? Why, with amazement in your eyes, do you make a long cross with your hand?" asked Jonas, as he added with evident satisfaction: "I have been with my father in Christ, Erasmus of Rotterdam. How often you may desire to say this of yourself: 'I have been, I have been with Erasmus.' 'Where?' you enquire. At Antwerp in Brabantia on the shore of the sea." Then Jonas went on to reveal the secret aspect of his journey: "I had with me letters in Latin by the Elector Frederick, Prince of Saxony, to which Erasmus also responded. The answer I have returned at the diet of the princes at Frankfurt."

This mission had also gained for Jonas a more cordial friendship with Spalatin, the Elector's chaplain and private secretary. In an undated letter that seems to fall into this period, Spalatin recalled a pleasant evening he spent with Jonas, sent him the most sincere greetings, and made cryptic allusions regarding Jonas' mission to Erasmus.

Meanwhile far-reaching changes had occurred at Erfurt. On May 2, 1519, during his absence, Jonas had been elected rector of the university. An entirely new mode of study was to make its appearance. His election as rector signified the complete triumph of the new learning and ushered in that two-year period which marked the very peak of the university's fame and popularity during its notable history. Some reforms had already been brought about before Jonas returned, since he remarked to his friend Melchior von Aachen in the aforementioned letter: "I find the school by far different from the one which I had left."

Aided by his colleagues, Eobanus Hessus, Draconites, Eberbach, and especially John Lange, Jonas vigorously inaugurated a thorough-going reform of the academic program. First of all, eight persons were appointed lecturers and given the task of promoting the study of the three basic languages of the Holy Scriptures, Hebrew, Greek, and Latin, and of introducing the study of the original philosophy and genuine theology. The frequent academic banquets and all the pomp connected with the formal promotion to the doctorate were discontinued in order that the funds thus saved might be used for the salaries of teachers in Greek and Latin. Only one general banquet was to be held annually. John Lange, the eminent Greek scholar, was given a responsible position in this department. The philosophical faculty was henceforth to be regarded as the most important one, and in fact was the one which was most thoroughly Humanistic in its program. All this was done according to the pattern set by the University in Wittenberg, for there a similar reform had been carried out. It required the reading of Aristotelian philosophy in the original without the aid of the scholastic commentaries; it gave an important place to the study of Greek, securing Melanchthon as professor in 1518; and it provided for suitable teaching in the Hebrew also. With unconcealed elation Jonas could therefore add in a postscript to the much-quoted letter written to Melchior von Aachen: "Our university has, during a hundred years or as long as it has existed, never been thus reformed." It was a tribute to Jonas' moral earnestness and keen interest in sound learning that during his term of office as rector these reforms were initiated, even though their success did not prove durable.

At that time young students from all parts of Germany were flocking to Erfurt and eagerly attending the lectures of the Humanist professors. Eobanus Hessus, the most popular teacher of the school, exerted a unique influence on the students and often had as many as fifteen hundred students in his lecture room, while others had to remain outside for lack of adequate space. The lectures of the other Humanists, including those of Jonas, were also well attended and gave proof of the immense popularity which the new learning enjoyed in the university.

Jonas had made a most favorable impression on the man whom he regarded as his "father in Christ." In his frequent and lengthy letters to Jonas, Erasmus showed a continued interest in the young Humanist and repeatedly directed his attention to the importance of the study of theology through direct recourse to the original sources. It was shortly after his return to Erfurt that Jonas received a letter from Erasmus in which Jonas was solemnly admonished to turn to the study of true theology and to discard the sterile Scholasticism of the day. In flowing sentences of flawless Latin Erasmus called upon Jonas to utilize his gifts so "that we reciprocally support one another in our various callings." At the same time he warned that no one ought to trust in himself more than is proper, since all gifts that man has are from God, who has desired "to bestow a large part of His benefits upon man through man." God has, continued Erasmus, given whatever ability a person might have "for a common usefulness." After such general exhortations Erasmus asserted—quite prophetically in the light of Jonas' later life—that Jonas ought to realize that God had some distinct mission for him, "that somehow God has destined you not to be concerned with unworthy causes, but indeed seems to have fashioned you as an elect organ in order to show forth the glory of His Son Jesus to the end that according to His desire the souls of mortals might be kindled; to this most wholesome office of all you may apply yourself fully and do this eagerly while the body is capable of enduring labor, while the mind is vigorous." He assured Jonas that God would prosper such endeavors and paid tribute to the intellectual ability, the moral purity and oratorical talent with which he could carry out this purpose. By avoiding all the inane subtleties of the Scholastics, Erasmus believed that Jonas could effectually instill Christ's philosophy into the minds of men by precepts and example. To avoid clamor and sedition, Jonas was to deal in civility and gentleness with persons of rank in state and church alike. "The human temperament is such that it is led more easily by civility than it is dragged along by austerity." Finally, concluded the great Humanist, the Scriptures were to be the source of his preaching, and true love of his office and living piety the necessary basis for "inflaming the souls of others."

The prevailing influence of Erasmus at Erfurt found expression in the subject matter treated in the lectures by the Humanist circle. Eobanus Hessus began a series of lectures on Erasmus' *Handbook of a Christian Soldier,* and in the preface, which was designed as an oration in honor of Jonas' new position as rector of the university, he held the ideals of Humanist learning and genuine morality before the students. This ideal was best set forth, according to Eobanus' opinion, by Erasmus of Rotterdam, upon whose *Handbook of a Christian Soldier* he was about to lecture and who as a Christian soldier "is not conquerable by any resources of his enemies." Referring to the new rector of the university, Hessus warmly praised his friend as "one of the most learned of good men, Jodocus Jonas of Nordhausen, a lawyer and above all a defender of Christian philosophy." As rector, said the poet-king, Jonas had done away with the old scholastic method and idle play with words in order to introduce true learning and Christian morals. Throughout this Latin speech Eobanus sprinkled Greek quotations, made special reference to the *disciplina Christi* which the New Testament enjoined, and concluded with an earnest admonition to the students to do battle valiantly as soldiers of Christ so that they might "as free men overcome the hostile army with Christ as leader and acknowledge Him alone as author of your liberty, Him Who alone has restored the lost liberty to the world, Jesus Christ our Lord and God."

While this preface proved indicative of the strong theological tone that pervaded the academic life, Jonas himself was weaned away more and more from his original profession and more irresistibly attracted by Christian learning, especially as it was made available in the original Greek sources, the New Testament Scriptures. Accordingly, he addressed himself to the challenging task of expounding the Apostle Paul's Epistles to the Corinthians in a series of lectures. The preface[2] to these Epistles, which preceded the lectures that were probably given in 1519 or 1520, has all the earmarks of Erasmian style and thought. Jonas began the preface by referring to the ancient rule of eloquence which affirms that only he who is himself fully permeated by the truth can persuade others of it. Jonas wished that he could say with Paul: "Our mouth is open to you, Corinthians; our heart is wide" (2 Cor. 6:11). However, he believed that his heart was as yet too impure. Nor did he desire to say anything about the method by which one may gain a true understanding of the Scriptures, since Erasmus had written so admirably and clearly on this matter. "You have Erasmus' method; now hold to the road by which entry was gained even into that broadest ocean of the Scriptures which is for sea-faring men who keep the course." The successful study of the Scriptures, he asserted, required a heart that had divested itself of all impurities and was burning to know the truth.

Then Jonas proceeded to paint a picture of the generally decrepit condition of the times. "The Christian commonwealth," he said with regret, "has fallen, the studies of all good things have lain neglected. As a result of these facts we have the tumults of wars by which the earth is agitated on all sides, as a result treaties are broken, as a result there is that internal and mutual hate which secretly gnaws at the vitals of the commonwealth." In every area of life degeneration and decay had taken place. A wrong education of youth had brought about the decline of the church and the word of Christ had been neglected. Jonas therefore called upon pastors and priests to be concerned again with the study of the Scriptures. Bishops, primates, and the ruling nobility seemed to have lost their concern for things spiritual and the education of the young. Instead, they had dealt with material matters, with the state of forests, with architecture, revenues, and the tracing of their ancestry. "These are the most important matters concerning which, sometimes with additional sternness, they deliberate with great gravity." But if they had relatives who had an inclination toward the study of theology, they dissuaded them from taking such a step. "And those same persons, if they see any one of their own or someone from the lowest rank of society who is one-eyed, or half-blind or lame, 'that,' they say, 'is a theologian to be made known to the Pope,' or 'the gait of the man indicates genius; here nature herself has fashioned a theologian.'" Thus the office of proclaiming the Gospel had been brought into disrepute, and monks had shown more concern for meat and drink than for spiritual food. In conclusion, Jonas ethusiastically endorsed the study of the Apostle Paul's writings and lauded his person. "Him receive with the Galatians as an angel of God, as Jesus Christ; read and retain his letters that burn like fire within a good heart. For he has read a thousand libraries who understands a single Paul."

When the half-year of Jonas' term of office came to a close, it was celebrated in a suitable fashion by staging one communal banquet on Michaelmas in the late fall of 1519. At that time the bachelor's degree was conferred upon fifty-seven students. Eobanus appropriately delivered the address for the occasion on "The Revival of Studies," in which he remarked with evident satisfaction upon the way in which Jonas had brought about this reform. Jonas had in a meaningful fashion placed at the head of his rectorial report the picture of the man who had inspired these ideals of reform and who had ever been his pattern in learning and Christian piety. It depicted Erasmus who was being approached by a group of admiring students; beside him stood the majestic figure of his patron, the Emperor Charles V; while on a preceding page there was represented the coat of arms of the rector: a whale spewing forth the naked figure of a man.

FOOTNOTES FOR INTRODUCTION

1. Paul Kalkoff, *Humanismus und Reformation in Erfurt*, pp. 32 ff.
2. The full title is: *Praefatio in Epistolas divi Pauli Apostoli ad Corynthios Erphurdiae ad christianae philosophiae studiosorum ordinem habita ab eximio viro Iodoco Iona Northusiano iurium designato d. Canonico ibidem apud divi Severi.*
Kawerau, *Der Briefwechsel des Justus Jonas*, Vol. I, pp. 40 ff.

Chapter 1

The Young Jonas

In the Prussian province of Saxony, thirty-eight miles north of Erfurt, lies the city of Nordhausen. Situated along the banks of the Zorge River on the southern edge of the Harz Mountains, it was one of Germany's famous cities during the Middle Ages. The possession of a royal palace as early as 874 greatly enhanced the city's prestige. Practically all the early kings of Germany and many Roman emperors resided there for various periods of time. Important plans of German rulers were conceived there, and this continuous association with royalty invested the city of Nordhausen with a degree of fame and conscious pride not enjoyed by many larger cities of Germany. Just when the city was founded is not definitely known, and the account that would make Emperor Theodosius or even King Merowig the city's founder is purely legendary. Although the city was destroyed by Henry the Lion in 1180, it rose phoenix-like from its ruins so quickly that it became a free, imperial city in 1253. During this century and the next it had the distinct honor of having several diets and other assemblies held in it. Until 1702 the protector of the city was the Elector of Saxony, which was an important factor in its acceptance of the Reformation in 1522. In the sixteenth century, when the Reformation swept over Europe, this imperial city, true to its exalted status, furnished the movement with men of ex-

8

traordinary ability and faith. They were men who were destined
to become forceful leaders and powerful interpreters of Reformation principles.[1] Among their number was Justus Jonas, who was to
tower over the rest in his brilliant achievements as a reformer.

The information about the parents of Justus Jonas is meager indeed. It would seem that his father's name was Jonas Koch. Moreover, we may infer that this name "Koch," according to the custom
of the day, referred directly to the occupation of Jonas' father, so
that "Koch" was not actually a family name in the proper sense of
the word. In a letter, written on July 6, 1530, to the Bishop of Strassburg, Count William of Honstein, Justus Jonas seems to confirm
the supposition that his father was a cook for the Stolberg family.[2]
In another letter in 1549, Justus Jonas reminded Count Wolfgang
of Stolberg of the fact "that my father, the old Jonas and alderman,
has always had gracious masters in your Grace's praiseworthy forbears."[3] Since it seems that the father of Justus Jonas had thus derived his name from his employment as a cook for a family of the
nobility, it need not surprise us that this appellation is later given to
Justus Jonas himself. We may surmise that Jonas Koch was a highly
respected and influential citizen of Nordhausen. The documents of
this city make frequent mention of his name in the years 1473 to
1502 as one who eight or ten times was a senator or alderman there.
Melanchthon, though he had never known him, repeatedly referred
to and praised Jonas Koch as a man of ability and influence, on
the basis of reports he had heard from fellow-citizens. Especially did
he laud his oratorical gifts. "We hear," testifies Melanchthon, "that
he attained the highest position of authority in his native city on
account of his eloquence and civil prudence, as one who, when
opportunities arose, was not unskilled but especially concerned lest
vigor be lacking in an oration."[4] On another occasion he writes, "I
have often heard that the Nordhausen senator by his counsel and
his ability to speak supported the government for a long period of
time, and that leading men often called upon him in case of very
grave deliberations."[5] While Melanchthon felt justified in designat-
ing Justus Jonas' forbears as "a family with oratorical ability," Luther,

too, referred to Jonas' eloquence as belonging to the sphere of "hereditary gifts."

Jodocus Koch or Justus Jonas, as he later called himself, the son
of this well-known Nordhausen senator, was born on June 5, 1493,[6]
in this free, imperial city which during his entire life he considered
"no mean city." Nothing is known about his mother. It may be
assumed that she died when Jonas was quite young and his father
apparently remarried. His second wife was a widow named Wolfhain
from Muehlhausen. She had two sons, Matthes and Berthold, from
a previous marriage. Matthes, who was given the paternal inheritance
by his mother, died in 1524 as mayor of Muehlhausen. Jonas and
Berthold were named heirs in the will which led to an irksome
dispute between Jonas and his relatives with regard to the inheritance.
In addition to this, his step-brother Berthold caused him considerable
difficulty and vexation. We are also told about an older sister who
was married and resided in Nordhausen. Her two sons, Frank and
Lawrence Rebus, were matriculated as students in the University at
Erfurt in the years 1518 and 1519.

Under the supervision of his father Justus received the best training available in one of the schools of Nordhausen, and Jonas, possessed of unusual mental capabilities, made such astonishing progress
that at the age of thirteen he was in the position to enter the University at Erfurt. It seems likely that Jonas' father died before he was
privileged to witness, with what would have been justifiable paternal
pride, the academic achievements of his son. Just when Jonas' father
died cannot be definitely ascertained; but it would appear from an
incidental allusion made by Jonas in one of his printed sermons that
his death occurred while Justus was still in his early teens.

It need not surprise us that tradition soon surrounded the life of
the precocious boy who was to become one of the principal figures
in the work of the German Reformation, with a kind of halo. We
are told of an unusual incident that was supposed to have taken place
in his early life. Kindervater in his biographical sketch recounts it
as if it were a well-authenticated occurrence. Though it has no
foundation in fact, it shows the high esteem in which Jonas was held

by subsequent generations as one of the leading men in the work of the Reformation. The legend has it that Justus Jonas' father had fallen seriously ill of the plague in the year 1500. An onion was placed as a poultice on the boil caused by the plague in order to draw off the poisonous toxins. The father removed the onion and placed it on a bench near him. Justus, unaware of the purpose for which the onion had been used, came along and, without being noticed by his father, ate the entire onion. "Although everyone thought the poison would straightway infect him and kill him without delay, the Lord nevertheless graciously averted every disaster and the killing stuff he had eaten could work no injury upon him whom he (the Lord) had destined to become a great light of his church before he was born of his mother."[7]

The Student

Toward the close of the fifteenth century and at the beginning of the sixteenth the University of Erfurt enjoyed a reputation as a school of learning second to none in Germany. Formally opened in the year 1392 as the fifth university of the nation, it soon became known as a school which espoused the conciliar movement of the day. Especially John of Wesel, who taught there for twenty years as professor of the Holy Scriptures, lent his powerful and lasting influence to this movement for reform. At the turn of the fifteenth century the university was in the enviable position of possessing men of national reputation on its faculty. There was Henning Goede, a doctor of law, who was styled "monarch of law" by his contemporaries. In 1509 he left Erfurt because of the disturbances in the city, and was successfully pressed into the service of the University of Wittenberg by Frederick the Wise, who called him to become provost of All Saints' Chapter and lecturer on canon law at the university. Jodocus Trutvetter from Eisenach, under whose rectorate Luther matriculated in 1501, won such a degree of popularity as professor at Erfurt that he was designated "Doctor Erfordiensis." In addition, the names of Bartholomew Arnoldi from Usingen and Nicholas Marschalk served

to enhance the growing fame of the university. It was Nicholas Marschalk who, in accordance with the Humanists' ideal, introduced the
"study of three languages," and edited a Greek textbook and a simple brochure serving as an introduction to Hebrew. Lastly, Conrad
Mutianus Rufus, the noted Humanist of Gotha, exerted a very marked
influence upon the students who were flocking to the University of
Erfurt. Having received his first schooling with Erasmus of Rotterdam in Alexander Hegius' well-known school in Deventer, Mutianus
went to the University of Erfurt where he received his master's degree in philosophy and began to teach. He did so with immense
popularity, but soon gave up his professional duties in order to take
a trip to Italy, as was the custom of many Humanists of his day.
After his return to Germany in 1502, he was offered and accepted a
position at the court of the Landgrave of Hesse. However, his active
part in the affairs of state and all the pomp and honor connected
therewith soon lost their attraction for him and he turned his back
upon them in order to accept a modest prebend at Gotha in 1503.
Over the entrance of his dwelling were inscribed, in golden letters,
the words: "Beata tranquillitas" (Blessed tranquility).

Although Mutianus never attained this "blessed tranquillity" because of the completely different views and degree of learning on
the part of his fellow-canons in Gotha, he was fortunate in being
able to cement a warm friendship with Henry Urbanus and George
Burkhardt of Spalt, later called Spalatin. Both of these men lived in
the nearby Georgenthal Cloister and shared the Humanist interests of
the Gotha Canon. In their common quest for classical learning they
did not, however, fall prey to an anti-religious one-sidedness, but
preserved a genuine religious sincerity and moral integrity. This, in
turn, did not fail to attract the attention of and make an impression
upon the young Humanists at the University of Erfurt.[8]

A Humanist Education

Such, then, was the cultural setting when Justus Jonas, as a mere
lad of thirteen, came to this celebrated university in 1506 in order

to study jurisprudence. The wonder that arises when one considers his youthfulness is lessened by the fact that it was customary for boys between the ages of thirteen and sixteen to enter the university, because the universities of that day included in their curricula the upper grades of the classical schools. Simultaneously, two other youths from Nordhausen, John Ramme and Nicholas Ferer, and also the future friend of Jonas, Tilemann Pletener from Stolberg, who became the well-known reformer at Stolberg, were matriculated with him. Only two years previously, Helius Eobanus Hessus had entered the university. Thus the intimate friendship which later developed between these various men was made possible.

Jonas continued the rapid advance in his formal training. In 1507, one year after entering the university, he received his bachelor's degree and in 1510, at the age of seventeen, he obtained the master's degree. During this first period of his stay in Erfurt, Jonas became a member of that circle of Humanists of which Eobanus Hessus, the famous Humanist poet, was the recognized leader. He joined this group at the age of fifteen and took a prominent part in their various activities. Two poems by Jonas, which date from this period, show how much he had become a part of the Humanist cause. The first poem, written in 1509, sings the praises of his friend Hessus in the glowing and affectionate language of that circle. "Hessus has a name never to perish among mortals," cries the inspired young poet, and he goes on to laud Hessus as a German prophet who is making a lasting name for himself. The second poem, composed in the year 1510, is written in a much lighter vein. In spirited lines Jonas makes sport of a friend in Erfurt who had resolved once for all to renounce his love for the opposite sex. This group of Humanists was a jocund company indulging in occasional carousals; yet it is difficult to determine to what extent young Jonas took part in them. The moderating influence of Mutianus, who was their chief counsellor, was no doubt felt at all times. Jonas, however, did not enter into a correspondence or closer relationship with the Gotha Canon during this period. Nor can it be inferred that he was at this early date in any way acquainted with or influenced by Luther, for Luther had entered the Black Cloister of the Augustinian Hermits at Erfurt in the summer of 1505 and in the fall of 1508 had left for Wittenberg to fill the chair of moral philosophy at the university.[9]

The riots that fairly rocked the city of Erfurt in 1509 and 1510 were instrumental in breaking up this influential coterie of Humanists who had gathered under the aegis of Mutianus and whose leader was the poet-king Eobanus Hessus. A tension developed between the senate of the city and the citizens, and when the indebtedness of the city was made known by the senate to representatives of the citizens, a popular uprising ensued. The populace demanded the keys to the great tower and the city's seal and soon took matters into its own hands. The leader of the senatorial party was put into prison and after a trial sentenced to death. After this commotion a period of comparative calm followed. But on August 4, 1510, another incident produced a second riot. On the occasion of certain church festivities an argument took place between some mercenaries and a group of students of the university. This disagreement led to violence. When the mercenaries were being hard pressed by the students, the citizens came to the aid of the mercenaries. The students at first defended themselves bravely but were soon forced to surrender. The angry mob stormed the main building of the university, the "collegium magnum," into which the students had withdrawn, and demolished the furniture of the lecture rooms, destroyed the books in the libraries, and carried off whatever seemed useful as loot. However, only the reference library was pillaged. The library of the professors and the insignia of the school were preserved from destruction. To be sure, the riots did incalculable harm to the reputation of the university and caused a temporary, but sharp, decline in the enrollment of the school.

The first person to leave the university during these dark and foreboding days was Eobanus Hessus. On a chill day, in the late fall of the year 1509, he rode out of the gates of Erfurt in order to seek his fortune elsewhere. Others belonging to the Humanist circle followed his example. Crotus Rubianus went to Fulda; Henry Eberbach undertook a journey to Vienna; and Petrejus followed him to

the same city soon after. Jodocus Jonas, who was desirous of pur-
suing his studies in law, left for Wittenberg, attracted no doubt by
the widespread fame of Henning Goede as well as by the rising
reputation of this new school. In the summer semester of 1511 he
was duly matriculated in the University at Wittenberg as "Jodocus
Jonas de Northusen, Arcium magister, Erfordien. Magunt dioc," under
the rectorship of Andreas Bodenstein von Carlstadt. He obtained the
degree of a bachelor of both civil and canon law and came into contact with the new evangelical emphasis that was taking form there.
There is no traceable evidence that he was influenced by or came
to know Luther personally. In his later correspondence with Wen-
ceslaus Link, Jonas made mention of the notable fact that during his
stay in Wittenberg he, "being a youth of nineteen years" heard Link's
"most venerable and evangelical sermons" on festival occasions in 1511
in the plain and small Interim Church belonging to the Wittenberg
Augustinians. In addition, he made the acquaintance of George
Spalatin who, in a letter dated August 17, 1514, assured Jonas of his
warmest friendship and interest and recommended him to Provost
Kitzscher.

In the spring of 1515 Jonas was again in Erfurt. Eobanus Hessus
had returned the previous year, and before long the entire poetic
circle, guided by the ever watchful Mutianus Rufus, had reassembled
and in the years that followed, the University of Erfurt reached the
zenith of its fame as a center of the Humanist movement and all
that it stood for.

Theology and Law

Reuchlin's controversy with the theologians of Cologne marked
the turning point in the history of the conflict between Humanism
and the old Scholasticism. In opposition to Pfefferkorn, a baptized
Jew, who had secured an imperial mandate empowering him to con-
fiscate and burn all Jewish literature that was derogatory of Christ's
person, Reuchlin staunchly advocated the preservation of the Rab-
binic literature in the interest of scholarship. In 1510 the theological

faculty of Erfurt, loyal to the scholastic cause, took its stand with the Cologne theologians against Reuchlin. Mutianus felt compelled to come to the aid of Reuchlin and, therefore, by letter and personal advice, bent every effort in the direction of a victory for Humanism. After Jonas' return to Erfurt in 1515 Mutianus also sought to win Jonas' "true and holy friendship" by writing to him. Mutianus told Jonas that he was dissatisfied with the morals of the day and would have people conform more wholeheartedly to the "norm of Christ." In subsequent letters that Mutianus wrote to Jonas he admonished him not to become a jurist of the usual type and be desirous of vainglory and material gain but to make the study of true wisdom and art as well as the manifestation of genuine Christian virtues his chief concern. It would seem that thus the Canon of Gotha, with a sense of humor that was never lacking in his correspondence, continued to exercise an undeniable influence on the Humanists at Erfurt. He was finally privileged to witness the defeat of the Cologne theologians and the vindication of Reuchlin's Humanist position with the publication of the *Letters of Obscure Men* which made their appearance early in 1516. Crotus Rubianus and Ulrich von Hutten were in all likelihood the authors of this satire which dealt such a devastating blow to the opponents of Humanist learning. Jonas had no immediate connection with the authorship or publication of these letters, although he was well acquainted with Crotus Rubianus. This event was the prelude for the final triumph of the Humanist movement at the University in Erfurt.

Meanwhile, Jonas was beginning to show ever greater interest in theology. He himself designated the year 1516 as the one when he first began to preach. In 1517 he moved to Nordhausen and, as it would seem, was engaged in the work of an attorney for some time. Eobanus Hessus, writing to him, asked for the return of a coin of Hadrian and a letter by Reuchlin. Though Hessus had to decline Jonas' previous invitation to come to Nordhausen, he nevertheless assured him of his warmest friendship. "Wherever I shall be," he wrote, "I shall keep for thee that which I owe, the promise and unimpaired purity of friendship in the inmost recesses of my heart."

The intimate association between the various members of the Erfurt Humanist circle was thus upheld, although they were separated for various periods of time.

In a letter dated June 18, 1518, written when he had returned to Erfurt, Jonas told his Nordhausen friend, Melchior von Aachen, Canon at St. Crucis Church and town clerk, of the possibility of receiving a prebend at St. Severi Chapter in Erfurt. A few months later he invited von Aachen to be present on the occasion of the formal bestowal of the doctor's degree of both civil and canon law upon himself. Besides, Jonas could relate that the famed jurist, Henning Goede of Wittenberg, was pleading on his behalf in his effort to receive a prebend at St. Severi. Jonas held the public disputation for the doctor's degree on August 16. Soon after he also received the position as Canon at St. Severi, for he wrote to Melchior von Aachen, under the date of October 5, 1518, inviting him to come to Erfurt while Henning Goede was there, and signed his name, adding the title "licentiate of law" and giving his position as "Canon of Severus, the Blessed Weaver." Thus he was engaged in his profession as ecclesiastical jurist and was at the same time a lecturer at the university.

The Young Professor

The popular uprisings, which had taken place sporadically in Erfurt from 1509 to 1516 and which were commonly known under the name of "the Seven Years' Revolution," had brought about the complete collapse of senatorial rule in the city. Whereas Erfurt had until 1516 nominally been under the protection of the Elector of Mainz, the economic bankruptcy of the city had obliged it to turn to Electoral Saxony for help, and in the Naumburg Treaty of 1516 it ratified its new and close ties with the Elector of Saxony, Frederick the Wise. In a similar way, during these years, a crisis was taking place in the realm of learning and theology. Mutianus Rufus had lent his influence to the victory of the new learning; but the actual triumph was not to come until his proteges, Eobanus Hessus, Justus Jonas,

Crotus Rubianus, Draconites, and others, had assumed positions of leadership in the life of the university. Furthermore, these men were to find in Erasmus of Rotterdam their new hero and patron saint whom they fairly worshiped and whose ideals in learning, religion, and reform became their very own.

Camerarius remarked fittingly about the new Erasmus cult which had suddenly arisen at the university: "One clapped approval for him as one would for an erudite and artistic actor on the stage of learning. Everyone who did not want to be regarded as a stranger in the kingdom of the muses, admired, glorified, and praised him. One wished the age good fortune. If someone could elicit a letter from Erasmus, his renown was gigantic and a great triumph was then celebrated. But if someone had the good fortune of having a personal meeting and interview with Erasmus, then he regarded himself as blessed on earth."[10]

The manner in which a direct, personal contact between the Humanist circle in Erfurt and Erasmus was to be effected presented a strange intermingling of political, personal and ecclesiastical motives. John Lange, an outstanding Greek scholar in the Augustinian Cloister in Erfurt, associated himself around 1518 with the Humanist movement, especially with Justus Jonas and Eobanus Hessus, whom he instructed in Greek. By virtue of his acquaintance with Luther, Lange served as the intermediary who was to cement a brief but significant union between Humanism and the new evangelical theology that had arisen in Wittenberg. When Eobanus Hessus, in the fall of 1518, inaugurated the series of "pilgrimages" which the Erfurt Humanists were to make to Erasmus' dwelling-place, it was in reality the Prior of the Augustinian Cloister at Erfurt, John Lange, recently made District Vicar, who sent Hessus to Erasmus in Louvain. Frederick the Wise had made a solemn stipulation in a letter written on December 18 to the Pope that Luther's doctrine should be subjected to the judgment of independent scholars who were to be granted security by several universities. Lange, by authority of Frederick the Wise, had instructed Eobanus to report to Erasmus on the status of the controversy concerning indulgences. For Eobanus Hessus, however, the main object of such a journey was to get a glimpse of the famous Humanist scholar, and although Erasmus was at that time ill, Hessus was granted an interview with him and returned to Erfurt completely enraptured by this fascinating man. During the same year Jonas was honored with a letter from Erasmus. In this letter Erasmus rejected the excessive praises of his friends as well as the calumnies which monks and theologians were heaping upon him. "With how many violent reproaches of brethren and theologians the New Testament is being stoned," wrote Erasmus concerning his edition of the Greek New Testament. And yet, like a good Christian, he expressed his determination "to struggle manfully through glory and ignominy, through evil report and good report toward Christ's goal." Jonas was delighted by this letter and its assurance of Erasmus' friendship and interest in him. In a mood of exultant joy he wrote to his Nordhausen friend, Melchior von Aachen, and enclosed a copy of the letter written to him by the celebrated scholar.

The year 1519 was to be an exciting and important one in Jonas' life. The acquaintance with John Lange ripened into an enduring friendship of major significance, for it was Lange who eventually brought Jonas into contact with Luther. Jonas wrote to his friend, Melchior von Aachen, on February 4, 1519, telling him of an imminent celebration set aside for the bestowal of the doctor's degree on three theologians. Two of these candidates were still adherents of Aristotelian Scholasticism, but the other one was none other than the District Vicar, his instructor in Greek, John Lange. In a note appended to this letter, Jonas asked his friend to send some venison for the customary banquet that followed the solemn promotion and also remarked: "Lange is altogether mine." On February 14 this event took place and, it may be assumed, served to strengthen the ties of friendship between Jonas and Lange. At the same time Jonas gave proof of his enthusiastic discipleship of Erasmus by defending the latter against the attacks which a certain Edward Lee had made on the Erasmian edition of the New Testament. For this literary defense Mutianus warmly praised the young Erfurt Humanist in a letter written from his secluded prebend in Gotha.

FOOTNOTES FOR CHAPTER 1

1. Ernst G. Foerstemann, *Kleine Schriften zur Geschichte der Stadt Nordhausen,* pp. 14-15; John Henry Kindervater, *Nordhusa Illustris,* pp. 1 ff.

2. He says toward the close of this lengthy letter: "But I, therefore, while such an opportunity presented itself, have the more eagerly written to you, because, having the same paternal city, I have been permitted from my youth to examine your virtues more closely. It was at that time when my father, Jonas, was in genuine favour with the celebrated Stolberg family, whom I also in my boyhood heard talking frankly and highly about your admirable virtues and gifts." Kawerau, *Der Briefwechsel des Justus Jonas,* Vol. I, p. 443.

3. Kawerau, *op. cit.,* Vol. II, p. 273.

4. C. G. Bretschneider, Editor, *Corpus Reformatorum,* Vol. III, pp. 535-536. Melanchthon in the prefatory letter to his syntax dedicated to Justus Jonas Jr., pp. 530-535.

5. *Ibid.,* Vol. VIII, p. 936.

6. Kawerau thinks that Melanchthon seemed to designate June 6 as the day of Jonas' birth in a letter found in *Corpus Reformatorum,* Vol. VI, pp. 171-172. Kawerau, *op. cit.,* Vol. II, Introduction, p. viii; and p. 199.

7. John Henry Kindervater, *op. cit.,* p. 119.

8. Kampschulte, *Die Universität Erfurt,* Vol. I, pp. 78-93.

9. Heinrich Boehmer, *Road to Reformation,* trans. by John W. Doberstein and Theodore G. Tappert (Philadelphia: Fortress Press, 1946), pp. 33-46.

10. Th. Pressel, *Justus Jonas in Leben und Ausgewählte Schriften der Väter und Begründer der lutherischen Kirche,* Vol. VIII, pp. 4-9.

Chapter 2

The Commitment to Luther

It is significant that thus far this eager turning of the Humanists toward the study of theology and their moral zeal were the direct result of Erasmus' influence. Evidence of Luther's evangelical teaching, especially with reference to his controversy over the sale of indulgences, is lacking, so that though he may have been known, he exerted no influence and his guidance at that time was not sought. There was one man who, while closely associated with Jonas and Hessus, was an ardent follower of Luther. He was the well-known John Lange, Jonas' instructor in Greek. In the years 1519 to 1521 the intimate friendship between Jonas and Lange was therefore to be very consequential. Both men, the former as an Erasmian Humanist with theological inclinations, and the latter as an evangelical theologian with real Humanist interests, were to benefit each other and prove to be leaders in the new learning and the evangelical reform at Erfurt.

In a letter to Lange, under the date of April 13, 1519, Luther gave instructions to Lange to remember him to "the most learned and most dear Jonas."[1] It can therefore be surmised that Luther was somewhat acquainted with Jonas previous to this time. Soon after this cordial greeting to Jonas by Luther, John Lange, along with the Humanists Crato and Camerarius, accompanied Luther, Carlstadt, and other Wittenbergers to the Leipzig Disputation which began on

June 27 and ended on July 16. As a personal witness of this tremendous debate between Luther and John Eck, Lange took the official records of it back to Erfurt and had them printed there.[2] Moreover, Lange had communicated to his friend Jonas that John Eck had in his impudence not spared Erasmus but had severely criticized his *Annotations on the New Testament.* Characteristically, in a letter of July 19, replying to this information from Lange, Jonas expressed regret that Mutianus Rufus had withdrawn from the open. Moreover, he showed his resentment against Eck's attack on Erasmus. "Good God, what is the charming little doctor attempting," wrote Jonas with manifest disdain of Eck. "Erasmus," he continued, "has in the space of three years revived the church of Christ and even the world, and now, imagine, on account of the matters brought together by Eck and on account of his little *Summas* suddenly all things are silent, tongues will cease, the glory of the reborn cross will be made null and void, the Erasmian and evangelical knowledge will be destroyed." With a satirical thrust Jonas supposed that "the suave man" as a kind of super-theologian might conceivably go so far as to be able to establish "that all things which happen in Rome are to be imitated." We see that Jonas regarded Eck principally as Erasmus' enemy and seemed to care little about Luther's position in the struggle.

Eck himself made a personal appearance in Erfurt late in August, 1519, and had no difficulty in winning the theological faculty to his side, since Usingen and other professors belonged to the old scholastic tradition. Jonas' indignation over Eck's conduct in Erfurt was voiced in a subsequent letter.

Luther's Influence

Despite the divergent loyalties—Jonas being an Erasmian and Lange a Lutheran—their friendship was sincere and real because at this point of the struggle in church reform both Erasmian Humanists and Lutheran theologians stood upon the common ground of advocating a reformation of the church. In fact, a real union of forces was now taking place as a result of Frederick the Wise's astute negotiations between Luther and Erasmus. Jonas' lectures on the Epistles to the Corinthians, the preface to which has been considered, seem to have brought him to the realization of Luther's Pauline position. These lectures came off the press on August 28, 1520. Besides, the whole Humanist circle at Erfurt was now enthusiastically acclaiming Luther's stand, since Erasmus himself had written favorably about Luther. Jonas' transfer to theology, to which his lectures on Paul's epistles bore witness, caused Luther to write a congratulatory letter to him in June, 1520. Excusing his failure to write before, Luther did not hesitate to show delight over Jonas' change of occupation. "I rejoice," he wrote, "that you have fled from the stormy sea of jurisprudence into the haven of the Holy Scriptures. May the Lord, who has begun it, preserve you. Miserable men are raging, seeking my life; but Christ lives and reigns."[3] Then Luther went on to give Jonas some information about the status of his struggle with Rome. Eck was in Rome, according to the latest reports received from friends, and was there engaged in obtaining the necessary proceedings against the Reformer. Luther asked Jonas humorously not to "return silence for silence, or sloth for sloth," but to write frequently. He closed with a request that Jonas pray for him. After only several months, Peter Mosellanus, the Humanist professor at Leipzig and follower of Luther, similarly congratulated Jonas on his transition to theology. He believed the University of Erfurt could through Jonas attain a greater distinction than that enjoyed by Plato's academy. Moreover, he urged Jonas, by the Holy Spirit who had granted him this new insight to employ his talents for the salvation of his own soul as well as of the souls of many others. Yet he was always to bear in mind that he should exercise moderation and seek to keep peace.

Jonas' shift from jurisprudence to theology was hailed as such a significant event that Euricius Cordus, a member of the Humanist group, composed a short poem celebrating this fact. Jonas also took steps which showed that his real interest was a religious one. A letter to Draconites announced his intention to become a preacher. This was a natural procedure for one who had lectured with such absorbing interest on St. Paul's letters to the Corinthians. Since as a canon no lower order than that of a subdeacon must have been bestowed upon him, he had the right to step forth as a preacher, even though the academic authorities could have questioned the legitimacy of such an act. The most momentous expression of Jonas' religious inclination was his wholehearted approval of Luther's program of reform. This last step was connected with the attempt of John Eck of Ingolstadt to put into effect the papal Bull against Luther in Erfurt. Eck had secured this Bull, which condemned the teachings and writings of Luther as heretical, on June 15, 1520, in Rome. He felt confident that the mere publication of it in Erfurt without his personal presence would suffice, since the orthodox party in the theological and law faculties would insist on having the instructions of the Bull carried out. Still, in order to effect prompt publication of the Bull, he originally planned to come to Erfurt. However, fearing a repetition of what had just happened to him at Leipzig, where the students had sung mock-songs about him and had sent him such threatening letters that he had been forced to flee the city by night, Eck changed his plans. Instead of coming to Erfurt, he veered off toward Coburg, where he arrived on October 6.

The Rift Widens

In Erfurt the authorities were prepared to publish the Bull. No doubt the theological faculty as a whole approved of having it printed and sold. But under the influence of Lange and Jonas a momentary delay was arranged, which Luther in a letter of October 30 interpreted as meaning that the Bull was disregarded because it had not been introduced there in a legal fashion. Soon thereafter a riot broke out among the students, who seized almost the entire press which had been printing it, tore up the leaves already printed, and threw them into the Gera River, shouting: "It is a bladder, may it float on the water!" This action by the students had been incited by a tract known under the title: "An Erfurt Declaration on Behalf of Martin Luther." The senate of the city gave its approval to the action of the students by silent consent. The Declaration, in its audacious and forceful expressions, its compressed language and classical Latin, points to a Humanist author or authors. Whether Jonas was the author or had a part in the composition of it cannot be definitely ascertained on the basis of available historical records. Its composition and publication took place in the early part of October, 1520, and proved to be a powerful weapon in frustrating the whole purpose of the papal Bull in Erfurt and in breaking ground for Luther's evangelical doctrine.

It began in the form of an official document: "An admonition to each and all patrons and friends of the most holy Christian and evangelical doctrine among the members of our fair university at Erfurt."

Forsaking its official style, after this introduction, the admonition continued: "Fairest reader, after lengthy, impious, and heretical counsels by certain impious Scribes and Pharisees who by a mere wicked title appoint themselves theologians, it has been thus decided against Luther, a most acute theologian, so that a document has already been put up for public view by the inspiration of the devil, a document in which the satanic legates in a prophetic manner tried also to thrust Martin beyond hell by excommunication." It was claimed that the teachers and baccalaureates of the university as theological professors of truth "with discernment rightly teach and profess that—if the Gospel be true at all, if the prophets have written rightly, and if Paul has not lied, the Spirit himself having spoken through Paul— Martin has thus far written well and in an entirely Christian way." This general statement on Luther's teaching was followed by an exhortation to action—and even to violence "lest the belief which was lifted up from the dust to the light through him be again suppressed." Only by being on their guard could the posting of the papal Bull be hindered, and it was their duty to persecute this good-for-nothing generation of Pharisees. Eventually these enemies of Christ's truth, it was claimed, would fall into the snare which they had prepared for Luther. In a mood of triumph the Declaration finally called upon its readers to act and walk as "most sincere lovers" of Christ, since they would reign eternally with him after the end of this life. It then closed with a quotation of verses six and seven of the twenty-fourth psalm: "Such is the generation of those who seek him, who seek the face of the God of Jacob. Lift up your heads, O gates! and be lifted up, O ancient doors! that the King of glory may come in."[4]

The most important result of this brief tract was that the authorities of the university were unable to post the papal Bull. In addition, a clearly discernible cleavage took place between the supporters of Eck and the Bull and the followers of Luther. Eobanus Hessus, lamenting this occurrence in a letter addressed to Lange toward the end of October, expressed wonder over the fact that the older professors at the university were such persistent opponents of Luther.

In the midst of this general commotion and period of internal tension and disagreement among members of the faculties, the election of a new rector took place on October 18, 1520. Crotus Rubianus, who after an extended stay in Italy had incidentally come to Erfurt on his way home, was the person selected for this post. While his term of office has often been regarded as representing the acme of the Humanist triumph at Erfurt, it was in fact the temporary dilemma of the divided university staff which was responsible for the selection of a man, who because of his lengthy absence would be least of all opposed by the adherents of Eck and the old order. Crotus Rubianus, as a Humanist, did succeed in carrying through the reforms initiated by Jonas in the faculty of arts. He inscribed upon the pages of the official record of registration of the university beside his rectorial report a table of a number of coats of arms in heraldic colors. The table, artistically drawn, contained the names and the individual coats of arms of the most eminent members of the Humanist group. In the center was Crotus Rubianus' own coat of arms and above his was Eobanus Hessus'. The four corners of the page were decorated with the coats of arms of Reuchlin, Mutianus Rufus, Erasmus, and Luther. To the right and left of Eobanus' coat of arms were those of Ulrich von Hutten and Justus Jonas. The latter's coat of arms, used on the occasion of his own report as rector, was, like the others, reproduced in color.[5] In addition, the coats of arms of Justus Mucius, Philip

Melanchthon, Joachim Camerarius, John Lange, Adam Crato, Henry Eberbach, John Draconites, Urbanus Rhegius, and George Forchheim were represented. The common purpose of reforming the church had, as symbolized by this report, brought about a union between Humanism and the Reformation; but a parting of the ways of these two movements was soon to come.

In a letter dated November 11, 1520, Erasmus asked Jonas to cease his attacks against Edward Lee, "even though he merited harsher things." The noted Humanist wanted to avoid every appearance of causing factions, especially since Aleander, the papal legate, had made his appearance in the Netherlands and ordered Luther's books to be burned. He sensed that the storm was coming and had no desire of being embroiled in the conflict whenever it would arise. "I am in favor of sound studies, I am in favor of evangelical truth; still I shall keep silent about that, if it is not allowed publicly. Christ will grant more tranquil times to someone else." To Jonas whose heart was aflame with evangelical passion these words must have been deeply disappointing; for the truth of the Gospel, as it was sounding forth out of Wittenberg, was beginning to engage his attention more and more.

The Appointment to Wittenberg

On January 21, 1521, the famed jurist, Henning Goede, had died. This left a professorship in canon law at the University of Wittenberg and the provostship of All Saints' Chapter vacant. Carlstadt had the unabashed audacity to suggest that he receive one of the vacant offices left by Goede. However, Spalatin lost no time in calling the Elector's attention to Jonas as a suitable successor. Reporting the death of Goede to Frederick the Wise in a letter, he recommended Jonas very highly. "Most gracious lord," wrote Spalatin, "in Erfurt there is a Canon of St. Severi, a licentiate of both civil and canon law, who has become master and previously bachelor of law at Wittenberg, is called Jodocus Jonas who was born at Nordhausen, a young man and pious, a learned priest, and wonderfully eloquent in both

Latin and German, a fine young jurist known to the father-confessor
of your Electoral Grace." Spalatin was, at the same time, not unmind-
ful of the fact that Jonas had recently given up his lectures on law
and had become a theologian. This he reported to the Elector as well
as the fact that Jonas could lecture on theology and preach. Spalatin
consequently suggested that it would be possible to have Jonas lecture on theology, even while he was provost of All Saints'. Frederick
the Wise, however, first offered the vacancy left by Goede to the
Gotha Canon, Mutianus, chiefly, it seems, as an expression of deference toward the learned Humanist. Mutianus graciously declined the
offer and, like Spalatin, recommended Justus Jonas.

To Worms and Affirmation

While these negotiations were still under way, Luther began his
journey to the Diet of Worms. Jonas, impetuous and eager to be
at Luther's side, had left Erfurt in order to join him at Weimar.
He accompanied Luther to Worms where, in accordance with the
Elector's request, he was to assist the Reformer with his counsel.
He was also given the opportunity of bringing the negotiations regarding his appointment at Wittenberg to a conclusion. In later years
Luther gratefully remembered Jonas' act of loyal support at this critical juncture of the Reformation.[6]

Luther had informed his friend Lange about his coming to Erfurt
while en route to the Diet, and his arrival caused a feverish stir of
joyful expectation among the city's population. On April 6, 1521,
outside of his old university city, Luther and his entourage were
received by a delegation of forty horsemen led by Crotus Rubianus,
the rector of the university. Besides, an innumerable throng followed the delegation on foot in order to welcome the celebrated Wittenberg monk. In the city he stayed at the Augustinian Cloister with
his friend Lange. On the following day, Whitsunday, Luther preached
a powerful sermon in the overcrowded church of his order on the
Gospel for the day. The sermon was an eloquent exposition of the
doctrine of justification by faith. Luther remained in Erfurt two

days, during which time he was overwhelmed by tokens of honor and homage. The university staged a banquet and feasted in honor of the Word of God proclaimed by Luther, and the city's senate bestowed many favors upon him.[7] It was primarily this reception at Erfurt which caused Aleander, the papal legate, to remark in his dispatch of April 15 that "the knavish imperial herald (Caspar Sturm) had made a march of triumph out of Luther's journey."

On April 8 Luther left Erfurt. Crotus Rubianus accompanied him for a short distance and in parting admonished Luther to remain steadfast; the city gave Luther its able captain, Hermann von Hoff, as escort; and the university possessed in Justus Jonas a worthy representative who would accompany Luther.

Before the arrival at Worms, Jonas had preceded Luther and his party there, and after due deliberation with Luther's friends, rode out to meet the arriving company early in the morning of April 16 in order to tell Luther beforehand that all arrangements for his stay had been made.[8] At ten o'clock a trumpet blast from the cathedral tower in Worms signalled the arrival of Luther and his companions. A great crowd had gathered to witness this event. Caspar Sturm, the imperial herald, rode at the head of the train. Behind him and his servant was a little Saxon wagon drawn by three horses. Under a kind of canopy sat Martin Luther with his three travel companions, Friar Petzensteiner, Nicholas von Amsdorf, a theologian and colleague of Luther at Wittenberg University, and the young Pomeranian student, Peter Suaven. Immediately behind their wagon rode Justus Jonas, the young Erfurt professor. He was followed by about a hundred men on horseback, consisting of both nobles and commoners, who had gone out early on Tuesday morning to meet the procession. Because the crowd had grown to about two thousand the wagon could advance but slowly. At length it halted before the House of the Knights of St. John, where Luther was going to be lodged during his stay in Worms. One of the spies of the papal nuncio, Aleander, reported that after getting off the wagon and before entering the house, Luther paused and "looking around him with his demonic eyes, exclaimed, 'God will be with me.'"[9]

Just how much of the historic proceedings at Worms Justus Jonas witnessed personally, it is impossible to say. Perhaps he was among the group that was permitted to accompany Luther on the next day, Wednesday, April 17, at four o'clock, to the episcopal palace not far from the cathedral. After waiting about two hours, Luther was finally asked to appear in the court chamber. Beside him was his chief legal adviser, Jerome Schurpff.

With becoming humility Luther stood, his knees slightly bent, before the Emperor and the princes and other dignitaries of church and state. He was asked by Dr. John von der Ecken, an official of the Archbishop of Trier, first in Latin and then in German, whether the books placed on the table before him were his and whether he was ready to renounce them or part of them. When Luther was about to affirm that the books were his, Schurpff interrupted, exclaiming loudly, "Let the titles be read!" After this request had been granted and the titles had been read, Luther declared with a subdued voice that the books were his. In answer to the question about renouncing them, he requested time to think this over because it had to do with faith, the salvation of souls, and the highest treasure on earth, the Word of God. In answer to this request Luther was told that he would be given only one day for reflection and then he had to reply. Returning to his quarters, the Reformer wrote on that same evening in a letter to a Humanist friend, John Cuspinian of Vienna, "Assuredly, with Christ's help, I shall not recant one jot."[10]

On the following day, Thursday, April 18, shortly after four o'clock, Luther was again escorted by the herald Sturm to a larger hall in the episcopal palace where a dense throng awaited him and his advisers. Again they were kept waiting until six o'clock, at which time the Emperor's throne was set up and the princes came down the stairs into the hall. Meanwhile it had become so dark that torches had to be lighted. Dr. Ecken opened the proceedings with a short Latin and German address. He asked whether Luther was now ready to retract all or part of the books which he had on the previous day acknowledged to be his. To this question Luther replied in German with a clear and animated voice in an address of about ten minutes. He was then asked to repeat the same words in Latin, which he did at once. Thereupon the Emperor retired with his advisers for a consultation. On his return, the official was instructed to demand a brief and unambiguous statement from the Wittenberg monk. In a fairly long speech Dr. Ecken sought to badger Luther into submission, as he concluded with a direct challenge, "Answer straightforward and honestly, unambiguously and unreservedly, whether you will retract your books and the errors contained in them or not!" Luther replied in Latin: "Inasmuch as Your Majesty and Your Highnesses ask for a plain answer, I shall give one without horns [reservations] or teeth [backbiting]. Unless I am proved to be wrong by the testimony of Scriptures and by evident reasoning—for I cannot trust the decisions of either popes or councils, since it is plain that they have frequently erred and contradicted one another—I am bound in conscience and held fast in the Word of God by those passages of the Holy Scriptures which I have quoted. Therefore I cannot and will not retract anything, for it is neither safe nor salutary to act against one's conscience." Then he added in the German tongue, "God help me! Amen."[11]

The die was cast. Ecken vainly attempted once more to have Luther change his mind. The Emperor signaled to the imperial herald to take Luther away. Without incident he was led back to the House of the Knights of St. John where, stretching out his hands in the presence of his friends, he said, "I am through. I am through."

The Emperor Charles V was staking everything upon the vindication of the Roman Catholic faith and the preservation of the unity of Western Christendom, and although Luther was equally determined to uphold God's Word of truth, the negotiations continued. On April 23 Luther was summoned by two priests to appear for a new hearing. It took place on the following morning, April 24, in the quarters of the Archbishop of Trier in the House of the Teutonic Order. Elector Joachim of Brandenburg presided. In reality this hearing, in which Schurpff, Amsdorf, and Justus Jonas took part, turned out to be a friendly conference during which an attempt was made to persuade Luther to give up the position he had taken. How-

ever, with all deference to those who sought to have him change
his mind, he adhered to the principle that he could yield only to
the authority of the Scriptures and plain reason. Further conferences
followed on succeeding days, but they failed to alter Luther's position. Actually they constituted more of a test for him than the dramatic stand before the Emperor and the Diet, for these conferences
with their informal atmosphere were conducted in a very conciliatory spirit.[12]

An End and a Beginning

During the course of these meetings Justus Jonas came to know
personally Cochlaeus, one of Luther's determined foes.[13] Cochlaeus,
published a report in 1540 in which he told of his encounter with
the young Humanist and portrayed him as "a remarkable young
man, elegant, tall of stature and in no wise uncultured." Cochlaeus
had first met Jonas on the street, as he was coming toward him with
two friends. The three had just complained to Capito about Cochlaeus' unfair attitude toward Luther. On the basis of this complaint
a discussion with Cochlaeus ensued on the street. Jonas came to
Luther's defense by quoting certain passages from St. Paul. Then,
before they parted, Jonas admonished Cochlaeus not to publish any
polemics against Luther, since no less than forty erudite and eloquent
men would be willing to write against him.[14]

The entire proceedings from April 16 to 25 have been preserved in
an extensive Latin report known as "The Acts and Exploits of
Doctor Martin Luther" ("Acta et res gesta Doctoris Martini Lutheri").
While Spalatin has been thought to be the person who may have
written this report, Kalkoff in his thorough study of the Diet at Worms
has demonstrated that the report must have originated from the
intimate circle of Luther's advisers, Schurpff, Amsdorf, and Jonas,
and that of the three only Jonas, as a trained Humanist, could have
written Latin in such a fine Erasmian style. Jonas' personality remained in the background of the entire report, a fact which can
be explained on the basis of his comparatively recent adherence to

Luther's teaching and his own youthfulness. The report has the distinct marks of having been made by an eyewitness, and reveals the enthusiastic admiration and profound regard which the author had for Luther. In it we find a phrase describing Luther as "the most Christian father," which is reminiscent of Jonas' calling Erasmus his "father in Christ." The report ends with a sentence which is similar to the closing lines of Jonas' later letters and which indicates a deep concern and interest for the fate of Luther and the Gospel. "May God therefore always preserve together with His Word the most pious man who has arisen for the purpose of guarding and teaching the Gospel to his church. Amen."[15]

Before his departure from Worms Jonas prepared a somewhat shortened account of the "Acts and Exploits of Doctor Martin Luther" together with an introduction and a conclusion. This account he handed to Ulrich von Hutten, who had it printed by John Schott in Strassburg. On the morning of April 26, after the midday meal, Luther and his entourage left Worms without being escorted by the imperial herald Sturm. Jonas accompanied the Reformer as far as Eisenach. Luther was shortly afterwards, according to a prearranged plan made by Elector Frederick the Wise, taken captive by four or five horsemen who brought him to the Wartburg Castle where he remained in hiding for the sake of his safety. When Jonas returned to Erfurt the poet-professor, Eobanus Hessus, celebrated his arrival in the city with an elegy. "Thou also, our unconquerable companion of the high-minded Luther, art to be celebrated in song in this region. O Jonas, thou who hast dared to follow him who was hastening onward in his self-made destiny." He went on to praise the daring faith and selfless devotion of Jonas as well as his ability as a counsellor. "Great it was for Martin to conquer with Christ, the Redeemer, for thee to be an ally of so great a work. Farewell." Ulrich von Hutten also lost no time in sending a letter of high commendation to Jonas because he had appeared with Luther in Worms.[16]

Jonas' conduct in Erfurt and at Worms as well as his continued zeal in the defense of Luther's cause aroused the opposition of the Dean of St. Severi Chapter, Doleatoris. Together with the Dean of the Cathedral Chapter, Wiedemann, the decision was made to carry out the instructions of the papal Bull and excommunicate as heretics both Jonas and Draconites, a fellow-canon and also a follower of Luther. Before action could be taken against Jonas he had moved to Wittenberg; but Draconites was commanded to leave the prebend. The result of this animosity on the part of the leading clergy resulted in riots by the students who, aided by the people, stormed into the homes of the clergy and plundered their dwellings. Crotus Rubianus, the rector, with praiseworthy impartiality, had the instigators among the students punished, and tried to restore peace and calm. At the beginning of May he resigned his office and left Erfurt never to return. The golden age of Humanism was over, and Erfurt's star as a university city declined with amazing rapidity.

Jonas at this time received a rebuke from another quarter besides the action intended against him in Erfurt. Erasmus had been following events with very keen interest. He had noted with inward disapproval the prominent part Jonas had played at Worms, and made a determined effort to keep Jonas from following Luther. In a lengthy letter he tried to show Jonas what a bane Luther's tumultuous procedure was for the church and how nothing good could come of it. "There is now the constant rumor, most beloved Jonas, that you were continually supporting Martin at Worms," began Erasmus, and he could well understand that Jonas in his piety was induced to support Luther. But he believed that once the concord of the church was lost "the peculiar character of the church is lost. For what is our religion other than peace in the Holy Spirit?" Erasmus pointed out how the church even in early days was far from perfect. That the study of the Scriptures had been neglected and the morals of the day were appalling, Erasmus readily admitted. Yes, though he knew "that from the beginning Luther enjoyed a great deal of favor on all sides" he was at once afraid, after tasting his first short works, "that the matter would end in tumult." Composed civility and gradual insinuation of reform were the methods Erasmus advocated; Luther failed to use them. Erasmus tried to illustrate how in the New Testament Jesus', Peter's, and Paul's methods accorded with these principles of gentleness and civility. Voicing his regret that Melanchthon, "a youth furnished with so many eminent gifts," had also been won over to Luther's side, Erasmus still hoped to win Jonas back to the more gentle, peaceful occupation of disseminating the Christian philosophy among the learned.[17] But the letter failed of its purpose. Erasmus was retracting in the hour when stout hearts of strong faith in the Word of the Lord were marching forward, and Jonas had decided to march with them.

FOOTNOTES FOR CHAPTER 2

1. Enders, *Luther's Briefwechsel*, Vol. II, p. 13.
2. *Luthers Werke*, Weimar Edition, Vol. II, pp. 248-253; Enders, *op. cit.*, Vol. II, p. 281.
3. Enders, *op. cit.*, Vol. II, pp. 419-421.
4. Kalkoff, *op. cit.*, pp. 92 ff.
5. Jonas' coat of arms portrayed, on a golden background, the blue head of a whale spewing out a naked man.
6. *Luthers Werke*, Weimar Edition, Tischreden, Vol. IV, No. 4871.
7. James Mackinnon, *Luther and the Reformation*, Vol. II, p. 291.
8. Adolf Wrede, Editor, *Deutsche Reichstagsakten unter Kaiser Karl V*, Vol. II, pp. 850 ff.
9. Heinrich Boehmer, *op. cit.*, pp. 404-405.
   James Mackinnon, *op. cit.*, Vol. II, p. 293.
10. Enders, *op. cit.*, Vol. III, p. 123.
11. Heinrich Boehmer, *op. cit.*, pp. 404-415.
12. Heinrich Boehmer, *op. cit.*, pp. 419-427.
13. Kawerau, *op. cit.*, Vol. II, p. 346.
14. Enders, *op. cit.*, Vol. III, p. 187.
15. Kalkoff, *Der Wormser Reichstag von 1521*, pp. 329-331.
    Heinrich Boehmer, *op. cit.*, p. 415.
    Adolf Wrede, Editor, *Reichstagsakten*, Vol. II, pp. 568-569.
16. Kawerau, *op. cit.*, Vol. I, pp. 51-53.
17. Kawerau, *ibid.*, Vol. I, pp. 54 ff.

Chapter 3

The Emerging
Theologian

With his move to Wittenberg a new mode of activity lay in store for Justus Jonas. In Erfurt he had, under Erasmus' influence, become a Christian philosopher; in Wittenberg he was, under Luther's leadership, to become a teacher of God's Word. Although Erasmus was unable to dissuade Jonas from continuing his support of Luther, it is evident that Justus Jonas never surrendered his Humanist heritage. He continued to cultivate his friendship with the Humanist circle. Nevertheless, the cordiality and warmth of this friendship of former years waned noticeably. Even Jonas' intimate friendship with his compatriot Melchior von Aachen of Nordhausen suffered partial eclipse in the face of his ardent espousal of Luther's cause.[1] While the Humanists lent their enthusiastic support to Luther in the initial stages of the reform movement in Wittenberg, after the Diet of Worms a growing estrangement took place because of the deep-seated differences between the theological views and goals of Erasmus as Humanist and Luther as Reformer. Erasmus was concerned mainly with morality. He tried to raise the moral level of the church's life by calling attention to its existing faults and failings. His program consisted of teaching the philosophy of Christ and its ethical ideals so that all might be imbued with its truth. Luther's chief concern was theological. He had rediscovered the Gospel as the true treasure of the church and as the power of God for salvation in the life of every one who believed it. This Gospel, in the Reformer's view, had to be proclaimed and preserved from misrepresentation and adulteration at any price.

While Justus Jonas sought to maintain his ties with the friends and representatives of Humanism, the Gospel had taken him captive. Clearly discerning the difference between the Humanistic ideals of reform and the Gospel, he felt compelled by conscience to give his allegiance to the Word of God. Nowhere does Jonas express this profound conviction more forcefully and more beautifully than in a letter of June 19, 1521, to the Elector Frederick the Wise. In this writing Jonas was particularly concerned about being freed from the duty of lecturing on canon law because to him it no longer had any real significance in the light of evangelical doctrine. He wanted first and foremost to become a teacher of the Gospel. The authentic accents of its power and truth had been heard by him. "Out of Wittenberg the truth of God has sounded forth," he wrote to the prince with heartfelt sincerity, "and the Word of the Lord has come out of and from Saxony." He was on this account hopeful that his Electoral Grace would show that measure of insight and understanding so "that no injury may happen to the evangelical cause and action, which have so blessedly begun in your Electoral Grace's city, Wittenberg, as well as to the most pure and plain glory and honor of the truth of our Lord and Savior Christ."[2]

It need not surprise us that later Jonas sided completely with Luther in the controversy with Erasmus on the bondage of the will. Still, when he dedicated his translation of Luther's *Concerning the Bondage of the Will* to Count Albrecht of Mansfeld, he seemed, by reason of his past personal friendship with Erasmus and his admiration for him, to regret that the great Humanist had become embroiled in this theological dispute with Luther. For in that dedication he spoke of Erasmus as a "dear friend." He wrote, "For although Erasmus is otherwise a valuable and great man, such writing about the free will is offensive and contrary to the Gospel."[3] In earlier years Jonas had praised Erasmus very highly before Luther, inasmuch as he had been genuinely concerned in bringing about an understanding between the famous Humanist and the Wittenberg Reformer. However, his efforts had met with no success. Later Luther in his polemical writing, *Answer to the King of England's Libellous Pamphlet,* recalled Jonas' excessive commendation of Erasmus.

Naturally Erasmus no longer regarded Jonas as his ally when he saw how Jonas sided with Luther in the dispute over free will. In his defense against Luther's attack on his *Diatribe on Free Will* Erasmus came out with the first part of *Heavy-Armed Soldier* in 1526. In it he alluded to a jurist as collaborator with Luther. No doubt he was referring to Justus Jonas. When Erasmus published the second half of *Heavy-Armed Soldier* in 1527, he made a direct attack on Jonas by calling him a person unduly proud of his learning. Luther, he claimed, had made him believe that it was a meritorious work to attack the Humanist; and Jonas had thereby become a malicious person. These attacks on Jonas led to a complete severance of friendship between the two men.

In September of 1527 Justus Jonas, writing to his friend Lange in Erfurt, made it clear that his admiration for Erasmus, who was joining in the Romanist attacks on the evangelical churches, had diminished. The papists, he wrote, "see Germany growing cold toward the Gospel; they see that Erasmus, the old fox, who is equipped with all the wiles and arts of the Greeks, has become inflamed against Luther and now agitates only for this, that one oppress him, not convince him with arguments."[4] Luther, learning of Jonas' altered attitude toward the Humanist of Rotterdam, congratulated him "on the recantation." "At last," he wrote to Jonas, "you paint that Erasmus of yours in his true colors and recognize him as a viper with deadly stings, though you used formerly to speak of him in many terms of praise."[5]

However, that Jonas continued to hold the intellectual greatness of Erasmus in high esteem is proved by an utterance of Jonas made in the same year. Luther referred to it thus: "My dear Doctor Jonas gave me no peace by urging continually that I should attack Erasmus honorably and write against him humbly. *'Domine doctor,'* said he, 'you cannot imagine what a fine, venerable old man he is.' "[6] In 1542 Jonas, saddened by the news of the death of Urbanus Rhegius and Capito, said that Urbanus and Erasmus had performed a laudable service by summoning sleeping citizens to defend the holy church and the German nation.[7] On another occasion, in 1552, he called to mind the fact that besides Reuchlin, Luther, and others, Erasmus had achieved a great deal on behalf of the universities. So in spite of Erasmus' vicious attack against him, Jonas, in a spirit of impartiality and fairness, always valued the manifest contribution of Humanism and throughout his life remained loyal to his Humanist heritage.

Provost of All Saints'

On June 6, 1521, Justus Jonas was installed as provost of All Saints' Chapter in Wittenberg. It was a manifest disappointment for him that in his new position he was expected to discharge the time-honored responsibility of lecturing on canon law. Luther himself had declared in the year 1520 "that it were well if the canon law, from the first letter to the last, and especially the decretals, were utterly blotted out." The study of such matters, he believed, was a sheer waste of time and a farce because the Pope arbitrarily determined what was binding for him and what he could set aside at his own convenience.[8] In this matter Melanchthon was in full accord with Luther's opinion and with Jonas' scruples. Therefore, the day after Jonas' installation Melanchthon wrote to Spalatin, the Elector's secretary, and urged him to act courageously in order to secure permission for Jonas to lecture on theology at the university and to release him from his duties of lecturing on pontifical law. Thus Melanchthon, deeply desirous of retaining Jonas in Wittenberg, asked Spalatin to "turn every stone lest such a man as this be lost to us."[9]

Meanwhile Luther who was still in hiding at the Wartburg Castle, was by letter confirming Jonas in his resolve to refuse to lecture on canonical law. Luther felt certain that Jonas, guided by God's Spirit, would consequently not acknowledge the "pestilential decretals of

Antichrist" which he had been commanded to teach. Moreover, Jonas was to become an Aaron who, "clothed in sacred vestments, that is, armed with divine Scriptures," and "having laid hold of the censer of prayer," could go forth to meet his opponents. Luther was concerned that Jonas should not consider his ministry at All Saints' lightly but should proclaim "the salutary and life-giving Gospel of Christ" and be firm in his faith in "this Emmanuel."[10]

In the course of negotiations with the Elector of Saxony regarding Jonas' status as provost of All Saints', there was a time when consideration was given to selecting someone else. Finally, Jonas appealed directly to the Elector. Toward the end of June, Frederick the Wise directed Jonas to come to Wittenberg, where a solution congenial to Jonas' wishes would be worked out. In replying to this writing of the Prince, Jonas expressed great joy over this decision. He looked forward to going to the University at Wittenberg, the highest perfection of which, in his opinion, censured the incapability of other universities, while its course of studies was the fulfillment of what men had talked and dreamed about.

Around the middle of the month of July, Jonas at last moved to Wittenberg with all of his possessions. In a letter to Eobanus Hessus he lauded the "incredible treasures of learning and all good things." The academic life in Erfurt was, in his estimation, lifeless in comparison with the ardor for studies in Wittenberg. It seemed to him that the reactionary forces that condemned the new learning were responsible for that university's rapid eclipse.[11]

With the Elector's consent and Spalatin's assistance Jonas now made the necessary arrangements which freed him from the responsibility of lecturing on canon law. He paid twenty guldens a year out of his own salary to the man who in his stead would lecture on the decretals; but Jonas himself retained the provostship and became a regular member of the theological faculty of the university. In a letter to the Elector's councilors, Jonas laid bare the motives which prompted him to work out this arrangement. He knew that in 1440 Laurentius Valla had demonstrated the fraudulent character of the decretals. He was aware of the fact that throughout the Holy Roman

Empire people were singing the praises of the University of Wittenberg because there evangelical doctrine was being proclaimed and written in a genuine apostolic spirit. He furthermore believed that the study of the original languages of the Scriptures, Greek and Hebrew, was necessary for the right understanding of its message, and hoped that other universities would follow this example. He saw finally how the students in Wittenberg were being educated in a Christian way and was certain that this would result in an expression of Christian conduct in all walks of life. Jonas therefore desired to have a part in this meaningful program of reform.[12]

Though a professor on the theological faculty, Jonas felt that he lacked the necessary academic qualifications for teaching. For this reason he earned the degree of a licentiate of theology on September 24, 1521, and the degree of doctor of theology on October 14 of the same year together with his Erfurt friend, Tilemann Pletener. Mutianus heartily congratulated Jonas beforehand on his attainment of the doctorate. John Lange of Erfurt was unable to be present on the occasion, for which Jonas chided him in a letter.

Carlstadt and Radical Reform

This letter of November 8, 1521, is illuminating with reference to the progress of the reform movement during Luther's temporary absence from Wittenberg. Having promised Lange to write to Luther concerning the agitated state of affairs in Erfurt, Jonas related that on the Sunday after All Saints' Day he had preached the Gospel, after all pontifical insignia had been hauled down and thrown out of the church. He also revealed in confidence to Lange that the maintenance of personal chastity in his life involved a real struggle for him. He therefore wondered whether this was an indication that he ought to take a wife.[13]

Jonas, who was evidently keeping pace with Carlstadt's radical program of reform in the city, soon received a note of warning from Spalatin, who cautioned against any rash innovations, as they would be certain to incur the disapproval of the Elector. The radical steps that were taken in Wittenberg toward reform had originated in the Augustinian Cloister where the Augustinian Eremite Gabriel Zwilling had agitated for the Sacrament "under both kinds," that is, of both bread and wine, and had advocated the abolition of holding private mass. His preaching spread beyond the cloister walls to the inhabitants of Wittenberg. The unrest which was thus produced led to an investigation by Jonas, Carlstadt, Melanchthon, and others. They sent an Opinion (*Gutachten*) to the Elector in which they gave their advice concerning the abolition of the mass in the Augustinian Cloister and stated their case for the permission of the celebration of the Lord's Supper "under both kinds." The Elector gave an evasive answer to the effect that he would promote that "which might tend toward the honor of the divine Word and the strengthening of the holy, Christian faith." But he said further that circumstances were not favorable for the radical changes suggested in the Opinion.[14]

Carlstadt took over the leadership in the reform of the worship and the abolition of the mass, and although opposed by many fellow-canons, announced his intention of celebrating the Lord's Supper in evangelical fashion on the first day of the New Year, 1522. In fact, however, the plan was carried out on Christmas Day, 1521, in spite of the Elector's express prohibition.[15] The excitement of the populace was heightened at that crucial time by the coming of the Zwickau prophets, Nicholas Storch and two others, who added fuel to the fire of a revolt.

Jonas' attitude is reflected in a letter of January 1, 1522, to Capito in which he rejoiced over the report that Cardinal Albrecht had begun to preach. He revealed in the letter that he also thought of the Reformation in national terms, for he resented the avarice of the Italians who were seeking to gain possession of German gold, while they did not care in the least where Germany as a country was located or what the German people were like. Jonas would therefore like to have Christian rulers confess Christ and free themselves from the stranglehold of Roman domination by the Pope.

Regarding the progress of reform Jonas reported approvingly that Carlstadt had married "a girl of noble ancestry but poor" and that the same had already prepared an elaborate defense of priestly marriage.[16] Moreover, a large proportion of the citizens in Wittenberg had communed "under both kinds" on Christmas Day and on New Year's Day. Jonas believed that such a procedure was based on God's clear Word and could be defended, even if people outside of Wittenberg maligned such actions. "The whole matter rests in the hands of the Lord," said Jonas, as he recounted many of these events in a letter to Lange dated January 8. He expressed the belief that the reform, as it was taking shape, was based on Luther's own writings. Having told Lange about Carlstadt's recent marriage as well as the marriages of other priests, he put the question to him: "What do you think I should do?" The question was an indication that he had been occupied with the thought of getting married and had come to the conclusion that the "diabolical hypocrisy" of celibacy had to be overcome. "Do thou pray the Lord," Jonas entreated his friend, "that he may grant Christian wives to the priests."[17] On February 5, 1522, Melanchthon reported to Einsiedel that Provost Jonas had taken to wife a "Felkin," meaning Catherine Falk. However, the marriage did not take place until February 9 and Melanchthon must have been referring to Jonas' engagement.

With the arrival of the Zwickau prophets, Nicholas Storch, Thomas Drechsel, weavers by trade, and Marius Stuebner, a former university student, in late December, 1521, the entire reform movement in Wittenberg had begun to take on revolutionary proportions. Carlstadt progressed from a denial of any distinction between clergy and laity to a condemnation of all scholarship and learning as unnecessary for an understanding of the Word of God. His zeal was not held in check by wise moderation, and soon the populace without heeding its leaders, took matters into its own hands. They invaded churches, destroyed images and pictures, and smashed windows. The fanaticism could not be restrained as it seemed, so Melanchthon called upon Luther and asked him to restore order. Luther decided to return to the city in order to establish peace. On March 6 he entered Wittenberg and on the following Sunday, March 9, he began his series of daily sermons for a period of eight days. This resulted in the restora-

tion of peace and quiet among the inhabitants. Both Jonas and Melanchthon now realized that they had been too precipitate in their
actions during Luther's absence, and so they again readily placed
themselves under Luther's wise leadership and counsel.

Luther's Moderation

Luther's return to Wittenberg did not signify that the reform of
the mass was not to continue. As provost of All Saints' Jonas was
now to carry out the needed reform under the wise supervision of
Luther. Although the Elector had forbidden any further innovations, both Luther and Jonas were prepared to continue on the path
on which they had begun to travel, even at the cost of incurring
Frederick's wrath. As a result Jonas was soon classed with Carlstadt
by the Elector. Still he did not leave off preaching against the abuse
of the mass, although he expressly warned the people against violence
in the matter. Luther made certain recommendations to Jonas and
the remaining canons regarding the services in the church. These
recommendations became the basis of Jonas' letter of August 24 addressed to the Elector. Genuine personal conviction of the precious
truth of the Gospel was coupled with due deference and tact. Jonas
reminded the Elector that the tremendous happenings of the last
four years could not in any sense be interpreted as a human work
but were manifestly of divine origin. God's truth, then, having been
apprehended, must be obeyed. "To whomsoever God grants the
privilege of hearing the Word purely and clearly, yes, rather when
he awakens it in the heart, to him he has truly given something
great. For it is a most precious treasure through which God gives
his knowledge, Spirit, and all gifts and understanding to hearts."
In the world the Gospel was meeting with opposition and indif-
ference; but it was the plain duty of those who had the opportunity
of hearing it to defend it from all abuses. Accordingly, Jonas
enumerated the manner in which the truth of the Gospel could be
presented in the best and most orderly fashion. The abuse of the

mass had to be removed and a scriptural order of worship patterned according to St. Paul's writings was to be introduced. No matter how small the number of followers of Christ, it was incumbent upon them to pay heed to the truth of the Word of God. "For it is the nature of the Gospel to be a living voice." It was, then, in Jonas' opinion, the duty of all who heard this voice to obey it.[18]

The Elector's reply was not encouraging. He even toyed with the idea of depriving Jonas of his prebend at All Saints'. This would have meant the loss of Jonas' assistance at Wittenberg. For that reason Luther came to Jonas' aid in a letter to Spalatin, Frederick's court chaplain and secretary. Luther confessed that he was in reality the motivating force in the demand for certain reform measures in the chapter of All Saints'. Frankly and firmly the Reformer stated: "The manner of the Prince, who despises us, is known. Thus we honor the Gospel that we even on occasion begrudge his servants a prebend for life, while we gladly fling riches to others in order that they may blaspheme our God. Jonas, a man whom one should purchase with a good deal of money and preserve for our land, you estimate to be worth less than straw and hay."[19] Despite Luther's fervent plea Frederick the Wise did not give his consent to any innovations. In the face of this resistance, Luther and Jonas were able to correct only some of the worst abuses. In the spring of 1524 the two men made a new attempt to reform the chapter, but they had to be satisfied with compromises. Nevertheless, Jonas set forth an official Opinion in the matter of correcting the ceremonies in the Church of All Saints'. The order of worship corresponded broadly to the pattern laid down in his writing to Frederick the Wise. Emphasis was laid on reading the Scriptures, preaching, and prayer. Not till the fall of 1525, however, did Jonas, through patient endeavor, succeed in restoring the purified order of worship in his own church. At that time the entire chapter was duly secularized. This program could now be carried out, because Frederick the Wise had died and was succeeded by his son, John the Constant, who permitted the evangelical reform of worship which Jonas had introduced.

It is evident that an intimate friendship between Luther and Jonas had developed during this first phase of the reform movement in Wittenberg. For on June 13, 1525, Jonas was among the small circle of friends invited to witness Luther's marriage to Catherine von Bora.

Dean of Theology

As professor of theology Jonas played a no less significant role. He began by lecturing on the Epistle to the Romans and did so by insisting on a literal and grammatical interpretation of the text and on a practical application to the contemporary situation. In 1524 he lectured on the Acts of the Apostles. During the years 1523 to 1525 Jonas was chosen as dean of the theological faculty, an office he retained until 1533. Jonas felt the weight of increased responsibility when he was chosen rector of the university during the summer semester in 1526. At the same time he continued to lecture according to Luther's example, alternately in Latin and German, and to busy himself with the task of translating.

When a plague broke out in Wittenberg in August, 1527, Jonas and his family left for Nordhausen. He rejoiced over the opportunity of being able to stay in Nordhausen as the guest of Michael Meienburg, his father's successor as burgomaster of the city and a friend of the Reformation. In a letter of September 16, 1527, Jonas invited his friend John Agricola of Eisleben to the city of which he was so proud. He likewise sent a letter to John Lange of Erfurt, after he had been in Nordhausen for two months, and expressed his regret that he had been unable to come to Erfurt to see his friend. Conditions in the church caused Jonas some anxiety. He described the growing hostility of the papal church toward the Reformation and asked Lange to join in prayers for Luther's continued health and strength.

In a letter in late November of 1527 Luther asked Jonas to return to Wittenberg, since the plague had abated. In his reply of January 3, 1528, Jonas mentioned his willingness to comply with this request. He came back with his family early that year. In Wittenberg new responsibilities awaited Jonas. He was chosen rector of the university for the second time and filled this important office from October, 1530 to May, 1531.

Jonas worked with Luther, Melanchthon, Bugenhagen, and Cruciger almost continually in ordering various affairs in the evangelical church. In September, 1533, they encouraged the preachers of Erfurt to bear the affliction and slander of hostile papists. In October they advised the Nuremberg Senate to conciliation in the controversy over private absolution. Jonas joined in urging the evangelical Henry of Einsiedel to make peace with the Catholic Duke George of Saxony. In a personal letter he again admonished Henry of Einsiedel to patient endurance. He continued to write to Prince George of Anhalt and took time to write to the brother Prince Joachim of Anhalt in order to comfort him in his illness. Simultaneously Jonas suffered from periodic attacks of kidney-stone and its debilitating effects, while occupied with the many demands and duties of his work.

At the University of Wittenberg the year 1533 proved to be highly significant. During the course of that year Melanchthon drew up the new statutes for the university. The first statute prescribed that the pure evangelical doctrine, as set forth in the Augsburg Confession, be taught, preserved, and upheld. Another stated that it was no longer required of a professor to lecture on the Book of Sentences of Peter Lombard—a characteristic of medieval scholastic universities. Instead it was demanded that he lecture on the psalms and the prophets.

In the middle of June of that year Elector John Frederick came to Wittenberg with other Saxon princes in order to confer with the theologians on the proposed General Council. As a result, an Opinion by Luther, Jonas, and Bugenhagen was formulated. It stated the unequivocal evangelical position that would be maintained. Only if the council to be convoked would be directed and determined in its decisions by the clear teachings of God's Word could it be accepted by the evangelical church as constituting a true council of Christendom.

When the Elector was informed by Luther that the university was about to bestow the degree of a doctor of theology on three candidates, John Bugenhagen, Caspar Cruciger, and John Aepinus, according to the evangelical statutes recently introduced by Melanchthon, the prince desired to be present at the solemn occasion. As dean of the theological faculty, Jonas had the distinction of presiding during the disputation on the theme: "Concerning Faith, Concerning the Church, Concerning Human Traditions," and of conferring the doctor's degree on the three candidates. Jonas began the solemnities of June 18, 1533, at which the Elector and other princes as well as persons of rank were present, with a suitable address entitled: "Concerning Degrees in Theology."[20]

"I do not suppose that anyone in this most laudable assembly," Jonas began, "is unacquainted with the common duties of life to such a degree that he would censure our plan of promoting men to doctors of the Gospel, especially when one beholds in this gathering our most illustrious Prince. . . ." His presence, Jonas continued, gave the stamp of approval to this academic procedure. Not desiring, therefore, to defend the custom as such, Jonas declared the purpose of his oration to consist of examining the reason for conferring the doctorate. "For we also feel that the title 'doctor' in a most difficult profession should not be conferred rashly upon many. Accordingly, this title is a public testimony of erudition and piety, with which the unlearned and impious are in no wise equipped." For that reason this honor was to be limited to a select few; for only upon those who through long association with qualified teachers had given proof of their learnedness, wisdom, and Christian character could this honor be bestowed. The men to be so honored, were, in Jonas' estimation, qualified in this respect. Retaining this custom, he said, would furthermore keep the ignorant away from the churches and would at the same time enable those who were called to the office of teaching to present a public testimony of their vocation and learning. Jonas believed that at no time in the church's eventful history was it more necessary to be watchful and to keep neophytes and the uninstructed from exercising a teaching office. Even Paul had commanded that those who were called to teach the churches were to be examined. He commended Timothy, not alone "because he had been nurtured by the study of the sacred Scriptures from very childhood, but also because he had been a companion in the struggles, the dangers, the controversies and deliberations of the Apostles. This experience, I think, ought to be required no less than insight and erudition." Nor was such experience easily gained, but could only be had after "vehement struggles." The doctor's degree in a school which was well organized did not only put a stamp of approval on the ability of those who received it, but also testified to their association with men of more seasoned experience and mature judgment. The claim that the unction of God's Spirit was the sole requirement for exercising one's authority as a preacher and teacher in the church was summarily rejected by Jonas. If Plato stated that he hoped finally in old age to come to the point where he could understand the doctrines of wise men, how much more did this hold true with reference to matters which reason cannot apprehend. Only by constant application and experience, therefore, could true discernment in spiritual matters result, and so the mere hearing of a lecture or the reading of any small book was not enough.

Having stated that the qualifications of a person who was to receive a doctor's degree required genuine learnedness and living piety, Jonas pointed to the goal of theological studies as the glorification of the Gospel and the salvation of one's own soul as well as the souls of others. The three men, upon whom this honor was now to be bestowed, understood that the privileges thus gained were "not for riches, glory, pleasures, but for the greatest hardships, the most burdensome cares, and dangers of every kind." The future outlook for unmolested well-being, serenity, and peace was not promising, as far as evangelical Christianity was concerned. So while even rulers and princes in many localities persecuted the Gospel, Jonas could not but laud the Elector for the protection he had granted and the generous help he had given for the proclamation and spread of the Gospel of Jesus Christ.

The festivities were brought to their conclusion by a splendid banquet given by the Elector at the castle where eighteen to twenty tables had been prepared. Among the celebrated guests were the well-known Englishman, Robert Barnes, and the Scotsman, Alexander Alane (Alesius), both of whom had registered for lectures at the university.[21]

The Task of Mediation

In October of 1536 Jonas was elected rector of Wittenberg University for a third time and served in that capacity until May, 1537. During this term he was able to effect an increase in the salaries of the professors by personally appealing to the Elector. As rector he was called upon to settle a controversy between Conrad Cordatus, minister in Niemegk and successor to George Witzel, and Melanchthon and Cruciger. Cordatus had impugned the orthodoxy of Melanchthon's and Cruciger's view on justification. Melanchthon was the first to inform Luther, Jonas, Bugenhagen, and Cruciger of this attack, while Cordatus addressed an appeal to Jonas over a month later and asked that he as rector should come to his aid in this dispute. Cordatus, convinced that he was justified in his position, was unable to elicit an immediate response from Jonas. In April, 1537, fully three and a half months later, Cordatus requested that Jonas rectify matters in this dispute and call upon Cruciger to revoke his heretical view publicly. He begged Jonas to read his writings and convince himself of Cordatus' orthodox views. But Jonas, sensing that Cordatus was not disposed to settle the controversy amicably, wrote and admonished him to control his passionate zeal in detecting heretical opinions. "If your present activities, dear Cordatus," wrote Jonas, "were of God or of God's Spirit, you would listen to your superiors. You seem to me to be weary of the corner and the small church to the care of which God has appointed you." By virtue of his authority as rector Jonas desired that Cordatus settle the affair by personal talks with both Melanchthon and Cruciger. Although Cordatus replied indignantly to Jonas' letter that he had not begun this controversy out of hatred and that he would make an appeal to the theological faculty,[22] Jonas manifested a praiseworthy firmness and prevented an open strife over minor differences.

In the same year Jonas was involved personally in a dispute with Jacob Schenk, who had been called as chaplain to Duke Henry's court. Schenk had obtained his doctor's degree in theology at Wittenberg and as one of the younger men in the evangelical churches maintained an aggressive stand in his views and behavior. At the beginning of 1537 he had turned to Jonas, his former teacher, in order to obtain the latter's support with reference to a criticism he had made of the Visitation Articles of 1528. When Jonas did not comply with this request, Jacob Schenk felt slighted and began to act independently of the Wittenberg theologians in his work.[23] In addition to his unwarranted pride and continual efforts to win nobles, councilors, and princes for his own plans, he claimed that it was not necessary to proclaim the law, since it is known to man's reason. It is the preacher's duty, he maintained, to preach the Gospel alone. Luther rebuked Schenk's pride and obstinacy severely and prophesied his fall into heresy.[24] However, because Jonas was made the principal recipient of Schenk's attack, Jonas addressed a letter to the Elector in order to clarify his own position and to alert the Elector against the wiles of the would-be leading reformer. "For although David says of himself and speaks of other God-fearing men in the psalter who have an abundance of spiritual wisdom: 'I have insight above that of old men,' nevertheless, not all young doctors are Davids."[25] Jonas was not able to forget the overbearing behavior of Jacob Schenk so easily, and several years later, in May, 1540, when in the company of Luther, again mentioned how little he thought of Schenk's sermons. Luther's rejoinder was simply: "It is an old resentment. doctor!"[26]

Early in 1538 Jonas had, upon the request of the Princes of Anhalt, gone to Zerbst in order to draft a Church Order for that principality. At Pentecost of the same year the duties at the university demanded that Jonas return to Wittenberg. There he had the opportunity of working harmoniously with Luther for the university and the church at large.[27] The last year and a quarter of Jonas' stay in Wittenberg was mainly taken up by local work. To be sure, he did not remain in Wittenberg during this entire period, but he was not called upon as frequently as in previous years to engage in other tasks.

It seems likely that the oration "Concerning the Study of Theology"[28] was delivered by him at the opening of the winter semester in October, 1539. It is certain that the speech was made sometime in 1539. Its content gives a clear indication of the high importance that was attached to the study of theology at that time. In this brief oration Jonas defines theology as being that area of learning which has to do with the true knowledge of the wisdom and will of God. The basic source of such knowledge is Scripture, which has been received from the patriarchs, prophets, and apostles. These were holy men of God who communicated the content of the Bible, not as they were moved by their own will, but by the Holy Spirit. Through the study of the Scriptures the wisdom and will of God become known to us by faith, so that we might perceive in all creatures in heaven, on earth, and in the sea and in the entire structure of the universe the daily miracles, the divine omnipresence, the greatness of God's works and his manifold wisdom. On account of original sin man cannot believe all this. For that reason God has given mankind the Holy Scriptures so that men might daily grow in the knowledge of God, worship him, and eventually partake of God himself, his life, his glory, and eternal salvation. This is the highest good for which the philosophers and the world's wise men have striven without the use of the Scriptures. This highest good has become accessible to men in general in the Scriptures. "The living and true God himself" is the author of this religion and theology and not Mercury or any other hero or wise man.

"We know therefore that theology is not such a meager knowledge which only serves this mortal life, like the remaining arts, which nevertheless, as long as this life lasts, have their glory; but with that wisdom which comes from above, for the knowledge of which man has from the beginning been created . . . we have been thus endowed." No matter, then, how different the vocations of persons may be, whether they study law, medicine, the art of war, statecraft, or philosophy—if they do not combine therewith the study of true theology, they have fallen away from their divine origin and destiny in life. Amid all the vicissitudes of life it is therefore necessary to find in theology a haven of rest, for human life degenerates into animal-like conduct as soon as theology is no longer the very core and motivating force of living.

"And if we should perhaps inquire about the first student and at the same time doctor of theology, we know it to have been our great parent, Adam who had God himself as teacher, who before the fall was permeated by the Holy Spirit, was a truly illuminated theologian who, with the exception of Christ alone, had no peer in any man. . . ." If Adam had not fallen into sin, all men would by nature be theologians and earth would be a theological school in the midst of paradise, in which the angels would be fellow-students and God himself the teacher. The fall into sin, however, has been responsible for the misery and ruin that have come upon mankind. This original sin of Adam has been subsequently inherited by all men in the world, and only by virtue of the sacrifice on the cross are we enabled to pass from death to life, out of sin and darkness into the heavenly kingdom.

Jonas admonishes the young students, as they "enter upon their academic career, whether it be that of the fine arts, or law, . . . that they hold the study of the sacred Scriptures and of theology (without which no man can attain to the end for which he has been created) in highest honor." At the same time those who, like Jonas, have been called to teach the Gospel must discharge their responsibilities in the fear of God. They must give sincere thanks to God that he has delivered them from the blindness of Epicureans, hypocrites, and proud Pharisees; for no pleasure on earth can take the place of the true knowledge of God. "I truly exhort all pious souls, especially the youth, . . . that the dignity of culture and religion be upheld, that from the first they may accustom themselves to a reverence and a love for religion." For that reason profane voices are to be silenced. Derision and cynicism are to be avoided, since there is enough labor and struggle involved in training youth "so that they may retain their love for religion."[29]

FOOTNOTES FOR CHAPTER 3

1. Kawerau, *op. cit.*, Vol. I, pp. 90 and 101.
2. Kawerau, *op. cit.*, Vol. I, p. 63.
3. Kawerau, *op. cit.*, Vol. I, pp. 92-93.
4. Kawerau, *op. cit.*, Vol. I, pp. 109-110.
5. P. Smith, *Luther's Correspondence*, Vol. II, p. 416.
6. *Luthers Werke*, Weimar Edition, Vol. XXVIII, p. 50.
7. Kawerau, *op. cit.*, Vol. II, p. 68.
8. *Works of Martin Luther*, Philadelphia Edition, Vol. II, p. 148.
9. *Corpus Reformatorum, op. cit.*, Vol. I, pp. 390 ff.
10. M. L. de Wette, *Dr. Martin Luthers Briefe, Sendschreiben und Bedenken*, Vol. II, pp. 17-20.
11. Kawerau, *op. cit.*, Vol. I, pp. 63-67.
12. *Ibid.*, pp. 72-74.
13. *Ibid.*, pp. 74-75.
14. Hermann Barge, *Andreas Bodenstein von Karlstadt*, Vol. I, pp. 313 ff. *Corpus Reformatorum*, Vol. I, pp. 465-470.
15. Hermann Barge, *op cit.*, Vol. I, p. 357.
16. Actually Carlstadt did not marry until January 19, 1522. His engagement took place on December 26, 1521, and this is what Jonas was reporting. Hermann Barge, *op. cit.*, Vol. I, pp. 364-365.
17. Kawerau, *op. cit.*, Vol. I, p. 83.
18. *Corpus Reformatorum*, Vol. I, pp. 628-638.
19. *Luthers Werke*, W. A. Briefe, Vol. III, p. 173.
20. Kawerau assumes that the address may have been written by Melanchthon and delivered by Jonas, since it was printed subsequently with Melanchthon's declamations. But there is no real reason for assuming this, since Jonas as a trained Humanist was quite capable of composing an address in polished Latin. Kawerau, *op. cit.*, Vol. II, pp. xvi-xvii.
21. Koestlin, *Martin Luther. Sein Leben und seine Schriften*, Vol. II, p. 288.
22. *Corpus Reformatorum*, Vol. III, pp. 348-351.
23. Paul Vetter, "Ein ungedruckter Brief des Justus Jonas aus dem Jahre 1537," *Archiv für Reformationsgeschichte*. Edited by Walter Friedensburg. Vol. VIII (1909-1910), pp. 121-134.
24. *Tischreden*, Weimar Edition, Vol. IV, pp. 69-70.
25. Vetter, *op. cit.*, p. 133.
26. *Tischreden*, Weimar Edition, Vol. IV, p. 568.
27. Kawerau, *op. cit.*, Vol. I, pp. 296-307.
28. Philip Melanchthon, "Oratio Iusti Ionae Doctoris Theologia, De Studiis Theologicis," *Selectarum Declamationum*, Vol. I, pp. 15-30.
29. Melanchthon, *op. cit.*, Vol. I, pp. 15-30.

Chapter 4

Architect of the Church

With laudable consistency Justus Jonas exhibited a deep concern for peace and concord within the ranks of Protestantism. His role as mediator in disputes of various kinds makes it possible to designate him as a kind of pioneer ecumenist of the Reformation era. That the results of his efforts in this direction were not crowned with notable success does not nullify his praiseworthy labors on behalf of true unity in the faith.

The Sacramentarians

Jonas' ecumenical outlook manifested itself in the controversy with left-wing Reformers like Carlstadt and Zwingli over the doctrine of the Lord's Supper. While he was at Wittenberg, Carlstadt had propounded his symbolic view on the Sacrament. Zwingli, the Swiss Reformer, and the South German theologians also held to a symbolic interpretation of Holy Communion. They believed that the bread and the wine in the Sacrament merely signified or symbolized the body and the blood of our Lord. Christ's body, they argued, could not be present in the Lord's Supper because it is "at the right hand of God." This view differed markedly from Luther's teaching of the Real Presence. After Jonas and Melanchthon had studied the writings of Chrysostom with special reference to this doctrine, they came to the conclusion that Zwingli and his followers were quoting only that which suited them.[1]

At first Bugenhagen, town pastor at Wittenberg and a colleague at the university, defended Luther's point of view by engaging in a dispute with Oecolampadius and the Strassburg theologians. Luther and Zwingli refrained from attacking each other openly until 1527. However, in the years 1527 and 1528 they defended their respective teachings in a number of polemical treatises. Martin Butzer, the Strassburg theologian who inclined toward Zwingli's view in this dispute, was deeply impressed by Luther's *Confession Concerning the Lord's Supper*. It became clear to him from this writing that Luther was not arguing for an outward, physical presence in the Sacrament but a sacramental union of bread and wine with the glorified body and blood of Christ. In the light of this fact, Butzer was eager to achieve a doctrinal consensus on the Lord's Supper with the Wittenberg theologians.

From the very beginning of the dispute with the sacramentarians, that is, with those who held extremely subjective views, Jonas was desirous of reaching an agreement on this cardinal teaching of Christianity. When Caspar Schwenkfeld came to Wittenberg toward the end of 1525 in order to come to a common understanding with the theologians there on the interpretation of Jesus' words of institution in the Lord's Supper, Jonas proved to be ready to discuss matters with him. Schwenkfeld made special mention afterwards of the warmth and cordiality that had characterized his conversation with Jonas. He reported that Jonas had claimed that Luther's opinion was not at all definitive for him in matters of faith, since everyone must be sure of his own belief. Nevertheless, Jonas had taken Schwenkfeld to task for calling Luther a "stubborn" person.[2] But in spite of all attempts, in this instance no agreement was reached.

The year 1526 found Jonas bending his efforts toward reaching an agreement with the South German theologians, Martin Butzer, Oecolampadius, and others, on the interpretation of the Lord's Supper. In a letter of June 24 Jonas disclosed his personal feelings. "For so grave an offense are these disagreements in the churches of Germany, which have now had such a remarkable revelation of the Gospel, that I believe that through these parties a greater loss may result than anyone now believes." Jonas informed Butzer that he had carefully studied Zwingli's and Oecolampadius' writings on the Eucharist; he found their opinions good and plausible; but he felt that they had forsaken the sure foundation by departing from the simplicity of the scriptural word. Asserting that there was to be no respect of persons in the settlement of this vital issue, Jonas in his desire for unity wrote: "I would not even be unwilling to risk all my possessions and myself in order that a genuine peace might come about." To effect a better understanding on the Sacrament, Jonas translated into German Luther's Latin writing to the Waldensians which advocated the position of the Wittenberg theologians.[3]

Through the efforts of Landgrave Philip of Hesse, a Colloquy at Marburg between the Wittenberg theologians and the Swiss and South German theologians had been arranged. Philip of Hesse, with statesmanlike vision, saw the necessity of presenting a united political front against the Catholic princes. At the same time Philip possessed a keen interest in theological matters. Zwingli welcomed the Colloquy for political and religious reasons, while Luther, opposing alliances of a political nature for religious reasons, did not believe that force should be used in matters of faith and was for this reason not particularly enthusiastic about the proposed plan. Nevertheless, he agreed to participate.

The Colloquy began on October 2, 1529, and ended October 4, without achieving its intended goal. The only accomplishment of consequence was the formulation of the Marburg Articles, a confession in which a consensus with regard to fourteen articles was established. The one article on the Sacrament of the Altar showed that there was unanimity in accepting the doctrine of communing "under both kinds" and the words of institution to be used. The dissent concerned the belief as to whether or not the true body and blood of Christ were present in the Sacrament.

Jonas had participated in the Colloquy with Melanchthon, Cruciger,

Myconius, Menius, and Osiander against Zwingli, Oecolampadius, Butzer, Hedio, and Jacob Sturm. Jonas' acute observations have been preserved in a letter to William Reifenstein, who was a member of a converted Jewish family of Koenigstein and a friend of Luther. "Before the Prince, with all the councilors sitting around, was placed a table at which sat these four—Luther, Philip, Zwingli, and Oecolampadius. When the Colloquy began and arguments were advanced on both sides, Oecolampadius urged this argument for almost two whole days: 'Christ has a true body and is in heaven, but no true body can be in many places.' . . . Luther would not permit Christ's words about the Supper to be distorted, by force or craft, from the clear words of him who said, 'This is my body' and the words of Paul, 'This I received from the Lord.' This offended our opponents and almost in disgust they cried out that it was a *petitio principii.*"

Jonas related what persistent efforts were made by the Landgrave of Hesse and his councilors to seek some way of compromise; "but," he added in a discouraged tone, "the matter will not be patched up on anybody's account, and there will be no agreement."

Although his characterization of the opponents in this dispute was in this case decidedly subjective, it is nevertheless of interest and value. "Zwingli," Jonas thought, "is somewhat boorish and presumptuous; Oecolampadius is a man of wonderful gentleness of spirit and kindliness; Hedio is no less suave and broad-minded; Butzer has the craftiness of a fox, making a perverse pretense of wisdom and keenness." Yet Jonas significantly added to this somewhat unfavorable description of the prominent opponents "They are all scholars, of that there is no doubt; the papists are no opponents at all compared with them."[4] Jonas ended his letter by stating that Butzer and he had a long private conference and came to an agreement on almost all the chief articles of the faith. But the exception here too was the doctrine of the Lord's Supper. Later, in a letter to Agricola on October 12, 1529, Jonas expressed his belief that Melanchthon and Luther had treated the essential matters in regard to the Lord's Supper thoroughly "so that hardly anything remains which could be written concerning this affair."[5] In the opinion of Jonas, who had eagerly sought and worked for a complete consensus within the evangelical churches of Germany and Switzerland in matters of faith, the Marburg Colloquy had heightened the partition-wall that so tragically separated Wittenberg and Zurich.

Several years later two Augsburg ministers, John Frosch and Stephen Agricola, sought Jonas' advice in regard to Butzer's and Oecolampadius' doctrinal position on the Lord's Supper. Jonas felt constrained to answer their inquiry. "I am unable," he told them, "to answer your last letters satisfactorily on account of other duties, but still we do not want to leave you without comfort in the meantime in this important and valiant affair regarding the Sacrament." Butzer, Jonas conceded, had come to an interpretation of the Lord's Supper which was substantially in accord with the view held by the Wittenberg theologians. But he cautioned them against any premature conclusion in this matter. "If Christ desires to prosper this affair, he will indeed do it; he will turn the hearts and the will of teachers and hearers so that they will freely, courageously, and simply confess the truth in the open." Therefore Jonas encouraged them to pray that Christ might bring the desired unity to its completion. They were, however, not to act without Luther's counsel, or else wait until a public agreement had come about. Jonas finally cautioned them: "But if anyone desires to force you into a confused and dark agreement, then act wisely; Christ will prompt you as to what is to be done in such an event. He who is the supreme wisdom will deceive no one nor lie."[6]

The Wittenberg Concord

In 1536, while temporarily filling a vacancy in the Church at Naumburg, Jonas was called back to Wittenberg. His return was necessitated by the negotiations for an agreement between the theologians of Southern Germany, Butzer, Hedio, Capito, and others, and the Wittenberg theologians. The crucial doctrinal matter concerned the Real Presence in the Lord's Supper. As early as July, 1535, Jonas had written to the pastors of Augsburg and had intimated that an eventual agreement between them and the theologians of Southern Germany would in all likelihood take place. While he regretted that Butzer himself had not taken the initiative in furthering unanimity in doctrine more energetically, his hopeful outlook was to be fully justified in the future.

From May 22 to May 29, 1536, Wittenberg was the scene of a constant exchange of views between the various theologians represented there. Jonas was present at the beginning of these sessions, but on May 25 he left for Naumburg again. On May 29, Melanchthon informed Jonas by letter of the final ratification and signing of the document which signified a complete agreement on the part of all German Protestants and which came to be known as the Wittenberg Concord. Jonas later added his signature to the agreement. Addressing a letter to Butzer some two years later, he recalled what an important achievement the Wittenberg Concord was for the further progress of the Reformation. "We shall pray the Lord," he wrote, "that the agreement which was acted on over two years ago may be continually confirmed and widely propagated there, since in these difficult times (so furiously do the adversaries rage against the truth of the Gospel) in no other matter is anything more needful for us than sincere and constant harmony of doctrine."[7]

The Diet of Augsburg

Charles V, who had made peace with the Pope at Barcelona and with Francis I of France at Cambrai, had been crowned by the Pope in Bologna. He was now in a position to settle the religious problem in Germany. For the first time since the Diet of Worms the Emperor's hands were free so that he could go to Germany in order that he might preside personally at the Diet of Augsburg. The invitation sent out by him to the princes and estates had a friendly and irenic tone. He desired that "everyone's view, opinion, and mind be heard." Encouraged by this intended purpose of the Emperor, the Elector wrote to Luther, Melanchthon, Bugenhagen, and Jonas on March 14, 1530, and asked them to meet at Torgau to formulate articles that would set forth the disagreement in faith and practice with the Romanists. On the same day Luther informed Jonas about the Electoral request, and Jonas had to halt the work of the visitation in which he was engaged. Between March 14 and 20 the Torgau Articles were formulated by the evangelical theologians of Wittenberg. It has so far been impossible to determine what sections Jonas may have written in this composite work of the theologians. It seems likely that he was the author of some sections. The second part of the Augsburg Confession later written by Melanchthon was based on these Articles.

On March 21 the Elector dispatched a request to the Wittenberg theologians, Luther, Melanchthon, Bugenhagen, and Jonas, to come back to Torgau, because he believed that they were the persons best suited to present the evanglical cause before the Diet and the Emperor. On April 9 Jonas could report by letter to his friend John Lange in Erfurt, that Luther, Melanchthon, and he had left Wittenberg on the third of April to attend the Diet. "Bishop Bugenhagen was left at home in order that there might be someone who could look after the university and care for the church. The Emperor Charles V has now been crowned by the Pope at Bologna and will himself come to Augsburg. . . . A messenger has come to the Prince from Nuremberg, and says that the Emperor has already entered Trent on his way to Germany, and trustworthy men write that he is now certain to come to Augsburg."[8] Jonas went on to tell his friend that the Diet would discuss matters of greatest importance and that "no human wisdom can control or prosper them." He believed that the present situation imperiously called for prayers to God so that he might "captain and pilot our ship in this stormy sea." Jonas was confident that the Lord would hear the prayers of the pious and therefore commended the momentous affair to the prayers of Lange's church.

En route to the Diet, Spalatin, John Agricola, and Caspar Agricola joined the Elector and his accompanying theologians. Luther had to remain behind at the Fortress Coburg because he was still under imperial ban and for that reason could not safely enter Augsburg.

The remaining theologians entered Augsburg with the Elector on May 2. Jonas' contribution to the Protestant cause at the Diet of Augsburg was significant. During this time he kept in close touch with Luther by letter, and represented the evangelical point of view with indefatigable constancy when Melanchthon was inclined to waver.

On May 4 Jonas wrote to Luther's wife, Catherine, advising her of their safe arrival in Augsburg and Luther's stay at Coburg. On the same day he wrote to Luther, informing him that they had reached the city. There was amazement in Augsburg over the early arrival of the Elector, but Jonas thought this to be advantageous to their cause. He prayed devoutly and daily for the Diet and the evangelical cause and expressed the hope that he would soon see Luther personally.

Before Charles V came to Augsburg for the Diet, the Elector John had sent him a copy of the Schwabach Articles, a document setting forth the basic beliefs of the evangelical churches. It had been prepared in the summer of 1529 by some of the Wittenberg theologians, court lawyers, and princes. The Elector did not know that Charles V had previously obtained and read a poor Latin translation of these same Articles. Displeased with them, the Emperor asked the papal legate Campegio for advice in this matter. The latter counseled Charles to "exterminate these stiff-necked heretics with fire and sword."[9]

When the Emperor finally arrived for the Diet on June 15, Jonas eagerly transmitted the news to Luther and described his entry into the city of Augsburg. He related that Melanchthon was in a despairing mood and therefore in need of intercession on the part of Luther. With joyful satisfaction Jonas noted that neither the Elector, nor his son, nor Philip of Hesse, nor the Duke of Lueneburg had taken part in the Corpus Christi procession. In the face of the obvious threats of the Romanist party, Jonas could clearly discern that the prayers of the evangelical church were proving effectual.

However, it soon became clear to the Protestant princes and theologians that the Emperor was not at all disposed to accept their proposals for reform. Campegio, the papal legate, demanded rigorous suppression of the evanglical cause. Eck, the archfoe of Luther, published a pamphlet that listed more than four hundred heretical statements which had been made by the Protestants. So agreement in matters of faith was doomed to failure. To Melanchthon fell the task of writing a confession of faith that would adequately express the convictions of the evangelical princes and estates. In this undertaking the great scholar succeeded admirably because he was able to express clearly the basic teachings of the evangelical churches and to show convincingly that doctrinally they were in agreement with the true faith of the one, holy, catholic church throughout the centuries. His effort resulted in what became known as the Augsburg Confession of the Evangelical Lutheran Church.

The Grand Confession

On June 25, 1530, Jonas was privileged to witness the forceful reading of the Augsburg Confession in German by Chancellor Baier of Saxony before the Emperor and other notables in the Chapter Room of the Episcopal Palace. After the reading the Chancellor handed the copy together with a Latin duplicate to the Emperor. It had been signed by the Elector of Saxony and his son John Frederick, by George, Margrave of Brandenburg, the Dukes Ernest and Francis of Lueneburg, the Landgrave of Hesse, Prince Wolfgang of Anhalt, and the delegates of the cities of Nuremberg and Reutlingen. Jonas had constantly assisted Melanchthon in the final composition during the weeks that had preceded and had kept the irenic Humanist from making any concessions involving evangelical principles. Besides, while Chancellor Brueck was the author of the German preface to the Confession, Jonas had written the Latin preface.[10]

What a momentous event it was in the eyes of the keenly observant Jonas may be inferred from a letter which he wrote to Luther several days afterwards. Jonas had paid close attention to every movement and to the changing demeanor of the Emperor. He said that he had occasion to observe the countenance of the Emperor more closely than at the Diet of Worms. In Jonas' estimation, mildness, nobility, and innate kindliness were the chief virtues of the Emperor. Jonas urged Luther as "the chariot and horseman of Israel" to weigh everything very carefully, since he was convinced that the events of those days were of utmost importance for generations to come. Jonas also reported wistfully that Melanchthon was still ready to concede too much in his intense desire for peace and that he himself had had a disagreement with him concerning the jurisdiction of the bishops. "Here you should give counsel," urged Jonas, "lest all of posterity suffer therefrom and our consciences be burdened." The result was that Luther, aware of what the tragic consequences of concessions on vital points would be, wrote a letter to Melanchthon. It inspired comfort and courage when the latter's faith was wavering. "In private sorrows I am weaker," wrote Luther, "but you more courageous; contrariwise, in public matters you are what I am in private ones, and I in public ones as you are in private ones (if the private affair which is carried on between me and Satan must be spoken of)." With courageous faith Luther ventured to make the assertion that if they should fall, Christ, who was the true ruler of the world, would fall with them. Consequently, Luther desired rather to fall with Christ than to stand with Caesar.[11]

Jonas was soon convinced by what he heard and saw at Augsburg that the papal party was unwilling to be reformed according to the Word of God. "The Bishop of Salzburg was to have made this statement in a private interview: 'I wish,' he said, 'both kinds, that marriage be allowed, I wish the Mass to be reformed, I wish that there be freedom in eating and other traditions, and that the entire body take this stand; but that one corner ought to reform us all, that is a disturbance of peace, that is not to be tolerated.' "[12] Erasmus, when consulted regarding the most important articles of the Confession, answered, as Jonas reported, in true "Erasmian fashion." "To the Emperor he wrote that the cause is great, but not to be hastened. If a reformation ought to take place, it ought to begin at the head, the Roman pontiff."[13]

The encouraging note for Jonas was the noble and steadfast faith demonstrated by the Protestant princes. Especially did he observe the cheerful and upright spirit of the Elector John, who said to Dr. Cruciger on one occasion: "I desire that my learned subjects should not worry or concern themselves about me. Rather let us do what is right according to God's Word. I know the Lord our God will surely help us."[14] In view of this loyalty to the Word of God on the part of the princes, Jonas and three other prominent preachers and teachers of the Lutheran Reformation—namely, John Rurer, the cathedral preacher of the Markgrave of Brandenburg; Erhard Schnepf, the chaplain of Philip of Hesse; and Henry Bock, who had probably accompanied Duke Ernest of Lueneburg—transmitted to the evangelical princes a writing which called upon them to make their religious convictions clear to the Emperor. If means and ways were to be found to effect an agreement, it would be well, said the document, to point to those articles "which a Christian could in no sense abandon without the surrender of principle."[15]

Luther was especially pleased with the strong faith of the Elector and Jonas' unwavering position. "Philip is being molested by his philosophy, and nothing else; for the matter is in the hand of him who dares to say most confidently: 'No one shall pluck them out of my hand.' "[16] Luther was well aware that the papal party would oppose the demands made by the evangelical princes and theologians. For him it was a matter of staunchly confessing and standing by the belief in God's revelation in Christ Jesus. "First, and most important of all," he wrote to Jonas, July 9, 1530, "Christ has been publicly proclaimed through our glorious Confession, so that the great ones of the earth cannot boast that we have fled and were afraid to confess our faith. Only I grudge you the privilege of being present at the reading of this grand Confession."[17] A theological Opinion was drafted by Jonas, Agricola, and Melanchthon on the following day.[18] It was deemed inadvisable that any more articles of faith should be presented to the Emperor, because the opposing party would first have to reply to their statement of faith. They themselves had stated their position most moderately. Several days later Jonas was cautioned by Luther "not to be timid." The Emperor himself was reeling to and fro. "Do not hope for concord or concession, and I also have never prayed otherwise to God, since I know that it is impossible, but pray only that they might permit you to teach, and that they might grant peace," was Luther's advice to Jonas, Spalatin, Melanchthon, and Agricola.[19]

In the same month Jonas took a leading role in drafting another theological Consideration in regard to the abolition of the mass. Jonas denounced the private mass as the source of much error and abuse. The Lord's Supper had been instituted, he claimed, in order to bring comfort to terrified consciences and to exercise and strengthen a Christian's faith. The papal celebrants of the mass knew nothing of this practice; they looked upon the sacrifice of the mass as a good work, which the followers of Luther could not endure with a clear conscience. Moreover, the primitive church knew nothing about a mass without communicants, and so the abuse must have crept into the church at a later date. This abuse of the mass, in Jonas' estimation, consisted in the blasphemous claim of performing a sacrifice for the living and the dead.[20]

After the public reading of the Augsburg Confession, Charles V had ordered the Roman theologians to prepare a confutation of the Confession. The papal legate Campegio drafted about twenty papal theologians for this task. Among these were Eck, Faber, and Cochlaeus, who were the most implacable foes of the Reformation. The reading of this confutation of the papists took place on August 3 and lasted a full two hours. The Emperor, after hearing it read, declared the Augsburg Confession refuted. Jonas reported these facts to Luther several days later. The fate of the Lutheran churches still hung in the balance and Jonas implored Luther to pray without ceasing for their cause. "For we behold and with our hands almost touch the fruit and effect of your prayer and the presence of your spirit."[21]

The continual efforts to bring about a compromise and an agreement never met with the approval of Jonas, for he believed that a surrender of the evangelical principle was surreptitiously being attempted. In a disappointed frame of mind he prepared to leave Augsburg on September 13, after he had drawn up his "Opinion Concerning the Conditions of Making Peace."[22] In this writing he stipulated seven conditions necessary for an understanding between the Romanists and the Lutherans, and without hesitating or wavering in his convictions, he firmly advocated the specific scriptural beliefs and practices as set forth in the Augsburg Confession. Luther later commended Jonas for his exemplary stand in those critical days when a Melanchthon compromise was a very real threat to the young evangelical church of Germany.[23] On September 30, 1530, Jonas wrote to his friend, Abbot Frederick of Nuremberg, reporting his arrival at Forchheim as well as mentioning how hostile the Catholic theologians and rulers were toward the evangelical churches.[24]

Proposed Alliances

The Diet of Augsburg made it clear that neither the Emperor nor the Pope was going to relax his opposition against the Lutheran Reformation. Yet there were hopeful signs of alliances with other countries of Europe looming on the horizon, giving promise of a more extensive spread of the Reformation that Luther had begun. As early as 1533 King Francis I had sought to negotiate with the Wittenberg theologians. In August 1535 he invited Butzer and Melanchthon to come to his court to discuss certain reform measures in the church. Melanchthon, who had at first been reluctant about this project, became eager to go there, but the Elector refused him permission to undertake the journey. Jonas, who had looked very favorably upon the plan,[25] was as much disappointed over the Elector's refusal as Melanchthon. Later, however, in a manner similar to Luther, Jonas expressed his misgivings about the projected plans of the French king.

Robert Barnes, who had come to Wittenberg in the summer of 1531, subsequently returned to England where Henry VIII appointed him as his chaplain. In March of 1535 Barnes came back to Wittenberg in the name of his king. He discussed certain doctrinal points with Melanchthon and was successful in getting the latter to write to the English king. In July the Elector issued instructions to

Luther, Bugenhagen, Jonas, Melanchthon, and Cruciger about the reception of an official delegation sent by Henry VIII. But in the summer of 1535 a plague broke out in Wittenberg. Melanchthon and the students of the university transferred to Jena, so that the lectures might be continued there. Jonas and his family also left Wittenberg to stay with relatives of his wife in the small village of Schlieben for a time.

Toward the end of September the English delegation came to the Elector's court, and Melanchthon reported on the favorable reception accorded its members by John Frederick. Edward Fox, Bishop of Hereford, and Nicholas Heath, Archdeacon of Stafford, arrived soon after. At the end of December, after both Jonas and Melanchthon had returned to Wittenberg, a series of conferences between Luther, Melanchthon, Bugenhagen, Jonas, and Cruciger and the English delegation took place. Two obstacles barred an understanding with the English delegation. One was doctrinal and concerned private masses and the doctrine of justification by faith; the other was practical and had to do with the celibacy of the clergy and Henry VIII's action in putting away his first wife, Catherine of Aragon. The emissaries of the king probably advised Luther and the other Wittenberg theologians that Thomas Cromwell, the king's minister, was their best friend in London. This he was, although he too, like the king was chiefly motivated by the political advantages of an agreement with the German princes. In response to these negotiations, Luther wrote a letter to Cromwell on April 9, 1536.[26] A day later the English delegation left Wittenberg without accomplishing any noteworthy agreement. On April 13 Jonas also wrote to Cromwell in the hope of being able to further some form of collaboration with the English.[27] Jonas expressed the hope that some working agreement between the King of England and the German princes might eventuate. In such a case the intolerable tyranny of the Roman pontiff could be resisted and the Gospel could be openly proclaimed. Jonas believed that an agreement on the principal articles of doctrine might be brought about and that in this way a basis for a political treaty might be laid. The letter is an indication of Jonas' desire to fortify and extend the Reformation in Europe.

The ultimate failure to achieve a consensus in doctrinal and practical matters was indeed a disappointment for Jonas, who by his Latin translations of Luther's writings had sought to win adherents to the Reformation throughout Europe. Until 1539 the theologians of Wittenberg still nurtured the fond hope that some approximation of doctrinal unity might be achieved. In October of that year the four leading men in Wittenberg, Luther, Bugenhagen, Melanchthon, and Jonas, sent an Opinion to the Elector which clearly stated that further negotiations would be fruitless.[28]

The Schmalcald Convention

In 1539 the Frankfurt Armistice gave the promise of peace to the Protestants of Germany until negotiations concerning the religious controversy could be settled at an imperial diet. Meanwhile the Emperor was still in a precarious political situation because large sections of Germany had become Protestant and the Archbishops of Mainz, Trier, and Cologne were threatening to secularize their territories and become Protestants. The Emperor therefore tried to effect a compromise with the Protestants by inaugurating a series of religious conferences. By the end of 1539 the Elector John Frederick requested an Opinion from Luther, Jonas, Bugenhagen, Cruciger, and Melanchthon, with reference to such conferences. He stated that the ratification of the Frankfurt Armistice still depended on the Emperor's attitude and that they were therefore to prepare for the defense of the Augsburg Confession by sending theologians to the Schmalcald Convention. The Wittenberg theologians replied that a compromise with the Roman Catholic opponents could take place only in unessential matters. As far as the theologians were concerned, the teachings of the Gospel were clear, and they should be permitted to proclaim them unmolested. They agreed to submit an Opinion to the Elector on this question and to send representatives to the Schmalcald Convention. The Opinion was sent to the Elector eleven days later and, while lamenting the sinfulness of schisms and divisions, firmly upheld the doctrines of the evangelical Lutheran Church which, if accepted by the Romanists, could alone become the basis of an agreement.[29]

Jonas, Melanchthon, Cruciger, and Bugenhagen accompanied the Elector to the Schmalcald Convention in March, 1540. After the imperial legates had arrived, the outlook for some mutual understanding seemed promising. The papal legate, de Farneso, only twenty years old, arrived on the scene during the middle of the month. Jonas was surprised that the Pope had sent such a youthful person to deliberations of such a grave and important nature. In the midst of all discussions Jonas did not for a moment waver in his evangelical convictions. "Though we may be in an extremely dejected spirit," he wrote to Prince George of Anhalt when negotiations were beginning to break down, "we confidently say with Christ: We do not have a devil, nor are we heretics, but honor God, our Father, but you unjustly condemn Christ and us."[30] Luther exhorted his colleagues from Wittenberg by letter to put their trust in God and pray. "It is God who in the midst of death makes alive, and in the midst of his wrath has compassion, in the midst of a tumult laughs; so also in the midst of a denial of prayers he will grant the desired prayers, even as all his works are divine and marvellous and incomprehensible, for whom they exist and do not exist, happen and vanish away, stand and fall, and all things are as nothing for him, to whom alone be glory, because he is the only God, the only Maker, the sole Governor of all things."[31] At this same Convention Jonas, Bugenhagen, and others signed a declaration which condemned the teachings of Schwenkfeld, Sebastian Frank, and other enthusiasts who could not be regarded as followers of the evangelical doctrine.[32]

In April Jonas and the other theologians returned to Wittenberg. The tangible result of the Schmalcald Convention was that the Emperor believed that a series of conferences between the two opposing church parties could aid in working out some kind of a compromise. The political situation also seemed to compel the Emperor to take such a course.

Attempts at Compromise

In June, 1540, the first conference at Hagenau took place. These negotiations, however, resulted in a stalemate and the conference was dismissed. While this conference was in progress, the rumor of the Landgrave Philip of Hesse's bigamy reached Jonas. Jonas had been called upon by Duke Henry to assist in the visitation work that was being done in Meissen. "In Meissen," wrote Jonas to his friend, Prince George of Anhalt, in June, 1540, "there is a strong rumor—I know not by whom it has been brought forth—that the illustrious Landgrave (may God avert it) had entered a second marriage. . . . Oh, monstrous scandal." Jonas was very much upset by this recurring rumor. "If the Landgrave has truly been brought low by so sudden a fall, God will nevertheless preserve the doctrine of Christ and will turn the joy of the adversaries into sadness," he wrote several days later to another friend.[33] Jonas realized full well what a grievous blow this bigamous marriage was to the Protestant cause at that crucial hour; but his faith in the cause did not falter.

In November, 1540, the second religious conference at Worms took place. Besides the two Wittenberg theologians, Melanchthon and Cruciger, Calvin and Butzer were there to represent the Protestant cause. Melanchthon and Cruciger kept Jonas informed on the matters discussed and the progress that was made during the months of November, December, and January. The preponderant evangelical majority caused the papal legate, Granvella, ultimately to break off negotiations, and the conference, like the previous one, proved to be a failure. Jonas was very much dissatisfied with the papal attitude, for soon after the conference at Worms had been adjourned, another conference was planned at Regensburg. Jonas had now lost faith in these conferences because he believed that the subtle papal machinations would hinder any workable agreement that was based on the truth of the Gospel. "But on this account our Lord God will not retract his edict and decree, since he says through Isaiah: 'My counsel will stand. My will will be done.' We clearly see that the affairs of God, surpassing the thoughts of all men, are being directed and governed from heaven." And after Melanchthon and Cruciger had returned to Wittenberg and given the details of the debates at the conference at Worms, Jonas was fully persuaded that the conclusions he had drawn were completely justified. He sent an absorbingly interesting account of Melanchthon's debate with Eck at Worms to the Princes of Anhalt and triumphantly recorded the indisputable victory of the Protestants as far as the defense of their faith was concerned. When, therefore, Melanchthon and Cruciger left for the conference at Regensburg in March, 1541, Jonas was under no illusions as to the possibility of an eventual compromise or agreement with the Romanist theologians. "In the entire rule of the Pope," he wrote to his friend Lange, "there is nothing sound."[34] The reports which he received from Melanchthon and Cruciger at Regensburg and the final outcome of the conference substantiated Jonas' gloomy forebodings.[35]

FOOTNOTES FOR CHAPTER 4

1. Kawerau, *op. cit.*, Vol. I, pp. 97 ff.
2. Kawerau, *op. cit.*, Vol. II, Introduction, p. xxxiv.
3. Kawerau, *op. cit.*, Vol. I, pp. 99-103.
4. P. Smith, *op. cit.*, Vol. II, pp. 497-499.
5. Kawerau, *op. cit.*, Vol. I, p. 129.
6. *Ibid.*, pp. 181-183.
7. *Ibid.*, pp. 280-281.
8. *Ibid.*, pp. 145-146.
   P. Smith, *op. cit.*, pp. 526-527.
9. E. G. Schwiebert, *Luther and His Times*, pp. 700 and 721.
10. K. C. L. Franke, *Geschichte der Hallischen Reformation*, p. 261.
11. *Corpus Reformatorum*, Vol. II, pp. 153-157.
    Enders, *op. cit.*, Vol. VIII, p. 51.
12. *Ibid.*, p. 67.
13. G. Berbig, Editor, "Acta comiciorum Augustae ex litteris Philippi, Jonae et aliorum ad M. L.", *Quellen und Darstellungen aus der Geschichte des Reformationsjahrhunderts*, Vol. II, p. 29.
14. *Ibid.*, p. 20.
15. Kawerau, *op. cit.*, Vol. I, p. 166.
16. Enders, *op. cit.*, Vol. VIII, p. 48.
17. Margaret A. Currie, *The Letters of Martin Luther*, p. 232; cf. Enders, *op. cit.*, Vol. VIII, pp. 93-95.
18. *Corpus Reformatorum*, Vol. II, p. 182.
19. Enders, *op. cit.*, Vol. VIII, pp. 102-103 and p. 113.
20. *Corpus Reformatorum*, Vol. II, pp. 306-308.
21. Enders, *op. cit.*, Vol. VIII, pp. 175-178.

22. *Corpus Reformatorum*, Vol. II, pp. 368-371.
23. Enders, *op. cit.*, Vol. VIII, pp. 266-268.
24. Kawerau, *op. cit.*, Vol. I, p. 178.
25. Kawerau, *op. cit.*, Vol. I, p. 225.
26. Enders, *op. cit.*, Vol. X, pp. 324-325.
27. Preserved Smith, "Notes from English Libraries. I. An unpublished letter of Justus Jonas," *Zeitschrift für Kirchengeschichte.* Edited by Theodor Brieger and Bernhard Bess. Vol. XXXII (1911), pp. 111-114.
28. *Corpus Reformatorum*, Vol. II, pp. 796-800.
29. Enders, *op. cit.*, Vol. XII, pp. 351-371.
30. Kawerau, *op. cit.*, Vol. I, p. 390.
31. Enders, *op. cit.*, Vol. XIII, p. 17.
32. *Corpus Reformatorum*, Vol. III, pp. 983-986.
33. Kawerau, *op. cit.*, Vol. I, pp. 394 and 397.
34. Kawerau, *op. cit.*, Vol. I, pp. 421-426.
35. *Corpus Reformatorum*, Vol. IV, pp. 140-142; pp. 146-147.

Chapter 5

The Work of Reforming

The year 1525 found Justus Jonas increasingly active in the organizational and administrative work of the Reformation in and around Wittenberg as a collaborator with Luther, Melanchthon, and Bugenhagen. By virtue of his training as a lawyer he was often consulted in matters that involved legal questions, and in that capacity was instrumental in solving many practical problems that arose in the reform period. The idea of church visitations which later came to assume such an important aspect in ordering and organizing the churches of the Reformation in Saxony and other parts of Germany, gradually developed as the result of needed reform. This brought about a form of cooperation between church and state which Luther, in protest against the medieval confusion of the two realms, desired to avoid. This step was necessitated, however, by the fact that the ruling bishops were in most cases hostile to the Reformation. Nicholas Haussmann had been commissioned to investigate church conditions and to make a detailed report to the Elector on existing evils and certain proposals for their reform. This he did in May, 1525. Realizing that something had to be done, Luther proposed a church and school visitation to the Elector John in November, 1526. In addition, the university strongly urged the fast execution of such a plan. Jonas had been given a twofold task in this important program of making the Reformation effective. He was called upon to work out a plan of visitation and was chosen along with Luther, Bugenhagen, and several others from the ranks of the knights and citizenry to carry out the instructions of the Elector. From October 22, 1528, till Easter, 1529, Jonas was sporadically engaged in the elimination of the most obvious abuses in the churches of Electoral Saxony.[1]

Jonas' excellent qualifications for this task, involving legal entanglements with regard to marriages and property, were soon recognized, and Hans von Metzsch did not hesitate, in a writing of February 8, 1529, to suggest to the Elector John that Jonas should head another visitation.[2] Later when Luther was released from his duties as a commissioner of the visitation, Jonas assumed the leading role. In every parish the visitors recommended ministers who had thorough training as theologians and were capable of carrying out their duties. Throughout this visitation Jonas conscientiously discharged his duties as a member of the visitation commission; yet he never acted on his own authority but always in consultation with the other members of the commission and with their consent. Thus he felt obliged in 1530 to put off a decision when the senate of Colditz asked for specific help and counsel because the other visitors were not present with him at the time. He recognized his responsibility to God in this work of visiting the churches. In a report, justifying the procedure of the visitation in one instance, he wrote to the Electoral Chancellor Baier: "But this is not our affair, it is God's affair. He sees the hearts of men and will judge them righteously."[3]

The work connected with the visitation of churches did not come to an abrupt end, for Jonas was called upon time and again to rectify some local situation. In 1531 Jonas and Pauli, as members of the commission, sent instructions to the senate at Leisnig, requesting that the overdue salary of the pastor, Wolfgang Fues, be paid.[4] In 1532 arrangements were made by the members of the visitation commission to have Ambrosius Naumann become deacon in Leisnig, and the senate there was asked to retain its present deacon, Paceus, until he could be placed elsewhere. It is of interest in this connection that although the visitors were actually appointed only for a given period of time during which the visitation was supposed to take place, they retained their authority over the congregations and acted as a kind of unofficial consistory in the church.[5]

In May, 1532, Jonas' name, together with the names of Luther, Bugenhagen, Cruciger, and Melanchthon, was affixed to a document which laid down certain basic principles to be observed in any future religious peace. It maintained that any religious settlement was to grant free course to the Word of God. No supreme court could legally proceed against church doctrine, since such a court would be concerned with secular matters and should not be allowed to interfere with the doctrine and conduct of the church's own affairs.[6]

The Second Visitation

Meanwhile the Reformation was continuing to strengthen its hold. In August of 1532 the Elector John sent a communication to Luther, Jonas, Melanchthon, and Pauli of Wittenberg which requested that because of the sad state of the ministry, they should send him a written Opinion, stating the time and personnel suited for a second visitation. The Elector died before the plan of this second visitation was carried out.

John Frederick, the new Elector, who saw the necessity of continuing the visitation program inaugurated by his father at the close of 1532, had an instruction for a second visitation issued. Jonas was made a member of two commissions in this instruction,[7] but subsequently changes in these appointments were made, so that only the visitation of the province of Saxony was placed under Jonas' leadership. He was to be assisted by John Bugenhagen and six other men.[8] Jonas, in this responsible role, was instrumental in making the visitation effective in its purpose in the particular area assigned to him. The standards of the ministry were raised, the well-being and harmony of church life were promoted, and the moral and educational level of the church members in general was put on a higher plane. The Visitation Articles, drawn up in 1533, also stated that the Augsburg Confession and its Apology should be among the books provided in every parish.[9] In the same year Luther, Jonas, and Bugenhagen made subscription to the Augsburg Confession mandatory for all candidates of theology at the university who desired a public certificate of their qualification as ministers in the church.[10]

Early in 1535 Jonas reported with genuine elation on the successful work of John Bugenhagen in Pomerania. "In the whole duchy the Gospel has been accepted," he wrote enthusiastically, "and the Word of the Lord is spreading there mightily and is being glorified."[11] Even though Jonas was wholly occupied by this visitation program he followed with keen interest the progress of the Reformation in other areas of Germany.

The spread of the Reformation inevitably made increasingly greater demands on its leaders, and among these Jonas ranks as one who gave himself unsparingly and worked indefatigably for its continued success. In the year 1536 Jonas was assigned a task which was to take him into neighboring territory, the city of Naumburg. Naumburg had, through popular support, been able to introduce the Reformation even in the face of opposition on the part of the Catholic Bishop and his chapter. When their evangelical preacher, Gallus, died in 1535, the senate of the city addressed a request for a suitable successor to Brueck, the Chancellor of Electoral Saxony.[12] The Elector in turn wrote to the Wittenberg theologians, Luther, Jonas, Bugenhagen, and Melanchthon, and asked them to suggest a minister for Naumburg. On April 5, 1536, the senate wrote directly to Luther and mentioned the Elector's favorable response to their petition for a minister. Their need was very great, they contended, and they therefore desired that someone be sent them for the ensuing Easter festival.[13] The Wittenberg theologians decided that Jonas and Jerome Weller should go to Naumburg to supply the vacant pulpit temporarily. At the same time they sent the Elector a written recommendation that either Jerome Weller or Michael Coelius be called there as pastor. The Elector John Frederick approved of Michael Coelius as future minister for Naumburg. Meanwhile Jonas and Weller arrived at Naumburg on April 13. Both men preached in the city's cathedral on Good Friday and Easter Sunday. However, Jerome Weller's voice was not forceful enough in the spacious cathedral and he could not be well understood. Moreover, the innumerable demands of the large parish proved too much for him, and he was honorably dismissed by the city's senate.[14] But Jonas continued his labors in Naumburg until April 23, when he was called back to Wittenberg.

Since Jonas had told the senate of Naumburg that the pulpit would be supplied by Wittenberg theologians until a permanent minister had been called, it is not surprising that the senate addressed a letter to the Elector of Saxony, asking for the services of Jonas during the interim. Accordingly Jonas was granted leave to continue his labors on behalf of the evangelical cause in Naumburg. This he did from June 2 until September 8, 1536, in spite of persistent opposition by papal priests. Meanwhile Nicholas Medler, who had been put forward as candidate for Naumburg by Luther, proved acceptable to the senate and was called there. After Jonas' departure from Naumburg the senate sent a letter of thanks to Luther. In it special mention was made of the satisfactory and faithful ministry of Jonas. Jonas' interest in the church of Naumburg continued throughout the years, and with the enthronement of Nicholas von Amsdorf as the first evangelical bishop of Naumburg in 1542 he witnessed the complete triumph of the Reformation in that city.[15]

A Church Order for Anhalt

Early in 1538 Jonas had, upon the special request of the Princes of Anhalt, gone to Dessau to draft a Church Order for the principality of Anhalt. Although the Princes had undertaken a visitation with the help of their own local ministers in 1534, they realized that the enterprise had been only of a provisional and preparatory nature and had not been satisfactory. So Jonas went to Zerbst where he conducted services and began to write the proposed Church Order. This work was interrupted by the Brunswick Convention in North Germany, which Jonas attended instead of Luther, who was prevented from undertaking the journey because of illness. At the convention Jonas was very favorably impressed by King Christian of Denmark. He believed him to be endowed "with excellent and truly royal virtues." By May Jonas had returned to Zerbst where, by the permission of the Elector of Saxony, he continued the task of drawing up a Church Order. On June 1, Jonas could report to Prince George of Anhalt that he had completed the first draft of the Church Order and that he intended to submit it to him for approval.[16] The phrase "order of the churches" seems to indicate that this Church Order was designed for the entire principality of Anhalt and not only for the local church in Zerbst. Nothing definite can be said regarding its ultimate fate, but it would appear that this Church Order was one of the first to be put into use in the principality of Anhalt. There is reason to believe that it became the basis for further church orders which were later developed.[17]

After indicating the provisional character of the Order in the title, Jonas recalled Jesus' command in the last chapters of Matthew and Mark where his Apostles were enjoined to preach the Gospel of the kingdom. "Therefore in things pertaining to God's glory and true worship it is above all highly necessary to see to it that chiefly the office of a shepherd, minister and teacher is well provided for." Jonas set up a high standard for the educational as well as the spiritual qualifications of the chief pastor and of all other pastors in Zerbst. Practical details concerning the salary, the administrative duties, and the relationship to the teachers and council were inserted. But a primary emphasis was laid upon the teaching responsibility of a pastor and the maintenance of proper ecclesiastical discipline. The evangelical church was concerned that the ministers of the Gospel guard the purity of doctrine and be diligent and God-fearing pastors who seek the salvation of souls and who uphold proper reverence, discipline, and order.[18]

First Consistories

Before the year 1538 was over Jonas, by virtue of his legal training, was called upon to word an Opinion that was to embody the necessary organization for judicial procedures in the evangelical churches. Hitherto the judicial authority of the visitors had been limited and the need for some kind of permanent organization to be empowered to act in grave legal matters was needed. On the suggestion of the Elector, Jonas, with the assistance of Luther, Melanchthon, and Jerome Schurpff, came out with "An Opinion of Theologians with Regard to Consistories."[19] The detailed work of this Opinion is proof of the concern for proper organization and discipline in the evangelical Lutheran Church and the prominent part which Jonas played in the initial creation of such machinery.

Jonas first of all demonstrated the need for the proposed consistories by pointing out that after abuses had been put aside, vice and unseemly conduct, blasphemy of religion and other gross offenses against Christian morality ought to be guarded against and properly punished. The function of the consistories would be to exercise authority over the purity and uniformity of doctrines and ceremonies and to safeguard the dignity of public worship and the Sacraments, to watch over the conduct of church officers and school teachers, and to defend these against unjust accusations. All matrimonial and legal disputes as well as public church discipline were to be handled by the consistories. They were also to care for the temporal possessions of the church, its places of burial, buildings, and holdings. The members of the consistories were to install pastors in their respective parishes and prevent unnecessary changes in the employment of church officers.

Jonas proposed that the consistories be set up at four places in the Electorate and that each consistory be headed by a commissary who should have both legal and theological training. The University of Wittenberg was to function as a kind of final court of appeal for these consistories.

The sentence of excommunication was again to be introduced, not in a worldly sense for temporal advantage, but in accordance with scriptural principles. In defending the sentence of excommunication, the Opinion read: "The ordinance of the Apostles and of the Scripture no creature is to abrogate; the world has taken this freedom from it; but a Christian church cannot exist in conjunction with coarse, licentious living." The sentence of excommunication was to carry with it temporal punishment, such as deposition from office and forfeiture of employment. It was to be used in the case of persons who espoused heretical views, or who were guilty of immorality, or who had flagrantly violated the Ten Commandments.[20]

The Opinion was, in its main outlines, accepted by the Elector, and after numerous deliberations a provisional consistory was set up in Wittenberg in 1539, while the proposed plan of similar consistories in Saalfeld, Coburg, and Gotha was temporarily dropped. The introduction of the Consistorial Order for Wittenberg was delayed until 1541, after Jonas had left Wittenberg, and the original plan was never adopted completely. Nevertheless, the basic ideas and features, as put forth in the Opinion, constituted the groundwork for the future organizational development of the evangelical Lutheran churches of Germany.[21]

Reform in Meissen

The death of Duke George of Saxony, who had been a very determined opponent of the Reformation in his territories of Meissen and Thuringia, meant that this opposition was to cease. Duke Henry, his brother, had already introduced the Reformation in his own small land, and since Duke George had no son, Duke Henry fell heir to his brother's territories and began his rule over them on April 17, 1539. As a member of the Schmalcald League, Duke Henry stood in a close relationship with the Elector John Frederick, his cousin, who exercised a considerable influence over the Duke and favored the plan to make the Reformation effective in Meissen and Thuringia.[22] The Bishop of Meissen, who was a loyal Catholic, tried to persuade Duke Henry that as bishop he be allowed to carry through a reform program of his own without any interference whatsoever from Electoral Saxony. But the Elector had already promised Duke Henry the aid of his own theologians and promptly made the necessary arrangements so that they might introduce the Reformation in these lands.

In May, 1539, Luther, Melanchthon, Jonas, and Cruciger accompanied the Elector of Saxony to Leipzig, one the principal cities of the land.

"We entered Leipzig with the illustrious Elector May 23," wrote Jonas to Prince George of Anhalt. A dense throng of people had come to the city's gate to witness their arrival and especially to see Luther. On Saturday, May 24, Jonas preached in St. Thomas' Church "whither an innumerable multitude of people had come."[23] The next day, being Pentecost, Jonas, at the command of the Elector, preached in the Church of the Benedictines, while Frederick Mecum and Paul Lindenau, chaplain of Duke Henry, preached in St. Nicholas' and St. Thomas' Churches respectively. Again great throngs came and listened attentively to their preaching. The Bishops of Meissen and Merseburg protested against the entire procedure and wrote to Duke Henry that they were still desirous of carrying out a reform of their own; but their protest was of no avail.

During their brief stay in Leipzig, the Wittenberg theologians apparently drew up a workable plan for the reform measures that were to be affected. It was entitled: "Luther and Colleagues: Regarding the Appointment (of preachers) for the Churches of Leipzig and Regarding the Visitation." Nicholas von Amsdorf and Michael Caelarius of Frankfurt were asked to come to Leipzig to preach the Gospel in the various churches, and no one was supposed to preach or assist them without special injunction or permission.[24] With reference to the projected visitation there was unanimous agreement that "Dr. Jonas, who had previously been present at the visitation[25] and has been long acquainted with such matters, is to be employed." It was claimed that Jonas possessed the necessary respect of priests and people alike in order to do the work thoroughly. The tremendous scope and the many details of the visitation were lastly pointed out, no doubt for the purpose of revealing the necessity and gravity of the task.[26] Luther, Melanchthon, and Jonas departed from Leipzig with the Elector, while Caspar Cruciger and Frederick Mecum were left behind to continue to preach and teach in the city.

On June 20, 1539, Spalatin received a letter from the Elector appointing him as one of the visitors of Saxony and informing him that Jonas and Melchior von Creitzen had also been designated as members of the visitation commission. The appointments had taken place in consultation with Duke Henry of Saxony, who intended to issue a special instruction for this visitation. Jonas informed the Elector of his readiness to undertake the work and to appear with Spalatin and Melchior von Creitzen at Dresden on July 8 to await further orders from Duke Henry. With becoming modesty Jonas acknowledged his limited capabilities in such a highly important task and assured the Elector that he would spare neither labor nor diligence in those areas where the door for the Gospel had been opened for them.[27]

Meanwhile the Bishop of Meissen, clinging tenaciously to his own plan of reforming the churches, had published a book which he had sent to the Elector. The Elector asked his theologians to draw up an Opinion on the book. By July 1 Luther, Jonas, and Melanchthon had embodied a criticism of this book in an Opinion which they sent to the Elector. The book was condemned as heretical on four counts: (1) There was no express rejection of the private mass. (2) Communion "under both kinds" was not advocated. (3) Celibacy of the priests was retained. (4) There was no clear presentation of the doctrine of justification by faith.[28]

Duke Henry's Instruction for the visitation in Meissen was issued to the visitors, Justus Jonas, George Spalatin, Melchior von Creitzen, Caspar von Schoenberg, and Rudolph von Rechenberg, on July 10 in Dresden, and on July 21 they began the visitation. In all they visited fourteen cities and towns, including Dresden and Leipzig, and returned to Dresden on August 26. The chapter of Meissen had proved impervious to demands that it too receive the visitors. Julius Pflug, the Dean of the Cathedral, remained especially adamant in resisting anything like a reformation of doctrine and ceremonies.[29]

Almost everywhere the members of the visitation found popular support in their efforts to spread the Gospel. Jonas could state that the people "are very much inclined and willing to receive the Gospel." Their main task was to abolish private mass, to prohibit communion "under one kind," to forbid monastic vows, and to permit priestly marriage. In the matter of regulating salaries, the minimum, first set at 200 guldens, was reduced by Duke Henry to 150 guldens, much to the disappointment of the visitors. They believed that thus vacancies were sure to result and the real work of the Reformation would be hindered.[30]

While the visitation was being hurriedly carried out, Jonas reported to the Elector. He complained about the brevity of the time in which the work had to be done and urged that the task be followed quickly by a second visitation. He related how the priests were convened in groups of twenty to thirty and so cursorily examined with regard to their knowledge of the Gospel and their own convictions that the visitation could not prove to be very effective.[31]

After the conclusion of the visitation its members addressed a lengthy report to Duke Henry. They explained the incomplete nature of the work they had done and drew attention to the fact that the number of papistical priests, especially in the rural areas, was still very great. Delay, they claimed, would be dangerous, and so a thorough introduction of evangelical teaching must be attempted by means of a second visitation. Public offering-boxes should be set up in the various parishes so that the ecclesiastical possessions would not be dissipated. The entire report was characterized by a conscientious concern for the souls of men and the welfare of the church.

In a personal report to the Elector, Jonas again reviewed in some detail the activities of the visitation. He urged the confiscation of Witzel's books, which had been printed in Leipzig. Jonas' elation over the reception of the Gospel in Dresden was great. "Most gracious Lord, although it is a new city, having been a forest about forty years ago, a large, fine people have gathered there from various lands." Jonas claimed that never, during the twenty some years that he had preached, had he preached before such immense throngs. He estimated that he had had well over six thousand listeners to his sermon on one occasion.[32] Jonas commended the many thousands of souls, who were eagerly waiting for the Gospel message, to the Elector's Christian conscience and asked him to continue to care for them out of divine compassion, particularly since the bishops did not cease to persecute Christ and the divine truth. It becomes more apparent why the princely rulers were, under the circumstances, so closely connected with church affairs and why they in effect became the chief bishops (*summi epis-*

copi) in evangelical territories. Jonas' genuine concern for souls is clearly in evidence here, as it is also in a subsequent letter to the Elector
in which he wrote: "I reasonably shrink from molesting your Electoral
Grace with writings so often, but the tremendous need of vacant
churches, of so many hundreds of ministers (where there are thousands
of souls to be cared for), all of whom still complain and cry out daily
under the rule of evil papists, compels me to supplicate and to write."

The Halle Church Order

Luther also favored a second visitation, and Duke Henry followed
the first visitation with a second one. But none of the former visitors
was asked to serve again. Perhaps it was done by the Duke in order to
show his independence from Electoral Saxony. At any rate, Jonas was
indignant over the fact that a second visitation was begun without his
knowledge and without previous consultation with the members of the
first visitation.[33] He had the more reason to feel thus because he was
very probably the author of a provisional Church Order for Meissen.[34]
He had drawn up this Order during the visitation and had adapted
it to the local situation.

The Order breathes the evangelical spirit of the Reformation and
reveals an alert sensitivity to the needs of the churches throughout
the territory. Special attention is given to the qualifications and duties
of the ministers. The document lays down the necessary rules for the
unhampered and orderly proclamation of the Word of God and the
frequent use of the Sacraments. The Order is important because it was
freely used in other territories and frequently became a pattern for
later church orders.[35]

The insistent demands for a more permanent organization in the
church at Halle compelled Jonas to draft a Church Order for that
church early in 1543.[36] His previous experience in the field of church
polity, notably the church orders he had drawn up for Duke Henry
of Saxony and the Princes of Anhalt, was an indication that he was
eminently qualified for this particular task. It is possible that his visit
to Wittenberg early in 1543 was made in connection with this work.[37]

While there he may have secured a copy of the Church Order for Wittenberg which had been drawn up in 1533. At any rate, he used the Wittenberg Church Order as a pattern for the Order which he wrote for the church at Halle. This Church Order was not, as has often been supposed, only a provisional one, but it was clearly intended as a permanent feature in the organization of the church at Halle. The senate in Querfurt asked Jonas for a copy of this Church Order in 1547 so that a similar order for its own church might be patterned after it. The title Jonas gave it was: "Church Order for the Christian Church at Halle."[38]

At the beginning of the Order the Apostle Paul's injunction that all things are to be done decently and in order is given as the principal reason why a form of organization is necessary for the church at Halle. This is followed by a brief reference to the main doctrines of Christianity, true repentance, faith in Christ, good works, and Christian love, the Sacrament of Baptism, and the Sacrament of the Lord's Supper, as these are found in the eighteen Articles of the Book of Visitation of the Elector of Saxony, in the Augsburg Confession and the Apology to it from the year 1530. The superintendent and all ministers of the church in Halle are urged to be especially concerned that the sublime and chief article of the Christian faith concerning justification by faith and the true knowledge of Jesus Christ be presented as the foundation upon which any superstructure is to be raised.

The Order also deals with the various services which are to take place on Sundays and weekdays, with the office of the ministry, the administration of the Lord's Supper, the sermons to be preached on the Catechism, the Sacrament of Baptism and its proper use, marriage, burial, and the selection of suitable hymns for the worship service. This Order with needed revisions, improvements, and additions was reprinted in 1552 and three times in the seventeenth century.[39]

Jonas' active participation in the visitation programs in the various territorial churches and his creative efforts in providing proper organizational machinery for the emerging evangelical Church of Germany show that he stands in the front ranks as a churchman in that critical period of church history.

As Friend of Princes and Rulers

From the very first the Reformation under Luther's leadership called forth both the support and opposition of various petty princes and rulers over small territories within Germany. And it was in fact the loyalty of many of them to the Gospel of Jesus Christ, as proclaimed by the churches of the Reformation, that resulted in the formulation of the Augsburg Confession and its adoption as a standard of faith in their respective lands. Their continued support of and interest in the work of the Reformation were most important. For this reason their good will and understanding meant much to the leaders of the reform movement.

Whenever the opportunity presented itself, Justus Jonas sought to establish a personal friendship with those princes who supported the evangelical cause. At the request of George Helt of Forchheim, a well-known friend, Jonas was induced to begin a correspondence with Prince George of Anhalt in November of 1532. George Forchheim had been the tutor of the Princes George and Joachim of Anhalt when they were attending the University of Leipzig. Later he became their friend and adviser at the court of Dessau.[40] Jonas, acceding to this wish of his friend, was by means of his letters able to lay the foundation for what became an enduring friendship between Prince George of Anhalt and himself. At first Jonas acted as a kind of correspondent for the Prince and related all important happenings at Wittenberg to the Prince. Later the letters took on a more intimate form and contained many personal references.

In the summer of 1534 Jonas had Melanchthon serve as a substitute for him in the work of the church visitation. Thus he, together with Luther, was able to spend some time at the court of Prince George of Anhalt in Dessau.[41] After his return to Wittenberg he reported in frequent letters to the Prince on the progress he was making in a historical study of the use of "both kinds." In spite of interruptions which were occasioned by illness, he indicated that he hoped to complete within a short period of time the small work on the Sacrament which, he believed, would prove "useful and consoling to many consciences."[42]

Late in 1536 Luther had asked Jonas to become a mediator in a lawsuit dealing with Anton Schoenitz and involving Jonas' friend, Prince George of Anhalt, and the Catholic Cardinal Albrecht. Luther was concerned that Jonas thereby defend the evangelical cause.[43] It seems the Cardinal for no apparent reason had his friend Hans Schoenitz killed. At any rate, the extant correspondence does not offer any explanation for this peculiar action of the Cardinal. The lawsuit, as can be seen from the correspondence between Jonas and Prince George, was treated in a dilatory fashion by the Cardinal, and Jonas seemingly was unable to obtain justice for Schoenitz' widow and her son Anton Schoenitz.[44]

When late in 1539 the hope of a Protestant alliance with England faded away completely, another territory in German lands was opening its door to evangelical truth. It was the Electorate of Brandenburg. To support the ruler in the work of the Reformation, Jonas wrote a most appropriate letter of commendation to Elector Joachim II. In it he presented a lucid and well-reasoned statement why kings and princes should further the cause of the Gospel. He maintained that the world did not show any concern for the Gospel and its blessings and was unable to discern its true value. Nevertheless, it was a great gift of God when the true treasure of the Gospel was apprehended in God's Word. "For that kingdom or land or person that has come to a knowledge of the true God, has received eternal help." "Yes, for that reason it is by far a greater treasure when God grants a land the Gospel than when He suddenly permits a rich mine to be discovered, even as also Christ compares the kingdom of heaven with a treasure or a mine concealed in the earth." Jonas rejoiced that the teachings of the Gospel had been so willingly accepted in the Electoral lands and that the door had been opened for the Lord Christ. He implored God's blessing upon the Elector's land during his rule and expressed his essential agreement with the Church Order which had been submitted for approval.[45]

On May 16, 1544, Prince George had been named coadjutor of the Bishopric of Merseburg by Duke August of Saxony. Jonas, rejoicing over the news of this appointment, congratulated the Prince most heartily and sent, as a modest gift for the occasion, one of his transla-

tions of a writing by Luther.[46] In September of the same year he celebrated the official beginning of the Prince's duties as coadjutor in Merseburg with public prayers in his church at Halle.[47]

On August 2, 1545, Jonas traveled to Merseburg to participate with
Melanchthon and others in the ordination of his beneficent friend,
Prince George of Anhalt. Luther had willingly fulfilled Prince George's
request that he should come to Merseburg in order personally to ordain
the Prince, because he was then seriously thinking of leaving Wittenberg permanently. He performed the rite of ordination with becoming
solemnity.[48] Melanchthon made out the certificate of ordination, which
had his personal signature, as well as those of Luther, Jonas, and six
other ministers, affixed to it.[49]

Before the catastrophe of the Schmalcald War, Jonas had the opportunity of beginning a correspondence with King Christian III of
Denmark (1536-59) who, in the years to come, was to bestow many a
benign favor upon him. Jonas believed that the Danish King would
be interested in hearing in greater detail about Luther's death, and
since a well-known friend was leaving Halle to return to Denmark,
Jonas entrusted to him the report of Luther's death together with a
personal letter addressed to the king. In this letter of April 15, 1546,
Jonas laid special stress on his intimate association with Luther over
a period of some twenty-two years and on his continual presence with
the Reformer during the last three weeks of his life. He commended
Luther's widow and her children as well as his own family, especially
his son Justus, to the king's favor. To this letter King Christian III
responded some months later. He sincerely thanked Jonas for writing
to him and for the report and, assuring him of his genuine sorrow
over Luther's death, promised to remember the Reformer's widow
and children. Similarly, the king indicated his willingness to extend
his favor to Jonas' eldest son, Justus, if he should happen to come to
Denmark.

In later years, when Jonas' second wife died, Prince George of Anhalt
conveyed his sincere sympathies to Jonas and showed himself ever
ready to help his friend.[50] The kindness of the King of Denmark also
brought rays of hope and comfort to Jonas during these dark days.

The king sent Jonas a purse of money in September of 1549, in order to assist him in his financial distress.[51] In his correspondence with Christian III, Jonas did not shrink from telling about his personal difficulties and burdens and he kept the king informed about the situation in the Church of Germany and found him to be a most gracious man.[52]

On January 2, 1550, Jonas sent the Danish King heartiest wishes for the New Year and thanked him for the generous gifts of money which the king had often sent. Amid the dangers which the Protestant church was then experiencing, Jonas in this letter called special attention to the steadfast courage of Duke John Ernest of Coburg, to whom the Pope and bishops had sent the Interim three times. Refusing to obey its injunctions, he faithfully shielded his ministers from harm and oppression. It was Jonas' sincere desire that the consolation derived from the reign of similarly pious Christian rulers and princes might be granted to the true church of Christ everywhere. He believed that neither council nor bishops would further the truth in Germany because "the light of the truth" had struck them in the eye too forcefully, and "like bats" they were now fluttering toward places of darkness and concealment.[53]

Thus Justus Jonas cultivated the friendship of princes and rulers with a due sense of deference for their position and a keen realization of their importance in the furtherance of the cause of the Gospel. Especially in his long and cherished friendship with Prince George of Anhalt, he revealed, in the intimate sharing of joys and sorrows, successes and disappointments, a human warmth and steadfastness of affection which evoke admiration.

FOOTNOTES FOR CHAPTER 5

1. C. A. H. Burkhardt, *Geschichte der sächsischen Kirchen- und Schulvisitation,* pp. 3-29 ff.
2. Kawerau, *op. cit.,* Vol. I, pp. 121-122.
3. Kawerau, *op. cit.,* Vol. I, pp. 125, 132 and 143.
4. *Ibid.,* pp. 179-180.
5. *Ibid.,* pp. 184-186.
6. *Corpus Reformatorum,* Vol. II, pp. 592-595.
   Walch, Editor, *Luthers Sämmtliche Schriften,* St. Louis Edition, Vol. XXI a., pp. 1747-1750.
7. G. A. H. Burkhardt, *op. cit.,* pp. 123-124.

8. *Ibid.*, p. 125.
9. Richter, *Die evangelischen Kirchenordnungen des sechzehnten Jahrhunderts,* Vol. I, p. 228.
10. *Corpus Reformatorum,* Vol. XII, pp. 6-7. An address by Melanchthon in 1553.
11. Kawerau, *op. cit.,* Vol. I, p. 221.
12. Felix Koester, "Analekten Beiträge zur Reformationsgeschichte Naumburgs von 1525 bis 1545," *Zeitschrift für Kirchengeschichte.* Edited by Theodor Brieger and Bernhard Bess. Vol. XXII (1901), pp. 279-280.
13. Enders, *op. cit.,* Vol. X, pp. 319-321.
14. *Ibid.*, pp. 320-322.
15. Koester, *op. cit.,* pp. 285 and 308-309.
16. Kawerau, *op. cit.,* Vol. I, pp. 274-292.
17. Sehling, *Die Evangelischen Kirchenordnungen des XVI Jahrhunderts,* Vol. II, pp. 499-500.
18. *Ibid.*, pp. 544-547.
19. Sehling, *op. cit.,* Vol. I, p. 200.
20. *Ibid.*, pp. 200-209.
21. Burkhardt, *op. cit.,* pp. 201-204.
22. Sehling, *op. cit.,* Vol. I, p. 85.
23. Kawerau, *op. cit.,* Vol. I, p. 325, Vol. II, p. 367.
24. Kawerau, *op. cit.,* Vol. I, pp. 320-321, p. 326.
25. Perhaps a reference to the visitation conducted in the small territory of Duke Henry by Jonas and Spalatin from 1537 to 1538.
26. Kawerau, *op. cit.,* Vol. I, p. 321.
27. *Ibid.*, pp. 326-329.
28. *Corpus Reformatorum,* Vol. III, pp. 728-741.
29. Burkhardt, *op. cit.,* p. 235.
30. Kawerau, *op. cit.,* Vol. I, pp. 331-333.
31. Kawerau, *op. cit.,* Vol. I, p. 339.
32. *Ibid.*, pp. 350-357.
33. *Ibid.*, pp. 361, 363 and 377.
34. Sehling claims that Prince George of Anhalt expressly designates Jonas as author of this Order. Sehling, *op. cit.,* Vol. I, p. 89.
35. A. L. Richter, *Die evangelischen Kirchenordnungen des sechzehnten Jahrhunderts,* Vol. I, p. 307.
36. Richter assumes that the Halle Church Order by Justus Jonas was written in 1541. He calls it "Hallische Kirchenordnung von 1541." Richter, *op. cit.,* Vol. I, p. 339. Franke and Kawerau suppose the date of its composition to have been 1542. Sehling, however, believes that the Order was drawn up early in 1543. Sehling, *op. cit.,* Vol. II, p. 431.
37. Kawerau, *op. cit.,* Vol. II, pp. 101-102.
38. Sehling, *op. cit.,* Vol. II, pp. 430, 434.
39. *Ibid.*, pp. 434-436, p. 295.
40. Kawerau, *op. cit.,* Vol. I, pp. 186-187.
41. *Ibid.*, pp. 208-210.
42. *Ibid.*, pp. 218-221.
43. de Wette, *Luthers Briefe,* Vol. V, pp. 21-22.
44. Kawerau, *op. cit.,* Vol. I, pp. 246-247, 261-262, 266-268.
45. Kawerau, *op. cit.,* Vol. I, pp. 375-376
46. *Ibid.*, Vol. II, pp. 117-118.
47. *Ibid.*, p. 129.
48. Koestlin, *op. cit.,* Vol. II, pp. 619-620
49. Enders, *op. cit.,* Vol. XVI, pp. 274-277
50. Kawerau, *op. cit.,* Vol. II, pp. 289-290.
51. *Ibid.*, pp. 292.
52. *Ibid.*, pp. 292-294, 297-298.
53. *Ibid.*, pp. 297-298.

Chapter 6

In Defense of the Gospel

From its very inception the Reformation was vigorously opposed by those who adhered firmly to Roman Catholic tradition and practice. As a result, controversy between the adherents of Roman Catholic teachings and the followers of evangelical doctrines was an almost continuous symptom of the times. Luther as the leader of the Reformation was naturally the most deeply involved in the controversies that revolved about his teachings. Nevertheless, his collaborators often ably assisted him in defending the truth of the Gospel. Jonas must be numbered among them.

Against John Faber

Jonas' theological comprehension and ability were given the opportunity of expression in a controversial writing of 1523. It was occasioned by a polemical writing by John Heigerlin, or John Faber, from Leutkirch, Vicar of the Bishop of Constance, who, though a Humanist by training and an admirer of Luther, believed it to be his duty to write against the Reformer. On August 13, 1522, he completed a polemical piece of writing in Rome and dedicated it to Pope Hadrian. Immediately after it had made its appearance, the first printing was quickly sold out and a second printing followed. Luther mentioned the "large Latin book written against me" in a letter to the Elector Frederick on May 29, 1523. Faber impatiently expected Luther's reply, but in this expectation he was to experience a disappointment. For Luther delegated the task of answering Faber's charges, especially his violent attacks on priestly marriage, to Justus Jonas, who had recently married.[1] Faber had contended that priestly celibacy was necessary, on the ground that "no one can serve two Lords," and that "the priests of God must be purer than all remaining Christians." To support his position Faber cited the authorities of the Fathers, the Councils, and the Pope. The biblical quotation "Be fruitful and multiply" he claimed was made invalid by this argument: "Matrimony indeed populates the earth, but celibacy heaven."[2]

Luther had written to Jonas: "I relinquish to you, Justus Jonas, this miserable compiler and accuser of matrimony, John Faber, Vicar at Constance, in order that you might exercise the preludes of your theology and transfix this Hector, who has already been overthrown by me, with arrows. . . ."[3] Jonas entered the conflict with youthful ardor and in the writing which resulted gave evidence of his thorough biblical learning as well as his skill in polemics. The little book, entitled *Against John Faber of Constance*,[4] appeared in 1523 and was prefaced by a dedicatory letter to William Reifenstein.

In this writing Jonas began his attack by remarking on the "gigantic and monstrous bulk" of Faber's work and "the splendid patchwork" he has done. However, Jonas contended, it is only an insatiable thirst for glory which has prompted Faber to write this defense of sacerdotal celibacy, for he despises the Christian doctrine and neither sufficiently understands nor acknowledges it. "Christ calls those who impugn the doctrine of God a brood of vipers, hypocrites, sons of the devil. Stephen Martyr in Acts 7 calls the enemies of the Gospel traitors and murderers. And we shall challenge you, Faber, with sacred Scriptures in such great and grave matters. . . ." After indicating that Scripture would be the armory for the supply of his weapons of truth, Jonas expresses wonder that Faber dares to write against Luther. In the face of Faber's attack, Luther is silent. Yet "not in all things is Luther silent, not in all matters is he thus quiet." Because of Luther's failure to reply, Faber accuses him of discourtesy; but this is not the case.

After these preliminary remarks Jonas proceeds with unconcealed enthusiasm to praise the revelation of God as it now shines forth in his Word with a brightness not experienced since apostolic times. Now it has become clear why God had brought about the invention of movable type in printing; it is here to serve the propagation of the Gospel. "Barbarism has been done away with, the sophists have been driven out of the schools of the theologians, from day to day the proclamation of a genuine theology and of the pure Gospel is progressing."

Faber has written his ponderous tome in barbarous Latin and has quoted heathen writers in order to make light of marriage. But at the very beginning of the Scriptures which deal with the creation of man, marriage is viewed as a divine institution. "God created man in his image and similitude, a man and a woman he created them." This passage Faber seems to have overlooked. "What the most high God has done, ought therefore to remain thus. Away, therefore, with the blasphemous and satanical opinion that 'the woman is a necessary evil,' as we find it stated by heathen philosophers and in heathen writings. Moreover, after God had created man and woman he blessed them and said: 'Grow and multiply.'" The Scriptures are clear on this point. They desire that man and woman be united in marriage. "And these words of God," says Jonas in reverence and faith, "are so powerful and efficacious that no creature whatsoever on earth or in heaven can make this natural order different." Jonas argues that there would be many more examples of celibacy in the Scriptures if the Spirit of God had desired such chastity. Jesus himself in Matthew 19 was aware that celibacy was not the natural order but an extraordinary gift. Nor does Paul advocate this rare gift of chastity for all, as it would appear from passages like 1 Corinthians 7, where he says that he wishes that all men were as he is. Many of the best and greatest men of Scripture, such as Abraham, Isaac, Jacob, Joseph, and Moses, were married.

God foresaw before all time that the future apostles and bishops such as Faber would hypocritically advocate celibacy, and so the Scriptures exalt marriage. "A bishop ought therefore to be blameless, the husband of one wife." What do the priestly celibates make of this Pauline admonition? "Behold," says Jonas triumphantly, "therefore we have here the sanction and ordinance of Paul, yes of God, even the

Holy Spirit and the most high Majesty." We must hold to the plain, grammatical sense of the Scriptures and not prate about a spiritual marriage to the congregation. Faber is thus trying to elude the simple meaning of Scripture, but must surely find that its truth is inescapable; for Jonas concludes: "You see, then, that heaven and earth might sooner collapse than this Word of God."

Responsibilities as well as blessings attend human marriage. Faith on the part of the marriage partners can transform "the water of vexation into the wine of consolation." Faber exaggerates the disadvantages of marriage. Its advantage is that it makes for purity of morals, which, Jonas says, is so conspicuously absent among the Romanist clergy. Yes, even Homer, Aristotle, and Demosthenes—and here Jonas shows his Humanist background—oppose immorality. Christians have the clear revelation of God's Word and will to guide them. Jonas finally reveals a total of sixteen flaws in Faber's argument and closes with a masterful summary of his own position.[5]

This effective little book by Jonas came off the press in rapid succession, first in Zurich, then in Hagenau, and lastly at some unknown place. Faber later replied to it and Jonas wrote an *Apology* with a preface by Luther in defense of his earlier book.[6] It was Jonas' first polemical work on behalf of the evangelical truth, and even thirteen years later he looked back with evident satisfaction upon his early, courageous exploit in literary warfare against the enemies of the Reformation.[7]

The Exchange with Witzel

The many difficulties and duties connected with the consolidation of the evangelical cause in the various churches in Electoral Saxony were in no small measure shouldered by Jonas. In the midst of these responsibilities as provost and professor, as visitor and adviser in church affairs, he was involved in a fierce controversy with a former adherent to Lutheran doctrine, George Witzel. Jonas had become acquainted with Witzel in Erfurt in the winter semester 1516 to 1517. After completing his studies, Witzel entered a cloister, only to leave it in order

to go to Wittenberg for a half year and attend the lectures of Luther
and Melanchthon. He was implicated in the Peasants' Revolt in 1524
and 1525, but, upon Chancellor Brueck's intercession, was acquitted of
the charges preferred against him. In 1526 he was, on the basis of
Luther's recommendation, given a parish at Niemegk, not far from
Wittenberg. There he carried on his work as a married minister of the
Lutheran Church.[8] Jonas had met Witzel personally again while engaged in the program of visitation in the district of Belzig.

In 1529 Witzel had written two essays expounding his particular
desires in the matter of reforming the church and had sent them to
Wittenberg. Melanchthon had answered him in a friendly manner, but
Jonas did not so much as reply to his suggestions. Because Witzel had
supposedly sheltered the anti-Trinitarian Companus in his parish, he
was suspected of heterodoxy and imprisoned in Belzig in 1530. After
his release he left Niemegk in the fall of 1531, embittered by what
seemed to him a harsh and unjust treatment of his person and completely alienated from the Lutheran cause. He rejoined the Catholic
Church and became a staunch protagonist of its doctrines.[9] He spent
two years in his home at Vacha and tried to secure the position of a
professor of Hebrew at the University at Erfurt; but Jonas, through his
influence at the university, was able to thwart his efforts in this direction.[10] Luther had at the same time written to three evangelical ministers at Erfurt and warned them against the sinister methods of
Witzel and his attack on the doctrine of justification by faith.[11]

In a letter of June 25, 1532, to Jonas, Witzel complained about the
former's unfair attitude and his incessant hostility. In Belzig, Witzel
claimed to have been treated unjustly and arbitrarily by Jonas, and in
Erfurt, Jonas wrongly spread the rumor that he was an Arian. Witzel
then gave the reason which caused him to return to the Romanist fold.
It was the result of a more thorough study of the Fathers. He also
staunchly defended his writing on good works.[12] The title of this
treatise was *In Defense of Good Works Against the New Evangelicals
by the Author George from Vacha*. The first copies of the book had
come off the press on May 20, 1532, and after it had reached Wittenberg
later in the year, Jonas lost no time in framing a reply entitled:

Against the Three Pages of George from Vacha, George Witzel, in Which Lutheranism Has Almost Been Cast Down and Devoured, Justus Jonas' Reply.[13] In November, 1532, Jonas was happy to be able to send a copy of his reply to Witzel's work to Prince George of Anhalt.[14]

In his polemic against Witzel, Jonas was unsparing and vehement. Making the issue almost entirely a personal one, he hurled a regular torrent of abusive epithets at his opponent, denouncing him as untrustworthy and unstable in his words and actions. "For first of all, when the Gospel appeared among us and it had now sufficiently come to light what an abominable, unchristian thing papal clericalism was, and he, too—Witzel himself—let it be known without concealment that he was opposed to such an abomination on account of the recognized truth, he nevertheless, contrary to the recognized truth, permitted himself to be daubed as a papal cleric at Erfurt at the hands of a bishop suffragan in Erfurt, whom he is wont to call a bishop of refuse, although he had not thought much of it and had known well in advance how he had to agree to deny matrimony and consent to other papal abominations." The Romanists were unable to effect anything, and Witzel himself was not the man to do any damage to the Lutheran cause, since he was after all only "a worn-out, wet fly" in his attacks against Luther.

By November 8, 1532, Witzel had framed an answer to Jonas' attack. In 1533 it came off the press at Leipzig under the title: *A Refutation of the Most Malicious Reply of Justus Jonas, That Is of Jodocus Koch Together with a Defense of Good Works by George Witzel.*[15] Meanwhile, Jonas' attack had done incalculable damage to Witzel's position, for in a letter the latter complained that more than one thousand copies had been distributed and that they were found in the possession of all heretics.

At that time another Protestant pastor, Balthasar Raida, of Hirsfeld in Hesse, had come to Jonas' aid in attacking Witzel in a writing entitled: *Against the Blasphemous and Lying Booklet of Agricole Phegi named George Witzel.* Luther had written a preface to the work and Jonas was also called upon to add a foreword. Early in 1533 the book appeared along with Jonas' preface. Jonas showed more moderation in his expressions in this brief foreword, but he did not let the opportunity pass by without accusing both Crotus Rubianus and Witzel of serious disability in theological discernment. Nor were they in any sense capable of teaching the truth of Scripture. "The holy divine truth will not permit itself to be stifled by much writing or yelling, much less by the heckling of those who can neither talk nor write," concluded Jonas.[16]

After a brief intermission in the controversy Jonas brought out a booklet in 1534 written in German which was skillfully calculated to show up the untenable position of his opponent and to prove the immovable biblical foundation of the Reformation concept of the church. It was entitled: *Which Is the Right Church and Contrariwise Which Is the False Church—A Christian Answer and Comforting Instruction Against the Pharisaic Prattle of George Witzel.* On April 9, 1534, he had announced the speedy publication of this writing in a letter to Prince George of Anhalt, so that the book must have made its appearance sometime in May.[17]

After beginning with a sharply worded reprimand of his opponent, Jonas explains the threefold purpose of his book. First, it is designed to set forth the distinguishing marks of the true church and of the false church; secondly, it shows what value the salutary teaching thus blasphemed by superficial talk has; and thirdly, it is to divulge information about Witzel's life. With remarkable clarity Jonas points out that every Christian must be aware that there are two kinds of churches on earth. The one is a godless multitude, by far the largest, under the rule of the Pope, priests, and monks; and though these rule by force, they simultaneously teach the divine law, as did the Pharisees in Jesus' day. But they persecute the Gospel and true worship, branding these as lies and heresy, while they shed the innocent blood of Abel. The other church consists of God-fearing people scattered throughout the world who hold to the true and pure Christian teaching, "rightly believe in Christ, rightly employ Baptism and the Sacrament, who call upon Christ earnestly and sincerely, confess Him, and suffer persecution for Christ's sake." This true church must always exist, for the Creed expressly testifies to this fact in the words: "I believe in the holy Christian church." It is necessary for every person to examine himself conscientiously whether he faithfully hears and obeys God's Word and makes use of the Sacraments. The true church cannot be found where a false sense of security and pride coupled with a disregard for Christ's words holds sway.

In the face of the accusation so frequently made that the evangelical Lutheran Church has separated itself from the one true church, which Christ founded, it can be truthfully said that it has marvelously preserved an unbroken continuity with the true church of Christ, because it has held to and continues to uphold the chief articles of the Christian faith, namely, belief in Christ and forgiveness of sins for Christ's sake through faith. There is no room for a false trust in personal merit. An unadulterated faith in Christ has been of the very essence of the belief embraced by all saints of the church, like Augustine, Jerome, Ambrose, Bernhard, and others. These may have observed different traditions, but such traditions belong to the unessential, outward nature of the church. The true church is one. In a spirit of an all-embracing charity Jonas even claims oneness with God-fearing, believing Christians under the rule of the Pope, although their adherence to many traditions divides them as far as their external allegiance is concerned. Ceremonies and traditional observances may vary, if only the Gospel can be truly preached. But the opponents, to whom Witzel now belongs, would not and do not acknowledge the Gospel as taught by Scripture, and so they constitute the false church.[18]

A biography of Witzel, appended to this treatise, was in the nature of the case colored by personal animosities and bias. It was intended to discredit Witzel's position as controversialist. The very purpose for which it was written invalidated its reliability as a source for true biographical information, although it was used as such by certain Protestant writers in decades to follow.[19] Thus Jonas sought to demolish the entire defensive wall behind which Witzel had tried to find security.

Polemics and Personalities

Later in 1534 Witzel replied in German to Jonas' last writing and
had it published under the title: *Concerning the Christian Church
Against Jodocus Koch.*[20] In it Witzel sought to clear himself of the
charges leveled against him, especially of those referring to his conduct
during the Peasants' Uprising in 1524 and 1525. This he was able to
do quite successfully.[21] But Jonas was afforded two more opportunities
to strike some devastating blows at his opponent; and when these last
two attacks had been made, the controversy subsided almost entirely.

The first opportunity came when Jonas was asked to write a preface
to a pungent satire entitled: *A Play by Sylvanus Hessus on the Defec-
tion of George Witzel to the Papists.* Since the author of this play
assumed the pseudonym Sylvanus Hessus, it has been difficult to
determine the true name of the writer. It seems that Antonius Corvinus, a Protestant minister in Witzenhausen since 1529, was the author
of this drama that proved to be a most potent weapon in prostrating
the papal opponent and rendering him innocuous for a future struggle.[22] In the preface Justus Jonas claimed that this dialogue painted
Witzel in his true colors, and as he went on to recount some incidents
in Witzel's life, he even impugned his motives for going over into the
camp of the enemy. In writing the preface Jonas was in the position
to reiterate and emphasize certain points in his polemic which the
satirical play would hold up for ridicule. On October 18, 1534, Witzel
wrote that he had neither read the "most vain babblings" of Sylvanus
Hessus, nor even seen it from a distance, but he promised to write an
energetic reply to Jonas' preface to the play which the latter was said
to have written.[23] This promise Witzel kept, and he wrote in a pro-
foundly agitated state of mind because of the evil motives which the
satire imputed to him and the bad name with which it branded him.[24]

Only a very short time after this Jonas followed through with another attack which, on account of its peculiar circumstances and
character, must have proved very annoying and disconcerting to his
opponent. A letter written by John Cochlaeus to George Witzel on
August 15, 1534, had come into Jonas' possession. In this letter Coch-

laeus expressed his regret over the persecutions which Witzel had to endure. Asking him to be of good courage, Cochlaeus advised him not to enter into a discussion about his matrimony, but to keep it secret. The remainder of the letter treated various themes of interest to both men, such as Witzel's book on the church written against Jonas, Cochlaeus' plan to publish four books against Melanchthon, and Erasmus' accusation that Cochlaeus and Witzel were in part responsible for the raging controversy. Jonas published the letter in Latin and German, after he had furnished it with appropriate notes which ridiculed and found flaws in the opponent's position. Jonas asserted in the preface that a papist had handed him the letter in spite of his unwillingness to take it. The papist had done so in order to intimidate Jonas and the remaining Wittenberg theologians with its promise of four polemical books by Cochlaeus against Melanchthon. A forged letter of October 1, 1534, which this papist was to have written to Witzel, was appended. In this letter the papal follower related how he had been with Witzel in Leipzig on August 24 and had returned to Eisleben, where Witzel was then preaching, on the next day. When he had come to his quarters, a violent tempest had arisen; soon after a lad had come to him with a letter which had been blown out of an open window. After reading the address and Cochlaeus' signature, the papist decided to return it forthwith to the addressee. He had, however, given a copy to one of a number of Lutherans for the express purpose of frightening them with Cochlaeus' "terrible threats."[25]

In the first of three written complaints under the general heading *Concerning the Robbery of a Private Letter* Witzel related that he had left the above-mentioned letter on the window sill in a room and that he accidently pushed it out of the window with his elbow in the darkness of the night. Evidently the letter had dropped into the yard of the Lutheran preacher at Eisleben, John Agricola.[26] Thus it came into Agricola's hands. Instead of returning it, Agricola sent it to Luther, who thankfully acknowledged its receipt and wrote: "We shall edit the same with annotations, because it has not been obtained by theft, as was mine once by Duke George, but was carried to us by a blowing wind."[27] To what an extent Jonas was assisted by Luther in editing this letter cannot be said. Since Jonas was chiefly concerned in the controversy with Witzel, he was undoubtedly the primary instigator in the entire undertaking. Cochlaeus later designated Jonas as editor of this letter and claimed that Jonas had done this to avenge himself on Cochlaeus as well. For Cochlaeus had at one time put various pointed questions to Jonas in a letter.[28]

Unfortunately suspicion and uncharitable representations as well as the use of excessive and abusive language entered into the controversy and caused it to degenerate into the realm of personal slander in many instances. Yet it must be said that it was difficult for Jonas to deal fairly with Witzel, since Witzel had become a religious renegade. On the one hand, Witzel had never understood the evangelical doctrine of justification by faith. Holding to the Erasmian ideals of reform, he was attracted to the Lutheran Church by the promise that in it he could realize those ideals. As a consequence his basic failure to understand the Lutheran Church became the ground for the bitter scorn with which he attacked it later. On the other hand, Jonas, unable to understand Witzel's strange behavior, was led into the error of attacking the person and questioning the sincerity of his motives.[29]

Osiander's Sophistry

After Luther's death, Jonas was involved in one more controversy which had broken out between two leading theologians in the Lutheran Church. The controversy between Osiander and Melanchthon afforded Jonas the opportunity of siding with Melanchthon in the defense of what was believed to be Luther's and the scriptural view of justification by faith. Osiander interpreted justification by faith as a process whereby Christ's divine nature dwelt in Christians by faith so that they were then pronounced just on the basis of the divine indwelling of Christ in the heart. In putting forth this claim, he believed that he was teaching a doctrine which was in harmony with Luther's position. He referred especially to chapters 14 and 17 of St. John's Gospel to support the claim that Christ dwelt substantially in the hearts of the believers.

Osiander's teaching was a confusion of justification—i.e. being pronounced just and blameless in virtue of faith in Christ's righteousness—with sanctification, i.e. becoming righteous on the basis of the new life begun in the heart by God's Holy Spirit. This obvious departure from Luther's doctrine of the righteousness that is granted by faith in Christ alone did not escape the notice of Jonas, who with keen theological discernment saw in Osiander's position a Catholicizing tendency, since the Council of Trent had condemned the evangelical teaching that the believer is declared righteous.[30] The disagreement between Melanchthon and Osiander over this disputed point produced a vehement controversy. Duke Albrecht of Prussia, into whose territory Osiander had gone from Nuremberg on account of the Interim, found that the dissension over Osiander's teaching was causing serious disturbances and disorders throughout the evangelical church of his land. Together with the Princes of Henneberg he sought to settle the strife by having their respective theologians formulate an Opinion and offer suggestions for an agreement. The Princes communicated to Duke John Ernest of Coburg their desire to have him permit Jonas to assist the Henneberg theologians with his counsel. The resulting Opinion, dated December 5, 1551, was signed by Jonas. Jonas likewise affixed his signature to the "Censures of the Theologians of the Saxon Princes at Weimar and Coburg Concerning the Confessions of Andrew Osiander on Justification by Faith."[31] Besides, Jonas wrote an Opinion of his own[32] which affords palpable proof of his theological capabilities and of his basic understanding of the heart of biblical revelation.

In the Opinion he states that the "splendid title" which Osiander has given his book, *Confession or Concerning the Sole Mediator Jesus Christ and Justification by Faith,"* makes it so much the more imperative to examine the spirits in order to ascertain whether they be of God. The biblical revelation is "clear, certain, simple, pure, unconfused and plain," so that no single, subtle, obscure paradoxes need to confuse or twist the teaching of Christianity. While Osiander rightly designates Luther as "the lion" whose sermons and lectures he has often heard in Wittenberg, he has evidently failed to understand him. Jonas, recalling his association with Luther for a period of twenty-five years, asserts that if Osiander had been privileged to enjoy a similar period of time with Luther, he would undoubtedly have remained an adherent of the apostolic doctrine and would not have resorted to all kinds of airy flights in reliance on his own ability. Instead he would have humbly lain down with the ox and the ass beside the cradle at Bethlehem in order to honor him who was of the tribe of Judah.

It is the opinion of ordinary folk, continues Jonas, that Osiander is engaging in subtle and confused sophistry which cannot be understood at all. Pious Christians with troubled hearts and consciences would not be able to find in Osiander's writings the comfort which they derive from the clear Word of God. For, after all, the real test of Osiander's views is whether they offer true comfort to the distressed and dying souls of men. Regarding his teaching they would probably say: "The preacher Osiander has need of a super-preacher. Oh, do not tell us about the sublime, incomprehensible indwelling of the Father, Son and Holy Spirit; tell me, as Paul says in Romans 8, how the Son has been given us as a gift and how with and in the Son, Christ, paradise and heaven have been brought down; yes, tell me, how through the blood of Christ and his obedience unto the death of the cross God is reconciled to us; yes, tell me, how the lion, Dr. Martinus, has for thirty years preached and taught before children, maids, servants, little ones, that hearts do not become pure except through faith."[33] Osiander's doctrine differs essentially from Luther's plain teaching. Jonas endeavors to make this apparent by asking: "Dear Mr. Osiander, whence do you derive the teaching that the righteousness of man or of a poor sinner is supposed to be the righteousness through which God the Father, Son, and Holy Spirit are righteous completely apart from the incarnation of Christ, when Paul, Peter, and all apostles point us to Christ, who has taken the form of a servant upon himself on our account, with streams and wounds has shed the precious blood on the tree for us? Who has commanded you that you should point us into the abyss of the divinity, into heaven? Go, then, to Osiander and soar suddenly above cherubim and seraphim, above all heavens, forget about the poor cradle in Ephratah."

In Jonas' opinion, Osiander's emphasis upon the presence of Jesus
Christ in the heart as the basis for justification belittles the objective
value of Christ's incarnation and death on the cross in human history.
In this point Osiander's teaching approaches the grossest error of the
papists, who, like Eck and Cochlaeus, have said that Christ, by his
suffering and death, merely made satisfaction for original sin. While
Osiander himself confesses that after birth we must be saved from
God's wrath and condemnation because we are not just, he departs
from the plain path of truth in his speculative flight. "A child ten
years of age, that has understood the Catechism well, could here conduct the seraphic Osiander to school and instruct him. Whoever has
been redeemed through Christ's blood and with that great price, is
he not sanctified, resurrected with Christ, translated into a heavenly
state? Where there is redemption from the eternal curse inherited
from Adam, is there not holiness, righteousness, divine sonship?"
Jonas and others, who have had the opportunity of hearing Luther's
sermons and lectures for twenty-five years, do not desire to indulge
in the abstruse speculations of an Osiander but abide by the Catechism. Christian righteousness is not hidden in the abyss of the God-
head, but has been commanded by God to be preached. It is the
righteousness "which is imputed to us if we believe that the Son of
God, true God and man, was sacrificed for our sin, and became our
ransom on the tree and arose for the sake of our righteousness." Outside
of Jesus Christ, of the seed of David, true God and man, no righteousness and no God are to be found.

Jonas now proceeds to show how the passages in John 17 are to be
explained: "That they may be one, even as we are one: I in them,
and thou in me" and "That the love wherewith thou hast loved me
may be in them, and I in them." These had evidently become the key
verses for Osiander's views. Ancient and present teachers have never
understood these words as an indwelling of the sublime, divine Spirit.
Jonas concurs with their interpretation which states: "that thou might-
est be efficacious in them through thy divine Spirit, support, illumi-
nation and truth." Christians should not suppose that they have to
ascend to heaven, but wherever they are, are members of the king-

dom of heaven. This precious treasure and wealth of heavenly possessions are given to Christians in the Word, and by faith in the heart
they experience the first fruits of Christ's Spirit, not the fullness of
the divine, which is reserved for heaven. For that reason the hearts
of all Christians should be the glorious temple and dwelling in which
God desires to work and dwell. But it is wrong to use the word
"substantial" in this connection, as does Osiander when he claims
that God is supposed to dwell in us on earth "in his entire indivisible
divine substance." Jonas illustrates the distinction that has to be made
in this way: While the sun exerts a definite influence on our bodies,
this does not mean that the sun in its entire substance is in all creatures. Similarly, we live and breathe the air, but the air as a whole is
not in us.

Jonas concludes that Osiander has through dangerous, obscure, and
complicated sophistry departed from the apostolic teaching, so that
his views might cause consternation, confusion, and the aberration
of many thousands of souls and consciences. "We, however, hold that
God will keep the same teaching of Luther which began in great
weakness and dealt a powerful blow to the huge mountain and rock
of the papacy . . . in accordance with this pure Word and in this
final age will preserve the sound doctrine and the Gospel which is
the word of salvation and comfort."[34]

With convincing earnestness and sharp satirical thrusts, Jonas attempted, in this Opinion of 1551, to guard against each and every
misrepresentation of evangelical doctrine. The main motive which
underlay the writing was the desire to keep inviolate the doctrine of
righteousness by faith as that apostolic doctrine which Luther had
again taught for the comfort and certain hope of Christian people
everywhere.

The Annotations on Acts

The theological productivity of Jonas was limited to several writings of an exegetical and instructional nature. In 1524 his *Annotations on the Acts of the Apostles*[35] appeared. These *Annotations* were

based on lectures he had delivered and afford a study of his terse, penetrating and practical exposition of Scripture.

In the dedication of this little volume to Duke John Frederick of Saxony, the nephew of the Elector Frederick, Jonas compares his own age with the apostolic era. Since it was his duty to lecture on something in the sacred Scriptures, he continues, he took it upon himself to explain this book and publish the brief annotations. In the Book of Acts, Jonas writes, the true church has been depicted for us. "For the true church is the congregation of the elect who believe in Christ and have the genuine and pure Word of God." To show its normative function for his own day Jonas remarks: "I ask, if we consider this account of Luke, where is that pompous and blustering life among the bishops? where the gilded temples, where that abominable celibacy, where so many factions of the monks?"[36]

The *Annotations* are introduced by an explicit reference to Christ as the Savior of men and to his office of helping and restoring men to fellowship with God. The purpose of the Book of Acts is to describe the true nature of Christ's church in which "the Gospel is of all things the most noble and certain symbol of the church." After giving a comprehensive summary of the contents of Acts, Jonas appositely comments on the practical implications of Christ's ascension and points out that his reign is not physical but spiritual. "By his ascension to the Father he has received this reign so that he fills all, which even now is understood by faith alone."

Jonas' exegesis is shot through with constant references to parallel Scripture passages which illumine the text he is treating. While there is a recurring emphasis on the righteousness which is ours by faith and to God's initiative in conversion, explicit mention of the fruits of faith and of the working of the Holy Spirit in dedicated lives is made. The primacy of preaching in the life of the church is shown to be fundamental. Moreover, the necessity of being chosen by God in order to be a minister of Jesus Christ is underscored. "True ministers of the Word know and are sure that it is not they who speak but the Spirit of the Father." Nor is the Christian life ever without a concomitant cross that exercises the believer in patience and hope. The author of the *Annotations*, at the close of his work, summons the reader to be incited to faith by God's providential dealing with the Apostle Paul. Thus throughout this brief exegetical treatise Jonas demonstrates conclusively his basic understanding of evangelical Christianity and his undeniable aptitude as a teacher of the Holy Scriptures.[37]

On Faith and Charity

In 1542 Jonas wrote a brief treatise for the avowed purpose of grounding the Christians of Halle in the evangelical faith. It was first printed in Wittenberg in 1542 under the title: "A Christian and Brief Instruction Concerning the Forgiveness of Sins and Salvation, by Justus Jonas, Doctor. Thereby You may Discover Some Principal Differences Between the Pure Christian Teaching of the Gospel and the Idolatrous, Papistical Doctrine."

The treatise begins by asking pointedly: (1) "Upon what is your salvation based?" and gives the succinct reply: "Upon the pure grace of God." For that reason, whenever the heart trembles because of God's wrath and is terrified by the divine judgment over sin, a person is to believe in God's mercy and the forgiveness that is granted for Christ's sake. (2) "How does this occur?" By virtue of the sin of our first parents, Adam and Eve, humanity merited eternal condemnation and would have been eternally lost if God had not conceived the unsearchable plan of sending his Son and through him reconciling the world to himself. Two sermons, dating back to the beginning of time, God has marvelously preserved for us through the patriarchs, prophets, and apostles. The one sermon preaches God's law and his wrath over sin; the other sermon proclaims that only Christ, the Son of God, could make reconciliation for our sins. "Whoever despises the wrath, also despises the sacrifice." God is at work continually in his church through these two sermons—on the one hand, punishing and giving knowledge of sin, on the other, granting forgiveness for the sake of Jesus Christ. The resulting faith in God's love and forgiveness must be attributed to the work of the Holy Spirit who alone enables us to know God, obey him, and become heirs of eternal life. (3) "Why do you base your hope on grace?" is the third question. The answer consists of three chief reasons. Salvation by grace alone gives to the Savior and Mediator, Christ, the glory that he deserves; he alone is the propitiation for our sins, so that we may be utterly sure that it is God's will to forgive us our sins; and such a faith enables us to worship God and pray to him in an acceptable way. (4) "How are you certain of this?" The certainty of faith has its origin in the express command and pledge of God, who sealed his promises by means of miracles and the resurrection. (5) In placing the question before us: "Is there also a difference in this article between the Christian teaching and papal error?" the reply is made that the chief distinction is found to consist in this: The Romanist Church, by demanding good works for salvation, induces doubt concerning the surety of redemption; the evangelical Church, putting forth Christ as the certain ground for salvation, obviates all needless uncertainty. (6) Since the problem arises at this point as to whether it is necessary to do good works, a clear-cut distinction is drawn between works by which we endeavor to earn forgiveness and works which are commanded and are pleasing to God. The former are rejected, while the latter are viewed as fruits of a living faith whereby we seek to glorify God. First, in doing good works, Christians are to be guided by God's law. "From this one should know that the human reason is not to devise its own works and worship, but shall abide by the rule which has been placed before us in the Ten Commandments and as they are explained in the Gospel." Consequently, all significant works are comprehended in the command to love God and one's neighbor. Secondly, because of human weakness and the temptations of the devil Christians must learn to depend upon Christ in doing good works, for he said: "Without me ye can do nothing." Thirdly, our works are not pleasing to God because of their perfection, but because they are done through faith in Christ and in obedience to God's command. Fourthly, we are to be incited to good works by three motives: God's will made known to us in his commands, Christ's vicarious suffering for us, and the desire to persevere in the salvation granted us. Lastly, Christians do not commit sin knowingly or purposely, but only out of weakness and insufficiency.

After this brief exposition of Christian doctrine, the importance of prayer as the principal way of exercising one's belief is discussed and a prayer by Luther is introduced. In conclusion, sixteen distinct differences between the doctrines of the papal and evangelical churches are enumerated with admirable precision and clearness. This treatment of evangelical Christianity is a gem of popular instruction motivated by fervent, evangelistic zeal.[38]

The small treatise proved to be very much in demand in Halle, so that Jonas had a second edition printed sometime in 1544. The short dedicatory letter that introduced this edition, in striking sentences made the aim and purpose of the author clear and pointed. "This life," says the author, "is the brief spring; that life is the beautiful, bright, living, and eternal summer, the true treasure, harvest, and fullness of the everlasting heavenly possessions and fruits." Human riches, honor, glory, the favor of the mighty and their disfavor pass away. "Here I ask: Is one then to jest about the welfare of the soul? Does it matter at all? Therefore, happy are they who hear the Word of God and heartily and earnestly embrace the right teaching, the true worship, in order to be sure of their soul's salvation."[39]

In the year 1524 Luther published the first evangelical hymnals. The second one that was published was entitled *Enchiridion or Handbook for Every Christian*.[40] This little book had been prepared by Luther to meet the specific needs of the day. It contained the Ten Commandments, which were followed by hymns written by Luther, Paul Speratus, and others. The versification of Psalm 124, consisting of eight stanzas, was the work of Jonas who, in this instance, gave proof of his ability as a hymn-writer. In the spirit of the author of the Psalm, Jonas extolled God's protective power and called upon him to come to the aid of his faithful people. Stanzas one, six, and eight are given here in translation.

If God the Lord's not on our side
When enemies are raging,
And he with us doth not abide
In highest heaven reigning;
If he is not Israel's defense
And doth not thwart the foe's pretense,
Then this is our undoing.

Lord God, thou comfortest so richly
Those who on thee depend;
The door to grace is open fully;
This reason cannot comprehend.
It says that all is now a loss,
Although the new birth through the cross
Is theirs who wait upon thee.

The heaven as well as all the earth
Thou, Lord God, hast well founded;
So may thy light be the bright hearth
At which our hearts are kindled.
Thus in true faith and charity
May we be ever loyal to thee;
Let the world be sore offended.

While the *Handbook* contained chiefly Luther's and Speratus' hymns, it is interesting to note that it was published by the printer at the Black Horn in Erfurt. It is therefore not unlikely that both Jonas and Lange were mainly responsible for this edition. Thus Jonas made a modest contribution to one of the first evangelical hymnals which, purged of unscriptural hymns of praise and prayer to Mary and the saints, became the basis for evangelical worship.

The crisis of the Schmalcald War elicited three hymns from Jonas' pen. The first hymn, "The Lord hear you in your distress," written during the early part of the war, was based on Psalm 20. The 14 stanzas of the hymn echoed the prayerful wish of the psalm-writer and, in its contemporary setting, became a prayer of intercession for the Elector of Saxony and the Landgrave of Hesse. Jonas had the hymn printed in order that the church in Halle might sing and pray it on behalf of

the Protestant cause. On October 26, 1546, Jonas had several copies of
the hymn sent to the warring Elector John Frederick through his son
Justus Jr.

Another hymn, based on Psalm 79, appeared in the same year. The
hymn interprets the Psalm in the light of the Protestant situation,
looking upon the evangelical Christians as the true Israel of God,
while the Pope and his supporters are viewed as the heathen mentioned in the Psalm. The first stanza of the hymn is:

> *Lord Jesus Christ, thine heirs are we,*
> *Thy holy church on earth below;*
> *Thine eternal people, blessed by God,*
> *We shall become in heaven's glow.*
> *May we who now thy Word do hear*
> *Be granted in thy presence there*
> *To rejoice, O Son of God, in thee.*

The hymn, after describing the believers who trust in God, tells how
Rome is attempting to abuse the Lord's temple by not permitting the
true worship of God. In the face of the many abuses in the Roman
Church evangelical Christians have become the object of scorn and
mockery and their plight seems desperate. After a prayer for forgiveness, a request for divine help and a petition to mete out a sevenfold
recompense to the foe, the final stanza of the hymn breathes the spirit
of trust in God.

> *We are indeed thy Church, O Lord,*
> *Poor lambs of thy green pasture;*
> *We'll thank thee through eternity*
> *That thou in fullest measure*
> *Hast promised us refuge and grace;*
> *So then both night and day we'll praise*
> *Thy wonder o'er all wonders.*

The last hymn, belonging to this period, was composed on the basis
of Psalms 22 and 71. It was intended as a prayer for the individual
Christian in time of distress and in the hour of death. It consisted of
four stanzas. The first and last stanzas are:

Lord Jesus Christ, true God art thou;
In extreme distress thou see'st me now;
When in her womb my mother conceived me
And carried me about thus hopefully,
Thou, Lord, didst protect me by thy might
And wast for me my life and light.

When I was very small and frail
And anxiously in danger and travail
I was born into this world of thine,
Thou didst become my Savior divine.
O dear Lord Christ, in this grave hour
I call upon thy matchless power.[41]

In addition to these three hymns, Jonas added stanzas four and five to Luther's hymn, "Lord, keep us steadfast in thy Word." These two stanzas, voicing the petition that God would destroy the counsels of the enemies of Christ's cause so that they might realize that God lives and does not forsake his people, were, to judge from their contents, written while the Schmalcald War was in progress.

Translations of Luther

Justus Jonas made his first venture as translator on behalf of the cause of the Reformation in 1521. Immediately upon his return to Erfurt, after attending the Diet of Worms, he translated into German Luther's Latin speech and reply before the Diet. He had Matthew Maler of the printing press at the Black Horn in Erfurt print his translation.[42] In 1524 Jonas translated Luther's German tract "That Jesus Christ Was a Native Jew" into Latin, and in 1525 he put into idiomatic and smooth-flowing German Luther's Latin treatise *Concerning the Bondage of the Will* which was directed against Erasmus.

During the tense and dramatic days at the Diet of Augsburg in 1530, when many demands were made on Jonas, he completed the translation of Luther's commentary on the Prophet Jonah from Latin into German. He dedicated this translation to Count William von Honstein, Bishop of Strassburg. Recommending Luther's exposition of the prophet to the Count, Jonas wrote that the glorious Gospel of Jesus

Christ shone forth luminously in the entire work. In the closing words
of this dedication Jonas stated that since both the bishop and he were
born in Nordhausen he was dedicating this translation to him.[43]

In 1533 Jonas dedicated a German translation of Luther's exposition
of the Book of Ecclesiastes to the Landgrave Philip of Hesse, and he
used the occasion to give counsel to the Landgrave in the fine art of
government. Since even heathen writers, like Demosthenes and Soc-
rates, realized that human wisdom was not sufficient for the high office
of government, Jonas heartily commended the study of Luther's exposition of this biblical book to the end that the Landgrave might
remain obedient to God, continue to fear him, and trust in him.[44] In
September of the same year Jonas was asked to make a Latin translation of Luther's exposition of the Sermon on the Mount. When
someone else undertook this work, Jonas proceeded with a Latin translation of Luther's *Summaries on the Psalms* and dedicated it to Duke
Ernest of Saxony late in 1533.[45] Early in 1534 Luther, rejoicing that
his German book *Regarding the Private Mass and Consecration of the
Priests* was so offensive to the papists, called upon Jonas to put it into
Latin. "But you, my Jonas, shall do well," wrote Luther, "if you render
this book, so odious to Satan's reign, but necessary for our brethren,
into the Latin language so as to be useful to most people. . . . But see
to it that you are mindful of my canon according to which I have
asked that you translate my thought in a free manner."[46]

In 1538 two translations by Jonas—one from Luther's writings and
another by Paul Jovius—appeared. The last mentioned was a translation of Jovius' Latin treatise: *Concerning the Origin of the Turkish
Kingdom,* and made its appearance in January 1538. In June of the
same year the translation into Latin of Luther's *Book of Ecclesiasticus*
was completed by Jonas and dedicated to the Princes of Anhalt.[47] In
1539 another Latin translation of Luther's brief treatise: *A Letter
against the Sabbatarians* came out.[48] Jonas believed that this labor of
translating furthered the cause of the Gospel. Consequently, he diligent-
ly performed this work, though ill health often interfered and many
other duties and responsibilities intervened.

In March, 1543, Jonas finished putting Luther's German writing

"Concerning the Jews and their Lies" into Latin. He was pleased to report to the Elector that this translation was bearing fruit in foreign lands.[49] In 1545 Luther was producing a writing against the Roman papacy. Though extremely violent in its polemic, it contained a very thorough discussion concerning the marks of the true and false church. Jonas had been informed by his son, Justus Jr., that Luther desired him to translate this piece of work from German into Latin. During a visit in Wittenberg in May Jonas was given this writing by Luther. Toward the end of May he reported to Prince George that he had completed translating most of the third and last part and that he hoped to give the entire translation to the printer very soon. This Latin translation probably came off the press in late May or early June. Jonas had a copy of the translation sent to a friend, Basilius Monner, later in the year.[50]

One translation by Jonas appeared during the years of the Schmalcald War and its ensuing upheaval. It was a translation into German of Luther's "Preface to the Entire Bible, How the True Church of God Had Its Beginning on Earth." Jonas completed the translation during his stay in Hildesheim. After it had been published, he addressed a letter to the Elector of Saxony in October 1547 and enclosed a copy of this translation, hoping to comfort the Saxon ruler who had been taken captive by the Emperor.[51]

After Luther's death Jonas began the Latin translation of Luther's "A Book Concerning the Councils and the Church." Evidently Jonas worked at this project sporadically for a number of years. During his last illness Jonas once more attempted to complete this translation. He wrote a letter of dedication to King Christian of Denmark and sent Latin versions of it and the book to Basilius Faber Soranus. Soranus, convinced that a thorough revision was necessary, undertook the same, so that the translation first appeared posthumously in 1556.[52]

Other Translations

Justus Jonas, recognizing in Melanchthon an important member of Luther's program of reform, also translated an impressive number of his writings. On February 3, 1528, Jonas sent a letter of dedication from Wittenberg together with the translation of Melanchthon's writing "Against the Doctrine of the Anabaptists" to Michael Meienburg, the friend with whom he had stayed at Nordhausen. Jonas revealed the motive which prompted him to translate this Latin work into German. He hoped that it would keep many "pious hearts and consciences" from falling prey to pernicious doctrines and would cause the readers of the translation to thank God for "such a mighty, gracious preserva-tion of the divine truth."[53] Only a year later he put into German Melanchthon's work *The Epistle of St. Paul to the Colossians.* In the preface to this translation he laid down the principles which guided him in translating this particular exegetical study by Melanchthon.[54]

In May, 1536, Jonas' German translation of Melanchthon's *Loci communes,* which treated the cardinal points of theology, appeared. He dedicated the translation to the Elector John Frederick of Saxony. In this dedication he gave the reason for translating this work. He believed that it set forth a clear and true summary of the Christian faith and desired that the German rulers and people read it in their own language. Jonas called upon the Elector to rule according to God's law and for the well-being of his subjects, and, in being mindful of his duties as a Christian ruler, to further Christian truth and virtue in his own land.[55] Jonas sent a copy of his translation of the *Loci* to the senate of Naumburg in the same year.

In 1540 a number of pamphlets and writings were translated by Jonas. The translations into German included a letter by King Henry VIII, a writing on the Turks, a letter of Philip Melanchthon to the Landgrave of Hesse, "Concerning the Church and the Old Church Fathers," a Melanchthonian declamation, "The Complaint of Lazarus" dedicated to Prince John of Anhalt, and Melanchthon's writing "Against the Impure Papal Celibacy and the Prohibition of Sacerdotal Marriage." The only translation into Latin was a Catechism which had been written for the churches of Brandenburg and the imperial city of Nuremberg.[56] This translation appeared early in 1539. In 1548 Archbishop Cranmer put this Catechism into English under the title:

Cathecismus, That is to say, a short Instruction into Christian Religion.[57]

Melanchthon's writing "Concerning a True Compromise and Negotiation for Peace in Matters of Religion," was translated by Justus Jonas and published in Wittenberg in 1541. A number of years later Melanchthon asked Jonas to translate his Latin treatise "Reasons Why the Churches. Which Confess the Pure, Christian Doctrine Have Accepted the Same . . ."[58] The translation was dedicated to the senate of Halle because Jonas felt that such instruction in the evangelical churches was timely and requisite. Jonas maintained that God's church could not be protected by human might but only by God's hand. "He himself will guard the ministry of the Gospel; that we ought to believe and in such a faith call upon him and not flounder about and faint for fear, but wait for help with peaceful hearts."[59]

In order to furnish the evangelical Christians at Regensburg with a better knowledge of their faith, Jonas translated the doctrine "Concerning the Church" from Melanchthon's *Loci theologici*. The translation was designed as an answer to the sermons of the Catholic preachers at the Cathedral in Regensburg. Jonas dedicated the brief treatise to the Protestant Christians at Regensburg whom he addressed specifically in a preface. Jonas called upon the Regensburg Christians to read this little book dealing so clearly with the distinction between the true and false church. For it had been put into German by him so that the pure gold and fine silver of God's Word might be differentiated from the dross, the clear fountain from impure and stagnant water.[60]

Equally important in the literary field was Jonas' participation in the revision of Luther's translation of the Scriptures. Every day during the years 1539 to 1542 Melanchthon, Bugenhagen, Jonas, Cruciger, Aurogallus, and the professional reader, Roerer, met several hours with Luther before the evening meal in order to perform this labor.[61] However, in 1541 the call of duty separated Jonas from this intimate circle of scholars and theologians and led him from Wittenberg to another sphere of service.

FOOTNOTES FOR CHAPTER 6

1. *Luthers Werke,* Weimar Edition, Vol. XII, pp. 81-88.
2. Kawerau, *op. cit.,* Vol. II, p. xix.
3. *Luthers Werke,* Weimar Edition, Vol. XII, p. 85.
4. The full title was: *Adversus Iohannem Fabrum Constantien. Vicarium scorta-tionis patronum, pro coniugio sacerdotali, Iusti Ionae defensio.* Printed in Wittenberg in 1523 by N. Schirleutz.
5. All quotations are from the original Latin print of 1523. Pages in it were not numbered.
6. Hasse, *Justus Jonas,* p. 144.
   C. L. Franke, *Geschichte der Hallischen Reformation,* p. 287.
7. Kawerau, *op. cit.,* Vol. I, p. 241.
8. Kawerau, *op. cit.,* Vol. II, p. xxxvii.
   Albrecht Ritschl, "Georg Witzels Abkehr vom Luthertum," *Zeitschrift für Kirchengeschichte.* Edited by Theodor Brieger, Vol. II, Third Part, pp. 387-388.
9. Otto Clemen, "Georg Witzel und Justus Jonas," *Archiv für Reformations-geschichte.* Edited by Walter Friedensburg. Vol. XVII (1920), pp. 134-136.
10. Kawerau, *op. cit.,* Vol. II, p. xxxvii.
11. Enders, *op. cit.,* Vol. IX, pp. 205-207.
12. Clemen, *op. cit.,* pp. 134-136.
13. *Ibid.,* p. 137.
14. Kawerau, *op. cit.,* Vol. I, pp. 186-187.
15. Clemen, *op. cit.,* p. 138.
16. Kawerau, *op. cit.,* Vol. I, pp. 188-189.
17. *Ibid.,* p. 205.
18. Hasse, *Justus Jonas Leben,* pp. 170-173.
19. It was entitled "Georg Witzels historia."
    Kawerau, *op. cit.,* Vol. II, p. xxxviii.
20. The full title: *Concerning the Christian Church Against Jodocus Koch Who Calls Himself Justus Jonas by George Witzel.* 1534, Leipzig, Nickel Schmidt.
    Clemen, *op. cit.,* p. 139.
21. Kawerau, *op. cit.,* Vol. II, p. xxxviii.
22. The proof for Corvinus' authorship is given by Otto Clemen. Clemen, *op. cit.,* pp. 139-140.
23. Kawerau, *op. cit.,* Vol. I, pp. 214-218.
24. Clemen, *op. cit.,* pp. 143-144.
25. *Ibid.,* pp. 144-152.
26. *Ibid.,* p. 145.
27. Enders, *op. cit.,* Vol. X, p. 70.
28. The published letter was entitled: "Epistola D. Coclei ad Georgium Vuicelium ne tristetur propter abnegatum coniugium sacerdotale et hactenus frustra ex-pectatos XXX. argenteos Iudae Iscarioth. Wittembergae 1534."
    Kawerau, *op. cit.,* Vol. II, p. xxxix, Vol. I, pp. 443-445.
29. Ritschl, *op. cit.,* Vol. II (1887-1888), Third Part, pp. 386-417.
30. W. Moeller, *Lehrbuch der Kirchengeschichte,* Vol. III, "Reformation u. Gegen-reformation," revised by G. Kawerau, pp. 221-222.
31. Pressel, *op. cit.,* p. 101.
32. Kawerau, *op. cit.,* Vol. II, pp. 309-319.
33. Kawerau, *op cit.,* Vol. II, p. 311.
34. Kawerau, *op. cit.,* Vol. II, pp. 314-319.
35. *Annotationes Iusti Ionae, in Acta Apostolorum* MDXXIIII bound in Reforma-tionsschriften Vol. IX. An original print made in Wittenberg 1524. A later edition in German came out in 1525 and another in 1567 in Wittenberg. Cf. Franke, *Geschichte der Hallischen Reformation,* p. 287; Th. Pressel, *op. cit.,* p. 46.
36. Letter of Dedication in *Annotations.* Cf. Kawerau, *op. cit.,* Vol. I, pp. 91-92.

37. This summary is based on *Annotationes Iusti Ionae in Acta Apostolorum.*
38. Based on a summary of the original document as found in Pressel, *op. cit.,* pp. 41-45; cf. J. M. Reu, *Quellen zur Geschichte des Katechismus-Unterrichts,* Vol. II, part I, p. 314.
39. Kawerau, *op. cit.,* Vol. II, p. 112.
40. The full title: *Enchiridion or Handbook for Every Christian Quite Useful to Possess for Constant Exercise and Concern for Spiritual Songs and Psalms, Rightly and Artfully Put into German.* A reprint of the original 1524 edition as extant in Strassburg was made in Erfurt in 1848. Cf. Hasse, *Justus Jonas,* pp. 146-147.
41. Philip Wackernagel, *Das deutsche Kirchenlied von der ältesten Zeit bis zu Anfang des XVI Jahrhunderts,* Vol. III, pp. 42-45.
42. Reference to this undertaking is made in Jonas' letter to Melchior von Aachen. Kawarau, *op. cit.,* Vol. I, pp. 53-54.
    Kalkoff, *Humanismus und Reformation in Erfurt,* p. 68.
43. Kawerau, *op. cit.,* Vol. I, pp. 437-443.
44. *Ibid.,* pp. 194-196.
45. *Ibid.,* pp. 197 and 201-202.
46. Enders, *op. cit.,* Vol. IX, p. 384.
47. Kawerau, *op. cit.,* Vol. I, pp. 269-272 and 293.
48. *Ibid.,* Vol. II, p. xxvi.
49. *Ibid.,* pp. 96 and 128.
50. The full title was: "CONTRA PAPATUM ROMANUM, A Diabolo inventum. D.Doct. Mar. Luth. E. GERMA. LATINE redditum, per Iustum Ionam. 1545." Kawerau, *op. cit.,* Vol. II, pp. 153, 168.
51. Burkhardt, "Neue Mittheilungen zur Korrespondenz der Reformation," *Zeitschrift für kirchliche Wissenschaften,* X Jahrgang 1889. Edited by C. E. Luthardt, p. 433.
52. Kawerau, *op. cit.,* Vol. II, pp. 337-343.
53. *Ibid.,* Vol. I, p. 118.
54. Kawerau, *op. cit.,* Vol. I, p. 129.
55. *Corpus Reformatorum,* Vol. XXII, pp. 15-18.
56. Kawerau, *op. cit.,* Vol. II, pp. 368-370, pp. xxvi-xxvii, Vol. I, p. 416.
57. A microfilm of this edition is in Yale University Library. A later edition appeared in Oxford in 1829 under the title: *A Short Instruction into Christian Religion being a Catechism set forth by Archbishop Cranmer in 1548: together with the same in latin, translated from the german by Justus Jonas in 1539.* Pressel, *op. cit.,* pp. 41 and 129.
58. *Corpus Reformatorum,* Vol. VI, p. 208.
59. Kawerau, *op. cit.,* Vol. II, pp. 205-206.
60. Preface to "Which Is the One True Church of Christ. Where It is Certainly to be Found. Which Is the False Church. Put into German from the Latin of Phil. Mel. by Justus Jonas, Dr." Kawerau, *op. cit.,* Vol. II, p. 324.
61. James Mackinnon, *Luther and the Reformation,* Vol. IV, p. 274.

Chapter 7

Early Work at Halle

The history of the spread of the Reformation to Halle and of its eventual triumph in that second largest city of the archdiocese of Magdeburg is characterized by two conspicuous features. First, the Reformation was embraced by the people in Halle who were won over to the evangelical faith by the Reformation writings of Luther. Secondly, it was providentially nurtured, strengthened, and extended by pious preachers of the Gospel.

The City of the Cardinal

It might well be regarded as the irony of history that the very person who was responsible for the enormous traffic in indulgences in 1517 should have to relinquish one of the strongholds of his spiritual rule and permit it to come under the domain of the Reformation. Albrecht of Brandenburg, Elector of Mainz, Cardinal and Archbishop of Magdeburg, was the most powerful spiritual prince in Germany at the time of the Reformation. By the purchase of the high ecclesiastical and worldly offices he held, he had incurred such a tremendous debt that a Plenary Indulgence was issued by Pope Leo X in the year 1517. According to a secret understanding the proceeds of the indulgence sale were to be divided between Archbishop Albrecht and the Pope. Ostensibly the money was to be used solely for building St. Peter's Church at Rome. The posting of the Ninety-Five Theses in 1517 marked the beginning of a victorious struggle against this corrupt practice, and the continued advance of the Reformation made Cardinal Albrecht an implacable foe of evangelical truth and its chief representative, Luther.[1]

As Halle was in the archdiocese of Magdeburg and therefore ruled by the Cardinal, at the beginning of the Reformation the city had a large number of heavily endowed and well-manned cloisters. Significantly, none of them belonged to the monastic orders which were known for their interest in learning, or their care of the poor and the sick. In addition to the ten or more cloisters and parish churches, there seem to have been around thirty chapels scattered throughout the city. It was, if the outward forms and expressions of worship are considered, a religious city. Innumerable altars in the churches were dedicated to several saints. The worship of these saints along with the Virgin Mary had assumed a more vital religious role for the people in general than God or Jesus Christ. Every Christian, every home, every guild, every locality and piece of land had a patron saint. St. Maurice was the patron saint of the city and was, for that reason, held in particularly high esteem. The Cardinal fostered this popular belief by purchasing relics of every kind and storing them in the new Cathedral Church he had erected.[2] Perhaps the Apostle Paul, passing through the city at that time, would have remarked, as he did at Athens: "I perceive that in every way you are very religious."[3]

In the spring of 1517 John Tetzel had also come to Halle and had sold indulgences in St. Martin's Chapel.[4] The proximity of Wittenberg, where Luther's Theses were posted in October 1517, was bound to result in the circulation of their content in Halle. In addition, the writings which Luther subsequently published came to be known, circulated, and read in Halle. The public edict, forbidding the reading of Luther's writings and ordering them to be burned, did not have the desired effect of suppressing the dangerous Lutheran "heresy." The Gospel message was eagerly accepted by the people of the city. In 1521 Cardinal Albrecht made a bold move. He instituted an indulgence sale in Halle to pay for the new Cathedral Church which he had begun to build. Luther courageously attacked the Cardinal in a writing entitled: "Against the Idol at Halle," and wrote a letter to Albrecht of Mainz in which he threatened to publish this attack if the sale of indulgences was not immediately stopped. The Cardinal sent a conciliatory letter in reply to Luther's vigorous and challenging protest and promised to put a halt to the indulgence traffic.[5] After that the stormy opposition from Wittenberg abated.

By 1523 the new Cathedral Chapter at Halle had been put into operation by the Cardinal. It was designed to act as a bulwark against the inroads the new Wittenberg doctrine was making into Albrecht's territories. A university was to be connected with it and the Cathedral was thus to resist heresy and preserve inviolate the Romish religion in Halle, the residence of the Cardinal and Elector.[6] Nicholas Demuth, hitherto provost of the Neuwerk Cloister, was selected as the first provost of the Cathedral; but in 1522 he left the cloister, embraced the evangelical doctrine and went to Saxony.[7] The minister appointed to preach in the Cathedral was George Winkler from Bischofswerda. In 1524 he began to preach the evangelical faith publicly in the Cathedral. Soon after he proceeded to abolish the corrupt ceremonies and to administer the Lord's Supper according to the New Testament practice "under both kinds"; lastly, as final proof of his complete break with Roman Catholic tradition, he also married. The people were attracted by Winkler's powerful and stirring evangelical sermons. Their presence put the stamp of public approval on his activities.[8]

The weapons forged for the abolition of evangelical truth in Halle were producing the very opposite effect from that which had originally been intended. With growing apprehension the Cardinal observed events. The Peasants' Revolt in 1524 and 1525 came close to the borders of his land; and after it had subsided he discovered, much to his dismay, that popular sentiment was against him in Halle. Accordingly, in order to placate its citizenry he promised to hear all complaints brought forth by the senate, his own councilors, and the people themselves. A number of articles were drawn up. One of these stated "that our gracious lord permit the Word of God to be preached purely and plainly and would have the most worthy Sacrament administered and given to us according to the institution of Jesus Christ." This was indeed patent proof of the popular desire for the Reformation in the city; but in dishonorable fashion and with inexcusable deceit the Cardinal broke his promise.[9]

Albrecht's Treachery

Throughout this time Winkler had continued to preach his evangelical sermons until he was accused before the Cardinal by a canon of the Cathedral and was enjoined in 1527 to appear before his superior in Aschaffenburg. The Cardinal dealt mildly with Winkler, the chaplain of his new Cathedral in Halle, for he imposed no penalty upon him for his conduct and permitted him to return to the city. The canons of the Mainz Cathedral, however, were hatching a sinister plot against Winkler. They were able to effect his delay in Aschaffenburg until their plans had fully matured. They were even successful in persuading Winkler to send his servant ahead of him on his return journey. After he had traveled scarcely two miles from Aschaffenburg, he was overtaken by several disguised and armed knights in the Spessart Forest and cruelly murdered on August 25, 1527.[10]

The news of Winkler's death spread rapidly. Popular sentiment blamed Albrecht of Mainz for the murder. Luther felt constrained to write a letter of comfort to the Christians at Halle. Recalling his intention of writing to them previous to this occasion, Luther felt that even though he was in poor health, it was his duty not to keep silent about "such a perfidious murder" but to bear witness to God's Holy Word. He praised the faithful service of Winkler and fervently hoped "that Magister George's blood may be a divine seed, which although sown in the earth by the hand of Satan and his members, may bring forth seed an hundredfold, so that instead of the murdered George a hundred other faithful preachers may arise, who will injure Satan a thousand times more than the one man has done."[11]

In the same year a second incident occurred which left a marked impression upon the people in Halle. During the Cardinal's absence from Halle most of his councilors had partaken of the Lord's Supper "under both kinds." Among these was a certain John Krause. While on a journey his wife, who was with him, gave birth to twins, and both she and the newborn children died immediately after the birth. As a result Krause became extremely melancholy. When the Cardinal issued a command that the entire populace in Halle was no longer to receive the Sacrament "under both kinds," Krause, fearing the Cardinal's displeasure and being persuaded that the traditional mode of receiving only the bread in the Sacrament was right, complied with this order, while the other councilors remonstrated against it. Krause's depressed mental state, however, became worse and, in a fit of melancholy, he committed suicide. Luther, on being informed of this happening, interpreted Krause's tragic end as an example of how a person, by falling away from Christ, falls into the hands of Satan.[12]

During the Cardinal's absence of several years the evangelical cause continued to make progress. In 1531 he returned in order that he might, by his personal presence, repress the Reformation movement.[13] Yet his efforts to control or intimidate those members of the city's senate who espoused the Reformation proved futile. Attempting to make the Catholic religion the sole faith of Halle's inhabitants, he issued a mandate, requiring all Christians at Halle to receive the Easter Communion according to the Catholic tradition "under one kind." But this measure failed to achieve its purpose, and so it was followed by a severe edict which threatened to excommunicate those who did not conform to the Cardinal's injunctions. Even this sterner edict was ineffectual. A group of newly elected members of the senate who were of evangelical persuasion resigned their offices because of the edict, and when they were again admitted to the senate they responded with true courage to the overtures which were made. "Because they knew and sincerely believed that this was the true Gospel and genuine Word of God, which they, praise God, had received, they could in no way surrender it and also nevermore desired to deny Christ." As a result these members of the senate were forced to leave the city, since the Cardinal insisted upon the execution of the edict. Only one of them recanted and returned to Halle; three died in exile because of the dire distress of their situation; those remaining returned to the city in 1541.

The stern, repressive measures that were put into force did not succeed in winning the Christians at Halle back to papal authority. When the evangelical citizens were unable to hear the Gospel preached and to receive the Sacrament "under both kinds" in their own city, they flocked in large numbers to the neighboring territories of Mansfeld and Electoral Saxony in quest of spiritual nourishment. This, too, was at length forbidden and punished with imprisonment and other severe penalties. Nevertheless, many dared to defy these ordinances and continued their pilgrimages to neighboring evangelical lands; others sought to strengthen their faith by reading the Scriptures in German and Luther's writings in their private homes; while for all these pious souls the hymns of Luther and his associates became a source of comfort and inspiration during these times of affliction and difficulty. Eventually these evangelical hymns became so popular that even Roman Catholics joined in singing them.[14]

The forcible suppression of the evangelical faith was a manifest failure, but Cardinal Albrecht was not convinced that he could not eventually succeed. In 1540 he renewed his efforts in this direction by forbidding the importation of all books and writings that did not have the approval of an official. The singing of all hymns written by Luther and his adherents was supposed to cease and the people were to be forced to attend mass and to hear the Catholic sermons.[15] It was the final attempt of the Cardinal to stamp out the Wittenberg "heresy." Popular sentiment was soon to triumph over tyrannical rule.

The opportunity that permitted this triumph was connected with the dismissal of the provincial Diet at Calbe in January of 1541. The Diet had granted the spendthrift, luxury-loving Cardinal 500,000 guldens for the purpose of liquidating his debts, and determined that the money was to be raised by a special tax assessment. The city of Halle was expected to raise 22,000 guldens of this amount. When the deputies who attended the Diet returned to Halle with their report, the senate convoked the entire citizenry in order to have the syndic Philip Gossmann make known that this money was to be raised at once. The citizens, however, attached certain conditions to the fulfillment of this obligation and had a council transmit them to the senate. The conditions were that they should be allowed to have an evangelical minister, that the Sacrament be administered to them according to Christ's institution, and that an evangelical schoolteacher be employed by the city. Although the Catholic members of the senate, especially the syndic Gossmann and the two ruling councilmen, tried to evade the issue, the council, wary of evasions and insistent in its demands, finally succeeded in obtaining permission to have an evangelical minister come to Halle from Leipzig or Wittenberg.[16] A deputation was speedily dispatched to Leipzig in order to secure the services of John Pfeffinger, an evangelical minister there. The report that Archbishop Albrecht had sent out knights who were to prevent the coming of an evangelical minister as well as a threatening letter by the coadjutor of the Cardinal so intimidated Pfeffinger that he declined the invitation.[17]

The Call to Jonas

The deputation returned to Halle and made its report. The populace was in a very agitated state, while the senate, its allegiance divided between the Catholic faith and the new doctrine, did not know where to turn. A revolt threatened and action was imperative. At this crucial moment a delegation—whether they were members of the deputation or of the council is not definitely known—went to Wittenberg and asked that Jonas come to Halle. After these negotiations had been carried out in secrecy and the Elector had consented to having Jonas go to Halle temporarily,[18] Jonas, accompanied by the Wittenberg chaplain Andrew Huegel,[19] ostensibly left Wittenberg on April 13, 1541, to journey through Thuringia to Nordhausen. Actually their destination was Halle. In reporting the call to Halle, in later letters, Jonas purposely kept silent about these preliminary negotiations which had taken place in Wittenberg and related only the subsequent steps connected with his call, likely in order that he might not imperil the position of the Elector of Saxony and thus make his going to Halle a political issue.

While on his pretended journey to Nordhausen, early on the morning of April 14, on Maundy Thursday of Holy Week, a delegation of four men, two being members of the senate and two being representatives of the people, came from Halle to meet Jonas and requested that he remain in Halle for two months or more and preach the Gospel.[20] On Thursday, late in the evening, Jonas and Andrew Huegel arrived in the city and were hospitably received in the house of a certain Dr. Milde, a member of the council elected by the people.[21] The report of the arrival of these two evangelical ministers spread rapidly throughout the city, and while the Catholic members of the senate and their adherents were in consternation over the news, the evangelically minded citizens were gladdened by it and rejoiced that at length they would have the Gospel preached publicly in their city.[22] The Catholic element was compelled to acquiesce in the wishes of the evangelical majority, and consequently there was no other course open to the senate than to bid the two men welcome and give them leave to preach. Accordingly, early on Good Friday two men were deputed by the senate to go to Jonas and Huegel and to ask them to appear before it. Jonas and his companion readily complied. There the two consuls, Querhammer and Ockel, as well as the syndic Philip Gossmann,[23] in the name of the senate renewed the call that had been extended and asked Jonas to remain in the city for two months. Jonas, in response, indicated his willingness to stay there until Pentecost or even longer and asked that both the Elector of Madgeburg, Cardinal Albrecht, and the prefect of the city and coadjutor of the Cardinal be informed.[24]

On the same day, in the afternoon at three o'clock, Jonas preached the first evangelical sermon in Our Dear Lady's Church[25] before an immense throng of people who "crowded around and with their voices acclaimed the power and grace of God."[26] Jonas, with a due sense of moderation, exhorted the people to obedience to all duly constituted authority and to prayer. On the following day, the eve before Easter, he preached a second time, and on Easter Day delivered two sermons before large gatherings in Our Dear Lady's Church, while Andrew Huegel preached there once.[27] From that time on Jonas

continued to preach daily and to instruct the city's population in the
evangelical doctrine.[28]

On Monday, April 17, Jonas was informed that the Cardinal, who
was taking part in the religious Conference at Regensburg, had issued
a mandate which forbade the city to accept Pfeffinger as preacher.
Jonas sensed the peculiar peril of his own position, but with admirable
faith and courage was ready to stake all on what he considered to be
his duty as a minister of the Gospel. "Here at Halle I have been
preaching daily before as large a multitude as I have scarcely seen in
any other city . . . , " he wrote to George Forchheim on that same
Monday. "I am afflicted with stone and at the point of death; perhaps
God wishes me, a most unworthy and weak instrument, to take upon
myself this great responsibility before death to the glory of his name
and the glory of Jesus Christ, the Son of God. May God grant strength,
utterance and wisdom, he, whom the world can resist only at its own
peril."[29]

The Test of Opposition

It was not long before determined opposition to Jonas' resolute reform program made itself felt both in the city and outside of it. The
Cardinal, who must have been quickly informed about events in
Halle, did not intend to permit Jonas to continue his work. He therefore dispatched two men from his court and instructed them to seek
out Jonas and to command him to leave the city since he had neither
the permission nor the right to preach or teach publicly in Halle without the consent of the Elector or his coadjutor. In the face of this
obviously serious order Jonas firmly stood his ground. He replied that
he had been called to Halle by the senate and the people, that he had
been requested to preach God's Word in the interest of charity, peace
and concord, and that he had felt bound by his conscience to accept
such an unequivocal call. He was consequently unable to carry out
the Cardinal's and the coadjutor's command. Even if it were the Emperor himself commanding it and he would have to forfeit his life,

he was determined to obey God rather than man. Jonas asked that he be permitted by the authorities to remain in Halle; yet stay he would in any case because he had not deliberately sought to obtain the office which he held, but had been duly called.[30]

In the city the opposition of priests and monks to Jonas' activities began to increase. A certain Matthias Metz, the Catholic priest and pastor of Our Dear Lady's Church, was especially provoked by Jonas' reforming zeal. He publicly branded Luther as a heretic and Jonas an undesirable intruder. Jonas lost no time in answering these charges and resorted to uncouth invective against his opponent. He accused the Romanist clergyman of gross ignorance. Affirming that he had been called in a legitimate manner by the entire senate and by the people of Halle, he reminded Metz that he had dealt with far more able opponents in controversy on previous occasions and was not at all frightened by these attacks.[31]

The senate of the city was now divided into two opposing camps. The syndic, Philip Gossmann, and one of the two ruling consuls, Caspar Querhammer, were staunch papists and in every way opposed to the Reformation.[32] Soon after Jonas' arrival a violent conflict broke out between the Catholic members of the senate and the evangelical members of the council, who as representatives of the people had been most active in the matter of securing Jonas' services. The syndic became so wrought up in the course of the heated debate that, in the excitement of the moment, he ran to the window, opened it and cried out into the open court before the city hall: "Help, help, ring the signal-bell, call the community together." In order to avoid confusion and disorder, three members of the senate asked the syndic to leave the meeting and not to appear again until he was asked to come back. Gossmann's proud and sensitive spirit was so injured by this public humiliation that he was afflicted mentally. His condition became worse from day to day and, when the spasms of rage into which he fell periodically made him uncontrollable, he was put into chains and finally died in this sad state.[33] Although a bitter enemy of Jonas, Jonas had prayed for the syndic and felt compassion for his wife and children. Jonas and the friends of the Reformation interpreted this occurrence as a divine judgment visited upon a man who had persistently tried to prevent the preaching of the Gospel.[34]

Luther, who had been kept informed on developments, was concerned that an evangelical syndic be chosen in Gossmann's place and recommended either Schneidewein or Rosenecker as his successor.[35] Yet the election of the new syndic was delayed for some time. Jonas was finally successful in securing the election of Kilian Goldstein, who had been Jonas' colleague in the Wittenberg Consistory.[36] To this end he had written a letter to Chancellor Brueck which in cryptic symbols asked him to promote Goldstein's election.[37] Subsequently Goldstein was chosen for this position. Luther was highly pleased with this choice. "I personally wished him the best of success," wrote Luther to Jonas, "as he is a saintly man who is consecrated to Christ; I hope he will further your efforts a great deal."[38]

Since the delegation which the Cardinal had sent to Jonas to ask him to leave Halle immediately had not been able to make Jonas waver in his resolve to stay, the Cardinal, while at Regensburg, addressed a lengthy letter to Emperor Charles V, complaining of the improper way in which Jonas and his assistant had come to Halle as preachers. In the interest of avoiding schisms and disorder they should have asked the Archbishop and Elector for permission to come. Instead, they had entered Halle without permission from the proper authorities and were disseminating their heretical and sectarian doctrines. Cardinal Albrecht therefore called upon the Emperor, whose duty it was as "supreme patron, protector, and defender of the Church," to issue a mandate threatening these two foreign intruders with the imperial ban.[39] The Cardinal made this request on June 30, 1541, and on July 27 of the same year Charles V issued the imperial mandate. The tenor of this document was in complete agreement with Albrecht of Mainz's letter. In many instances it was worded in the same way. It demanded that Jonas and his colleague leave Halle within the space of an hour under pain of excommunication.[40] Although the Cardinal probably planned to make use of the mandate in the course of his efforts to rid Halle of its evangelical preachers and reformers, there is no evidence that it was ever put into effect by him.

Political considerations related to the Burgraviate, which the Elector of Saxony exercised over Halle, may well have prompted the Cardinal not to employ the imperial mandate.[41] Moreover, events in the city convinced him at length that all the measures which he had taken had not weakened the evangelical movement with its popular hold on Halle's citizenry. During Jonas' brief stay the movement which he had partially driven underground experienced a resurgence that fairly defied violent suppression. With poignant regret and in deep disgust he openly admitted his failure in trying to make the new Cathedral at Halle the stronghold of the Roman Catholic faith in the lands which he ruled. From Regensburg he went to Mainz in 1541, had the relics as well as all other valuables removed from the Cathedral at Halle and brought to Mainz where they were offered to the faithful for edification. On December 7, 1541, the doors of the new Cathedral were locked, a silent testimony to the triumph of the Reformation in Halle.[42]

Jonas' intrepid appearance in Halle as well as the undaunted courage with which he carried out the Reformation elicited the admiration of many of his friends and prompted them to encourage him in the task which he had so auspiciously begun. On April 21, 1541, John Spangenberg, the evangelical minister at Nordhausen, wrote to Jonas and wished him God's blessing in his work.[43] In May of the same year Frederick Myconius, to whom Jonas had reported the progress he was making in Halle, sent a congratulatory letter. "Continue, Lord Jesus Christ, to triumph over the proud, ancient foe," he exclaimed in a joyous mood. "May you, too, my Jonas, continue to wage the wars of the Lord!" Myconius regretted that he was unable to join him in the fray, and asked Jonas to send him detailed reports on the battle and the hope for victory.[44]

Jonas, well aware of the broad scope of his task, appealed to Nicholas Medler of Naumburg to send his deacon Benedict Schumann to assist him at Halle. Medler graciously consented to lending Schumann to Jonas until Pentecost.[45] At the same time Medler extended his best wishes to Jonas. He wrote: "Therefore, my most famous and excellent sir, doctor, and respectful patron, I rejoice with you and congratulate your church for which I never cease to pray. . . ." Medler encouraged

Jonas to continue his efforts and to be comforted in the Lord with the hope that he would witness still greater miracles in Halle. "I hope the Prophet Jonah will thus be liberated from the belly of the whale, that is from the stone, so that I may be richly provided for in Nineveh, that is that the vineyard of the Lord may bear fruit." Medler also extended the leave he had granted to Schumann by permitting him to remain with Jonas during the Pentecost season.[46]

George Major, a former student of Jonas in Wittenberg, wrote in September, congratulating the eloquent provost and professor of Wittenberg because a door had been opened to him at Halle and he was preaching the Gospel with notable success.[47] Lastly, Jerome Weller, a compatriot from Nordhausen and pastor at Freiburg, expressed his sincere joy over Jonas' successful venture in Halle and praised the populace of the city for rewarding their evangelical pastors so liberally for their labors. Begging his friend to keep him informed on all developments, he closed his letter by commending Jonas to God's perpetual care.[48]

A Measure of Progress

The extensive correspondence of Jonas with his benefactor and friend, Prince George of Anhalt, and with Luther permits us to trace, in many of its interesting details, the progress which the reform movement was making in Halle under Jonas' aggressive leadership. As early as April 25, only eleven days after Jonas' arrival in Halle, Luther advised him by letter to proceed cautiously with the restitution of the Lord's Supper according to Christ's institution. "Only insist vigorously that the Word and Gift of God be free and not bound," wrote Luther, "and neither Pope nor Emperor, nor any other creature has the right to forbid it in any place. For that reason one must disregard the threats, laws, and commands, like those of the devil himself, and obey God who will strengthen you and confound the adversaries."[49] On Thursday only three days later, the Lord's Supper was celebrated in true evangelical fashion.[50] Even at that early date Jonas believed that the forcible suppression of the truth of the Gospel might issue in open rebellion. Conflicts and contentions were not lacking from the very beginning, "so great [was] the malice and provocativeness and Phara-saic bitterness." Still, "exceedingly great multitudes" daily heard Jonas' sermons.[51] On May 29, 1541, Jonas could report to the Prince of Anhalt that two determined opponents had been marvelously converted to evangelical Christianity and that the one, formerly a loyal papist, had received "the whole Sacrament" from Jonas' hands.[52] Somewhat later three more eminent papists came over to the evangelical camp. This trend happily continued in the months to come.[53]

Jonas believed very strongly in a teaching ministry, for by the end of May he had completed a series of sermons on the Lord's Prayer and was about to preach on the Ten Commandments.[54] While his preach-ing attracted large numbers of people at all times, a strenuous opposi-tion also manifested itself. Instead of being frightened by any threats that were made, he was able to instill fear into the hearts of his foes by his fearless behavior.[55] The monks continued to do everything in their power to hinder Jonas' work. They called him "a heretic, a sedi-tious person"[56] and went about from house to house administering Communion "under one kind" and attempting to regain their hold on the people. Although Jonas' enemies were "breathing threats and murder," he continued to trust in the living Lord whom he believed to be present with him in the conflict and who endued him with all strength. "Here the Word of the Lord, through the blessing of God and the help of Christ's Spirit, is continuing its course favorably enough and is honored by God's elect and is glorified by the manifest works of God," he stated in a letter to his friend, Prince George of Anhalt.[57] "My life," he added somewhat later, "is not so dear to myself, even if I have five children and a most loving and faithful wife; nevertheless in this holy business no citizens of the world nor terrors of men will drive me out of here, unless they besprinkle the nearby walls with our blood. And still the will and counsel of the impious do not take place, but Christ governs all things. . . . My will shall come to pass, says the Lord God Almighty."[58]

For Jonas it was a matter of conscience that he should continue his work in Halle. He was at all times ready to obey the proper authorities in temporal matters. The senate and the people in Halle followed his admonition to do likewise. But Jonas could not and would not submit to any human ordinance that conflicted with the divine will. Hence he could not obey a command by which thousands of souls would be denied the Gospel "which God has commanded to be preached to every creature, to all mortals beneath heaven."[59] With praiseworthy steadfastness he clung to this conviction in the midst of strife and difficulties.

The Regensburg Conference had been in full progress during the first months of Jonas' stay in Halle. Reports on the negotiations there had reached him from time to time. In July he obtained a report from Caspar Cruciger, who had attended its sessions and had returned to Wittenberg.[60] A letter from Melanchthon, promising an oral report, followed several days later.[61] A more gloomy picture of the Protestant situation was painted for him in a letter by Spalatin, who had received a first-hand report from Amsdorf. Spalatin believed that true peace was being effectually blocked by the papal opponents.[62]

The few months that Jonas had been lent to the city of Halle soon passed, and it became apparent to him that his task was unfinished. A man of his capabilities was needed to make secure the gains of the past and to organize and extend the work of the Reformation. After the Elector of Saxony had given his consent, Jonas promised to serve the church in Halle for three more years as its superintendent and chief pastor. He retained his provostship and its annual income of 100 guldens, in return for which he was on occasion to lend his counsel and aid in matters relating to this office.[63] In the beginning of September his family also moved from Wittenberg to Halle, indicating that he had a prolonged stay in mind.[64]

Earlier Jonas had begun negotiations with Nicholas Medler in order that he might again obtain Benedict Schumann for the work in Halle. Medler's sickness prevented him from sending the reliable deacon at once.[65] In September Medler indicated that Schumann would soon be sent.[66] His coming was delayed until October, at which time Medler announced to Jonas that his "faithful co-worker in the vineyard of the Lord" was about to move to Halle.[67] After this additional assistance had been secured, the next task for Jonas consisted in finding churches which permitted the evangelical worship. Our Dear Lady's Church was proving to be far too small to accommodate the growing number of worshipers. By the end of the year the senate had succeeded in obtaining St. Ulric's Church for evangelical services. On Christmas Day, 1541, Jonas formally dedicated the church to its new purpose and Benedict Schumann became its first regular pastor. Simultaneously the senate addressed itself to the task of improving the dilapitated and neglected school system of the city by employing Emericus Sylvius, a learned schoolmaster. The education of children in the city was thus given due attention and the level of learning was raised considerably.[68]

The responsibility that had first claim on Justus Jonas and that always loomed large in his eyes, was that of bringing the redeeming Gospel of Christ to the souls of men. This primary duty he faithfully fulfilled in 1541, the year during which he introduced the Reformation in Halle.

FOOTNOTES FOR CHAPTER 7

1. Pressel, *op. cit.*, pp. 77-78.
2. Franke, *op. cit.*, pp. 9, 11-12.
3. Acts 17:22.
4. Franke, *op. cit.*, p. 23.
5. *Ibid.*, pp. 50-52; P. Smith, *op. cit.*, Vol. II, pp. 80-81.
6. *Ibid.*, p. 62.
7. Pressel, *op. cit.*, p. 78.
8. Franke, *op. cit.*, pp. 63-64.
9. *Ibid.*, pp. 70-71.
10. *Ibid.*, p. 81.
11. Margaret Currie, *The Letters of Martin Luther*, pp. 165-166.
12. Franke, *op. cit.*, pp. 87-88.
13. *Ibid.*, p. 101.
14. *Ibid.*, pp. 121-122.
15. *Ibid.*, pp. 129-131.
16. *Ibid.*, pp. 134-139.
17. *Ibid.*, pp. 139-140.
18. *Corpus Reformatorum*, Vol. IV, p. 173.
19. Kawerau seems to prove conclusively that the Chaplain Andrew referred to in Spalatin's *Annals of the Reformation* and other contemporary documents, is not, as has always been done, to be identified with Andrew Poach, a fellow-citizen of Nordhausen, who later was undoubtedly associated with Jonas in Halle. Rather he was Andrew Huegel, chaplain in Wittenberg. Furthermore, it has never been shown that Poach ever held the position of a chaplain in Wittenberg and so he could not have been the one who accompanied Jonas to Halle.
    Kawerau, *op. cit.*, Vol. II, pp. xliii-xliv.

20. *Ibid.*, p. 1.
21. J. C. Dreyhaupt, *Pagus Neletici et Nodzici oder diplomatisch-historische Beschreibung des Saal-Creyses,* Vol. II, p. 20.
22. Franke, *op. cit.,* p. 142.
23. All three belonged to the Catholic party.
24. Kawerau, *op. cit.,* Vol. II, pp. 1-2.
25. Franke, *op. cit.,* p. 142.
26. Kawerau, *op. cit.,* Vol. II, p. 2.
27. Franke, *op. cit.,* p. 142.
28. Kawerau, *op. cit.,* Vol. II, p. 2 and p. 13.
29. *Ibid.*, p. 2.
30. *Ibid.*, pp. 4-6.
31. *Ibid.*, pp. 6-12.
32. *Ibid.*, pp. 16-17.
33. Franke, *op. cit.,* p. 144.
34. Kawerau, *op. cit.,* Vol. II, pp. 17-18, 23.
35. Enders, *op. cit.,* Vol. XIII, p. 352.
36. Kawerau, *op. cit.,* Vol. II, p. xlv; Dreyhaupt, *op. cit.,* Vol. II, p. 21.
37. Dreyhaupt, *op. cit.,* Vol. II, pp. 28-29.
38. Enders, *op. cit.,* Vol. XIV, p. 34.
39. Kawerau, *op. cit.,* Vol. II, pp. 31-33.
40. *Ibid.*, pp. 41-42.
41. *Ibid.*, p. xlv.
42. Franke, *op. cit.,* p. 145.
43. Kawerau, *op. cit.,* Vol. II, pp. 3-4.
44. *Ibid.*, pp. 19-20.
45. *Ibid.*, pp. 20-21.
46. *Ibid.*, pp. 21-22.
47. *Ibid.*, pp. 51-52.
48. *Ibid.*, pp. 58-59.
49. Enders, *op. cit.,* Vol. XIII, pp. 315-316.
50. Kawerau, *op. cit.,* Vol. II, p. 10.
51. *Ibid.*, pp. 12-13.
52. *Ibid.*, p. 23.
53. *Ibid.*, pp. 24 and 56.
54. *Ibid.*, p. 23.
55. *Ibid.*, pp. 23-24.
56. *Ibid.*, pp. 57 f.
57. *Ibid.*, p. 23.
58. *Ibid.*, p. 25.
59. *Ibid.*, p. 37.
60. *Corpus Reformatorum,* Vol. IV, pp. 558-559.
61. *Ibid.*, pp. 569-570.
62. *Ibid.*, pp. 611-612.
63. Pressel, *op. cit.,* p. 84; H. A. Erhard, "Justus Jonas the Elder," *Allgemeine Encyklopädie der Wissenschaften und Künste.* Edited by Ersch and Gruber. Vol. XXII, Second Section, p. 401; Hasse, *op. cit.,* p. 190.
64. Enders, *op. cit.,* Vol. XIV, p. 64.
65. Kawerau, *op. cit.,* Vol. II, p. 41.
66. *Ibid.*, pp. 50-51.
67. *Ibid.*, p. 34.
68. Franke, *op. cit.,* p. 146.

Chapter 8

Pastor at Halle

Even though the close of the year 1541 found the Reformation firmly established in Halle, there remained one source of opposition to its progress within the city. The resistance came from the Franciscan and Dominican monks who did not shrink from employing any method of attack that would prove injurious to the Reformation. In their sermons they inveighed zealously against the evangelical doctrine; unbidden they made their way to the bedsides of the sick to administer the Lord's Supper according to the Romanist tradition. They continued to hold private mass in their cloisters, and they let no opportunity pass by to harm the evangelical cause and to hurl insults at its representatives.[1] Jonas was naturally perturbed by their behavior, and his invectives against them were always bitter.[2] He first looked upon their hostility as the special cross which the church of Halle had to bear, but at length he decided he would endure their continual antagonism no longer.[3] Since he knew that the citizens' council was on his side, he thought that the opportune time for launching a full-scale offensive against this interference had come. On January 15, 1542, he formally handed to the senate a written Opinion (*Bedenken*) concerning the question: "Whether the Cloisters at Halle Are to Be Abolished."[4]

In this Opinion Jonas pointed out that the people of Halle had, in the past year, graciously experienced an answer to their fervent prayers and had been granted preachers who taught the pure doctrine of the Gospel. He believed that the intercessory prayers of surrounding evangelical churches had in no small measure marvelously strengthened and supported this work and that much stubborn resistance had been successfully overcome. It was Jonas' sincere desire that the senate, in gratitude to God for this proffered grace, should endeavor to do away with all false doctrine and idolatry and maintain the purity of the Gospel. Two cloisters in the city had continued in their service of Baal during the past period of reform and were persisting in teaching their false doctrines and practicing their godless ceremonies. Further, Jonas wrote that although he and the other evangelical ministers had until now patiently endured such abusive practices, the writings of Luther and Melanchthon made it clear that it was the divinely enjoined duty of the ruling authorities to abolish this false worship of God. Since the activities of the monks in their cloisters were contrary to Christ's doctrine, the question could rightly be raised as to how the authorities might best deal with this problem. Jonas then proceeded to treat this question with regard to its doctrinal and canonical aspects and listed twenty-six reasons for the course of action which he advocated. The monks in Halle, who had gathered from the surrounding countryside, he contended were obdurate and impenitent idolaters of whom no change could be expected. They slandered Luther's German Bible, asserting that it was a forgery. They taught that evangelical Christians received the devil in the Sacrament, and they constantly threatened reprisals. Jonas believed that the proposal of the city's council to abolish the monasteries was fully justified, and he advised its execution.[5]

The senate, in response to the Opinion by Jonas, stated that it favored a policy of patient waiting. Although it was eager to see the removal of cloisters, the evangelical Christians did not participate in their activities and were not directly harmed by them. Since the preponderant number of the city's population adhered to the evangelical faith and practice, the senate held that it would be wise to wait with their abolition. After several months, however, the senate took definite steps in curtailing the activity of the monks by forbidding them to administer the Sacrament "under one kind," because even previous to the Reformation they had not possessed this prerogative. The archiepiscopal court protested that this procedure went beyond the senate's authority and interfered with the jurisdiction that rightly belonged to the ruling archbishop. In order to circumvent this legal barrier, the senate had its municipal servants go from house to house, prohibiting the citizens from attending the cloister churches and receiving the Sacrament from the monks.[6]

The Church Prospers

In spite of the unpleasant enmity of the monks, Jonas was privileged to see the proclaimed Gospel bear much fruit in Halle. Even the enemies of the Reformation had to admit this. The church was, to Jonas' satisfaction, enjoying comparative tranquillity. He resented the repeated, but unsuccessful, attempts of the monks to create disorder and their malicious misrepresentation of evangelical faith. He, in turn, seeking to silence them, attacked them audaciously in his sermons. He believed that the Pope was, in the last analysis, to be blamed for these perpetual attacks upon the churches of the Reformation, and in a letter to Prince George made so bold as to declare: "The Pope is, has been, and remains forever an instrument of the devil and a monster of crime."[7]

Toward the end of January, 1542, Jonas entertained the notion of remaining in Halle for many more years, perhaps even spending the remainder of his life there. He was fast approaching his fiftieth birthday and could not help noticing the signs of declining physical vigor.[8] Still he did not surrender any of his duties or seek to lighten the burdens of his work. He preached three times a week, as did his colleague, Benedict Schumann. The two subdeacons who were assisting him likewise preached from two to three times each week. A regular preaching program was inaugurated which was designed to acquaint the people with the Scriptures and the cardinal doctrines of the evangelical belief.[9] As superintendent, Jonas appears to have enjoyed the cooperation of his fellow-ministers, so that he was able to work with them harmoniously in the common service of the church. It is to his credit that during the time of his superintendency at Halle neither discord nor controversies arose among the various evangelical ministers.

In the month of August, 1542, the Reformation had advanced sufficiently so that another church in Halle could be set apart for evangelical services. Jonas wisely inaugurated a plan of action that was designed to secure St. Maurice's Church for the Reformation. He knew that the senate would support him in achieving the goal, if Luther and his colleagues would endorse the procedure. Jonas therefore had an official letter, which approved the plan of taking over St. Maurice's Church, sent from Wittenberg. Luther himself wrote the letter, which was signed by him as well as by John Bugenhagen, Caspar Cruciger, and Philip Melanchthon. The letter advocated that St. Maurice's Church should immediately be taken over for evangelical services and encouraged Jonas and the church at Halle in the reform program by mentioning how marvelously God was triumphing over his foes.[10]

Soon after this, the council urged the senate to approach the prefect of the city and to request of him that St. Maurice's Church should be opened for evangelical worship. On August 26 the senate attempted to carry out the suggestion of the council but without success, and when it became known in the city that the prefect had declined the senate's request, the inhabitants of Halle took possession of the church in spite of this refusal. On the same day of August, at three o'clock in the afternoon, Jonas preached the first evangelical sermon in the church. The Dominican monks, who looked upon St. Maurice's Church as their own possession bequeathed to them by the Cardinal, were very incensed over this action. On September 1, one of them, named Sebastian, with an ax in his hand, overtook Jonas on the street with the intention of splitting his head. Fortunately he was restrained. Later Matthias Wanckel was called to serve as the first evangelical minister of this church of which the people of Halle had so dramatically taken possession.[11]

An important step in conserving the gains which had been made in reforming the church at Halle was taken when the Elector of Saxony, by virtue of his Burgraviate, made a secret alliance with the city of Halle. According to the terms of agreement he promised to

protect the inhabitants of the city against any reprisals or attacks by
Cardinal Albrecht. The letter, guaranteeing this protection, was written
on November 6, 1542. In return for this promise of aid the city obligated
itself to pay annually the sum of 1,000 guldens to the Elector and his
heirs.[12]

The Dispute with Wolferinus

In the summer of 1543 a controversy had arisen in Eisleben, the city
of Luther's birth, among the three Lutheran ministers with regard to
the problem of how the consecrated wine in the Sacrament of the
Lord's Supper was to be properly disposed of after the celebration. A
certain Simon Wolferinus, minister of St. Andrew's Church, had
adopted a different practice from the usual one. Instead of using up
all the consecrated wine during the distribution, he had a deacon drink
what remained in the chalice after the administration of the Sacrament.
He defended this practice by asserting that afterwards the wine was
again ordinary wine. For this reason he also proposed certain theses
upholding his assertion. He subsequently defended them in a disputation. He was opposed by Frederick Rauber, the pastor of St. Peter's
Church in Eisleben, who believed that Wolferinus, by differing from
accepted practice, was treating the matter too lightly. The superintendent of the church in Eisleben and the chief pastor at St. Andrew's
Church, Valentinus Vigelius, sided with Rauber in the dispute and
appealed the case to Wittenberg. Luther, who did not wish that
scholastic speculation concerning the sacramental union of Christ's
body and blood with the bread and wine should arise, maintained that
the Real Presence of Christ continued throughout the administration
of the Sacrament. He did not want to create any doubt in the minds of
communicants as to when this union ceased because this would destroy
the value of the Sacrament for them. He believed that Wolferinus'
position tended toward speculation and perhaps eventually toward
doubt concerning the Real Presence of Christ in the Sacrament. For
this reason he wrote to Wolferinus, expressing dissatisfaction over the
provocative and uncharitable manner in which the latter disputed

with his fellow-ministers. By resorting to a practice differing from the accepted one, he was causing offense and open conflict in the church. He therefore begged him to follow the general custom of the evangelical churches in Wittenberg and elsewhere and to put an end to this unseemly quarrel.[13] John Bugenhagen added his signature to the letter with a postscript stating that he subscribed to Luther's opinion in the matter.

Jonas, as superintendent of the church at Halle, was also consulted by Vigelius concerning this controversy. Addressing a letter to Wolferinus, he implored him to stop the dispute and to follow Luther's advice.[14] Jonas believed that Luther's counsel in this specific case should be heeded because, like Luther, Jonas was earnestly desirous of avoiding divisions or disruptive controversies which might prove to be very detrimental to the future of the evangelical cause in Germany. At the same time, there is no denying that in this instance Jonas demanded such complete acquiescence to Luther's opinion that no room was left for ideas that differed in only unessential points.[15]

However, Wolferinus again explained his position in a letter to Luther. The Reformer replied on July 20, 1543, asking Wolferinus to make every effort that concord and peace might be restored between him and other evangelical ministers in Eisleben. Luther stated that he agreed with Melanchthon, who counseled that the accepted custom in the use of the elements of the Lord's Supper be continued in order to avoid offense, and so Luther hoped that the controversy would cease. "The Lord direct your hearts in accordance with the charity and patience of Christ," he wrote.[16] This prayerful wish was seemingly granted, for no further signs can be found of the dispute in which Jonas had assisted.

Halle or Wittenberg?

The church at Halle witnessed a steady growth in the year 1544. Jonas, anticipating a promised visit by his friend, Prince George of Anhalt, was delighted to be able to tell him that in one church five to six thousand people attended his sermons on the Catechism. He

hoped that the Prince himself would be able to witness the spectacle
of such a large multitude of worshipers. When the expected visit of
the Prince did not materialize, Jonas informed him, "I have taught the
Catechism for an entire month to an astonishingly numerous throng
of four, often five thousand or more listeners."[17]

The three years which Jonas had agreed to serve the church at Halle
had quickly elapsed. The return of the provost was being demanded in
Wittenberg. The church at Halle was loath to have him return; the
senate earnestly petitioned him to stay longer, and Jonas saw the need
of carrying on the challenging work he had begun. In the middle of
the year 1544, hoping that he could retain his affiliation with Wittenberg as provost and professor, he began to negotiate with Wittenberg
University and the Elector. Luther, Melanchthon, and Bugenhagen
had agreed that Jonas could be allowed to remain another year at
Halle, and the Elector gave his approval to this extension of his leave.
In order, however, to be able to effect a better understanding, Jonas
went to Wittenberg and submitted his wishes to Luther. Jonas desired
to retain the provostship in Wittenberg for several years more or for
life and would pay a substitute fifty to sixty guldens for lecturing in
his stead at the university.[18]

When Gregory Brueck, the Elector's Chancellor, was notified of
Jonas' plan, he strenuously opposed it and wrote a letter to the Elector
in which he criticized Jonas' attempts to retain the provostship. Brueck
reminded the Elector of his past generosity toward Jonas: that he had
given him the income of the provostship while he was serving the
church at Halle, that he had bequeathed to him as a possession the
hamlet Eutzsch near Wittenberg, and that in every way Jonas had
been remunerated above his due. Brueck then proceeded to minimize
Jonas' work in the church at large in a manner plainly evincing personal animosity and prejudice. Perhaps, he contended, Jonas had done
his work well as a professor at the university; that he did not know.
However, he felt that his presence at Augsburg in 1530 was super-
fluous and in no way helpful to the cause. He therefore made some
suggestions to the Elector as to how he might best rid himself of
Jonas. It might be that Brueck, as a jurist, mindful of how Jonas had

been successful in transferring the lecturing privileges of the provostship from the law faculty to the theological faculty, felt that Jonas had
tried to increase the prestige of the theological faculty at the expense
of the law school. In any case, with such feelings of animosity toward
Jonas, this evaluation of the latter's person was certainly not worthy
of a statesman of Brueck's stature.

Jonas addressed his request with regard to the final settlement of
his position in Wittenberg to the Elector on July 15, 1544. He expressed
the belief that in the interest of evangelical Christianity it would be
best for him to remain at Halle where the preaching of the Gospel
had been so richly blessed and where its divine influence was extending
to cities and villages near by. Besides, his personal health had improved
much during the years of his stay in Halle and his family was well
settled there. Simultaneously, he wished to retain his cordial connections with Wittenberg which, through long association, had come to
mean so much in his life. To that end he desired to retain the provostship at All Saints' Chapter.[19]

John Frederick of Saxony, in his reply, remarked how much it
pleased him that the Gospel of God's grace was being spread in Halle
in the face of much opposition; still he was not disposed to grant the
provost his request. If Jonas decided to go to Halle permanently, he
would have to demit his office as provost with all its privileges.[20] In
August of the same year Jonas declared that he would soon inform the
Elector of his decision. As late as November Halle's syndic, Kilian
Goldstein, was still trying to aid Jonas in obtaining his wishes by writing to Chancellor Brueck; and Luther, ever sympathetic and ready to
assist his friend, made a special effort to change the Elector's decision.[21]
The Reformer was persuaded that the Elector should permit Jonas to
retain the provostship because his position in Halle was not secure.
"The evil worm at Mainz," that is, the Cardinal, was still alive. Jonas'
repeated willingness to expose himself to danger and death deserved
reward. Jonas' relationship to the university would, Luther asserted,
prove advantageous, and as "one of the older servants of the church"
who had a growing family to support, he was richly deserving of the
position as provost.[22]

All efforts were of no avail. Gregory Brueck favored a settlement, granting 100 guldens each year to Jonas for eight years after his resignation as provost.[23] The Elector made a more generous settlement than Brueck advised—100 guldens was to be given to Jonas annually for life. Jonas was in turn to surrender the provostship, relinquish each and every claim in connection with it, and in addition pay the university 50 guldens, and put forth no further petitions. He was thereby released from all obligations to the church in Electoral Saxony.[24]

On December 11, 1544, Justus Jonas received the official call from the city of Halle to become its chief evangelical minister and superintendent. In reviewing the past years of Jonas' labors, the call regarded his coming to Halle and his uninterrupted preaching and teaching of God's pure Word as providential and divinely blessed. The city, represented by its senators, the masters of the guilds and parishes, extended to Jonas the call to become its permanent pastor and superintendent. The remuneration was fixed at 300 guldens per year, in addition to which he was to be furnished a home for his family. His chief duties would be to preach twice a week, read the Scriptures once a week and promote the orderly conduct of worship. Although called specifically as pastor of Our Dear Lady's Church, he was to exercise oversight over St. Ulric's and St. Maurice's Churches, introduce uniformity in worship, and to collaborate with the senate in effecting any changes, so that in all things a desirable harmony and Christian concord might be achieved and maintained.[25]

Two Loyal Friends

Jonas' visit in Wittenberg in May, 1545, was motivated by his desire to confer with Luther regarding "various matters."[26] No doubt the forthcoming Council of Trent and the general situation of the evangelical churches were included in the discussions. Yet it would seem that Jonas had gone to Wittenberg specifically to obtain Luther's advice on a matter relating to the church at Halle. The result of this conference with Luther and Melanchthon was that the latter two sent letters to the senate in Halle, supporting Jonas' program and policy in

the local churches. These two letters bear eloquent testimony to the
harmony of ideals and the spirit of mutual support and helpfulness
among the leaders of the reform movement. Since Melanchthon's letter
was written one day earlier than Luther's its contents will be noted
first.

With a tactful reminder that it was in no sense his intention to
meddle in affairs which were no concern of his, Melanchthon told the
senate at Halle that his writing to them was prompted by the Christian spirit of helpfulness. He had been informed that the senate had
planned to change the salaries of school teachers and other officers in
the church. If this meant that they were going to lower the salaries,
Melanchthon stated it would be a grave mistake. Even though it might
not be easy to remunerate the teachers properly, their work was of such
an essential and important nature that the existing authorities could ill
afford to decrease their wages. Their responsibility of educating youth
in the Christian religion was of such vital consequence that their work
should be ranked as most necessary.

The claim put forth by some that the standards ought to be relaxed
and that teachers with inferior qualifications could serve the schools
of Halle just as well was as fallacious as it was dangerous, because only
well-trained teachers could lay that foundation which would be essential for further education in advanced schools.

Besides, the education of well-disciplined youth, ready to serve the
church, not only constituted an ornament of a community but a divine
service. Lamenting the destruction of the many excellent schools in
Asia and Greece by the Turk, Melanchthon called upon the senate
at Halle to promote a proper Christian training in their schools. They
should also be grateful that they had "God-fearing, learned, sensible,
chaste pastors" whom the people loved and who could give Christian
counsel. They should therefore hold them in honor and not tamper
with the present scale of wages.[27]

Luther's letter, written May 6, sincerely commended the growth and
prosperity which the church in Halle had experienced through the
years. He was delighted that the people were conducting themselves
so well, that the teachers were laboring in harmony with one another,

and that the senate was favorably disposed toward the Gospel. He emphasized the precious nature of that unity which was in evidence in Halle but was so tragically absent in many churches of the land. Though in a joyous mood over the state of affairs in Halle, he deemed it advisable to admonish them to continue in the same path of concord "and, not to be weary in well-doing but ever to increase in strength." Satan was always lying in wait, so that he might do some damage, and therefore it was necessary for them to be on their guard and to pray in order to avoid his unexpected assaults. Luther referred to Moritzburg, the home of the Cardinal's coadjutor, and to Aschaffenburg, the Cardinal's residence, as the places from which emanated many subversive influences which ought to be repelled. On that account he pleaded with them that they should strive to keep the church, the council, the preachers and the schools closely united so that through faith and prayer the devil might be resisted. "I hereby commit preachers, sacristans and schools to your Christian love, especially Dr. Jonas, from whom we were most unwilling to part. I especially, for I would gladly always have him beside me."[28] The preciousness of faithful and sincere preachers, Luther maintained, ought to make the senate ready to accord them double honor. "And it is no small gift that God had given you the heart to call such men, and love, cherish and honor them." Luther's final advice was that the senate should acknowledge its rich, divine blessing in having pious pastors; though they might easily make changes in the ministry, the possibility of improvement seemed very dubious. Having said this, Luther invoked the blessing of God upon the senate so that, strengthened and preserved from all wickedness and cunning of the devil, it might be granted rest and peace.[29]

These two letters seem to have had the desired effect. After Jonas returned to Halle, there was no more mention of the contemplated reduction of salaries in the churches and schools of the city. With local difficulties adjusted, Jonas, ever watchful, could devote more attention to external matters, to the Emperor's activities and the papal plans that were being made for the General Council at Trent.[30]

The importance which Melanchthon attached to Jonas' encouraging friendship and good will is impressively illustrated in a letter which Melanchthon wrote in July, 1545. Melanchthon was being suspected of compromising the evangelical faith and he tried to assure Jonas that the suspicion was unfounded. In a letter he recalled the twenty years that the two had been most intimately associated, remarking how well they knew each other. It was not his nature, stated Melanchthon, to conceal anything from his friend. "Yes," he wrote, "I laid bare my entire heart to you, and all domestic and public affairs I was wont to confide to you." With God's help Melanchthon desired to maintain constancy of friendship in this life so that Jonas and he might enjoy it in a more delightful manner in eternity. This wish was the more heartfelt and earnest since Melanchthon believed that only a brief span of life on earth lay in prospect for him.[31]

Himself a Glass

In the summer of 1545 Jonas was in Merseburg on the occasion of the ordination of his friend, Prince George of Anhalt. After this event Luther returned with Jonas to Halle. On the next day Luther preached in Our Dear Lady's Church. At the beginning of his sermon he saw fit to remark that there was no real need for him to preach the Gospel in Halle, as the city was abundantly blessed with learned, diligent, and good ministers who preached the Word of God purely to its citizens. On this occasion the senate gave a golden cup as a special token of honor to the great Reformer who, while staying in their midst, had proclaimed the Word of God to them.[32] On August 16 Luther was back in Wittenberg.[33] At the beginning of October Luther again made his way to Halle with Melanchthon. There they were joined by Jonas, and the three journeyed to Eisleben where Luther had been asked to mediate in a quarrel which had broken out between the Counts of Mansfeld. Since the dispute was not settled, the Counts requested that Luther again come in December for further negotiations. In a letter written to Count Albrecht of Mansfeld on December 6 Luther consented to come, adding: "I must take a period of eight days for this, although I have so much to do; and I shall risk this in order that I may lie down joyfully in my coffin, after I have seen my dear lords and countrymen reconciled to each other with cheerful, harmonious hearts."[34] As previously, Luther and Melanchthon journeyed through Halle on the way to Eisleben. On the way back, January 6, 1546, on the festival of Epiphany, Luther preached in Halle.[35] In the course of his sermon he expressed his deep regret over the Council of Trent which had officially begun its work on December 13, 1545, and had condemned the Protestant doctrine.[36]

Not long after his return to Wittenberg it became necessary for Luther to undertake a third journey to Eisleben. He preached his last sermon in Wittenberg on January 17, and on January 23 he left the city, accompanied by his three sons and his servant. On the morning of the 24th they arrived in Halle, where they were compelled to stay at Jonas' home for three days because of a flood of the Saale River. In a humorous mood Luther wrote to his wife Catherine: "We reached Halle to-day at eight o'clock, but could not go on to Eisleben; for we encountered a great Anabaptist, with huge water-billows and great blocks of ice, covering the land, and threatening us with a baptism. . . . We did not risk embarking on the river, as we and our servants and the ferrymen were much afraid, and we did not wish to tempt God. For the devil is enraged against us, and he dwells in the water floods; and it is better to evade him than afterwards to complain of him; besides, it is needless to delight the Pope and his emissaries through our death."[37] During this stay at Jonas' home, Luther at mealtime presented his friend with an exquisite glass beaker, having inscribed upon it the words which Luther proposed as a toast to his host:

"To Jonas, a glass, Luther, himself a glass, gives a glass
So that both might be mindful that they are similar to fragile glass."[38]

On January 27, the day following the commemoration of St. Paul's conversion, Luther mounted the pulpit in Our Dear Lady's Church for the last time. He preached a stirring and eloquent sermon on Acts 9:1-10, and in addition to a general Christian instruction, he made specific references to the "fragile and wooden sanctuary" which had been reared by the late Cardinal, their erstwhile bishop and ruler. He also expressed amazement that the people still tolerated the "shabby monks, these rascals and blasphemers"[39] in the city.

On January 28 Jonas and his servant accompanied Luther and his three sons to Eisleben. As they were putting across the Saale River, which was still at flood stage, Luther remarked to his Halle friend: "Dear Dr. Jonas, wouldn't that please the devil greatly, if I, Dr. Martin, with my three sons and you should drown in the water."[40] They arrived in Eisleben on January 29. Luther, ably assisted by Jonas' counsel, mediated in the dispute between the Counts, and also preached four times in St. Andrew's Church at Eisleben.[41] Jonas was almost prevented from continuing his helpful assistance when he accidently injured his leg by bumping against a chest. He was, however, able to get about with some difficulty.[42] On February 16 an agreement between the Counts of Mansfeld was reached, and both Luther and Jonas signed the document which they had drawn up.[43]

We owe the faithful account of Luther's last days and death in Eisleben, as well as the details of his funeral, to Justus Jonas, who was aided by Michael Coelius, chaplain of the Counts of Mansfeld, and John Aurifaber, Luther's personal servant. Especially Jonas had the privilege of being in Luther's presence almost without interruption for the three weeks prior to Luther's death. In Eisleben he even shared the bedroom with Luther and his two younger sons. The account alluded to was published in 1546 under the title: "Concerning the Christian Departure from This Mortal Life of the Venerable Dr. Martin Luther. A Report by Dr. Justus Jonas, M. Michael Coelius, and Others Who Were Present."[44]

The Report relates the occurrences of Luther's life from January 23, when he left Wittenberg with his sons, until his death early on February 18. While the treatment of the time from January 23 until February 17 is brief, a great deal of space is devoted to the events and activities of the last two days of Luther's life. It is told how during those three weeks in Eisleben Luther uttered many fine and comforting thoughts, how he used to retire to his bedroom at eight each evening and how, turning toward the window, he would pray with such earnestness and persistence that Jonas and the others who heard him marveled.

Luther, the Report states, spent the morning of February 17 in his room resting and engaging in prayer. At the evening meal that day he spoke much of death and the future life. He had broached the question as to whether, upon being gathered into the Church Triumphant, Christians would recognize one another. Luther answered the question in the affirmative by drawing a parallel from the marvelous way in which Adam had recognized Eve in the Garden of Eden when he said: "This is . . . flesh of my flesh." Luther ventured to affirm that Christians would recognize father, mother, and one another even better in the life to come than Adam had recognized Eve.

After saying his accustomed prayers on the evening of the same day Luther began to feel ill. Everything was done to alleviate his pains and make him comfortable. By ten o'clock he seemed to be feeling better. So he asked Jonas and the others to go to bed. As Luther crossed the threshold of his room he said: "God grant it, I am going to bed. Into Thy hands I commend my spirit, Thou hast redeemed me, Lord, God of truth."[45]

At one o'clock in the morning Luther awoke, complaining: "O Lord God, how I am pained. Oh, dear Dr. Jonas, I suppose I shall remain here in Eisleben where I was born and baptized."[46] Though Jonas and Coelius tried to comfort Luther by assuring him of God's help and by asking him to call upon the Lord Jesus Christ, his High Priest and Mediator, he replied that his illness was becoming more severe and that he would soon breathe his last.[47] Thereupon he uttered this simple, moving prayer: "O my heavenly Father, the God and Father of our Lord Jesus Christ, thou God of all comfort, I thank thee, that thou hast revealed to me thy dear Son Jesus Christ, in whom I believe, whom I have preached and confessed, whom I have loved and praised, whom the Pope himself and all godless dishonor, persecute and blaspheme. I pray thee, my Lord Jesus Christ, let my poor soul be committed to thee. O heavenly Father, though I leave this body, and must be snatched out of this life, I nevertheless know for a certainty that I shall remain with thee eternally and no one can pluck me out of thy hands."[48] After that he repeated John 3:16 and Psalm 61:21 aloud. An attempt by the physician to help him by giving him some special medicine failed, and with that he repeated the words three times: "Father, into thy hands I commend my spirit, thou hast redeemed me, God of truth." Before death claimed him, both Jonas and Coelius asked him with loud voices, before all who were present: "Reverend father, do you wish to die steadfastly in Christ and the teaching as you have preached it?" The distinct and audible answer of the dying Reformer was "Yes." After this his voice was silenced by death.[49]

On the same day, February 18, Jonas sent a written account of Luther's death to the Elector John Frederick of Saxony. It related the last days of Luther's life in less detail than the Report. As one who had been a disciple of Luther for twenty-five years, Jonas believed it to be his duty to forward this account of Luther's death to the Elector at the earliest possible moment in order that the Prince might issue the necessary instructions relating to Luther's burial.[50]

On February 19, at two o'clock in the afternoon, the casket containing Luther's body was taken to St. Andrew's Church in Eisleben where Jonas preached the funeral sermon based on 1 Thessalonians 4:13 ff. In the first place, Jonas dealt with the person and gifts of Luther; then he treated the doctrine of the resurrection and eternal life; and finally he gave warning to Luther's opponents concerning the power which his death would have.[51]

Jonas used the occasion to impress upon his audience the undeniably abundant blessings that had been showered upon them through the person of Luther. He urged them to remain steadfast in their Christian faith and hope in the face of death, even as he demanded sincere repentance on the part of the entire German nation at this tragic hour. "So, too," he admonished, "will God's terrible punishment assuredly fall upon Germany after the death of the man of God, Dr. Martin, if it does not amend its ways."[52] Jonas believed to see a parallel between Augustine's fear lest his fatherland lose the Gospel and a similar apprehension expressed by Luther. Yet, said Jonas, for two hundred years the Gospel was preserved after Augustine's death in answer to prayer. He therefore concluded: "As we too are, at this time, so greatly concerned, lest we should lose the Word of God, let us also begin to live penitently, and earnestly pray that God would preserve His Word yet longer among us, after Dr. Martin Luther's death, as he did in the time of St. Augustine."[53]

Early on Saturday, February 20, Michael Coelius preached the second funeral sermon in St. Andrew's Church on the text taken from Isaiah 57: "The righteous man perishes, and no one lays it to heart." In the afternoon the impressive funeral cortege left Eisleben, as multitudes crowded the wayside to observe it. At five o'clock on the same afternoon the train reached Halle, where the concourse of people was so great that the procession had to come to a halt. The casket was brought into Our Dear Lady's Church at half-past six and throngs of worshipers sang Luther's hymn: "Out of the depths I cry to Thee, Lord, hear me, I implore Thee." Since it was so late a funeral sermon was not delivered.

In the early hours of the morning on February 21, the funeral procession left Halle, making its way to Wittenberg. On the following day it arrived at the Elster Gate of the city—the place where the papal Bull had been burned by Luther twenty-six years ago. In Wittenberg all preparations for the honorable burial of its most distinguished citizen had been made. Princes and professors, ministers and laymen— all classes of society were represented, as the funeral train made its way through the city to the Castle Church where the casket containing Luther's body was placed opposite the pulpit. Several thousands of people had gathered in the church to join in singing the funeral hymns and to hear Bugenhagen's sermon and Melanchthon's oration. "After the oration was over," the Report reads, "several learned teachers, chosen for this purpose, bore the corpse and let it down into the grave and thus laid it to rest; and so the dear instrument and vessel of the Holy Spirit, the body of the venerable Dr. Martin, in the Castle at Wittenberg, not far distant from the pulpit (from which, during his life he had delivered many a mighty, Christian sermon before the Elector of Saxony and the entire church) was laid into the earth." The

Report concludes with the express testimony of its authors that they recorded the factual occurrences which they had witnessed.[54] It had been made at the request of the Elector, and the obvious wisdom of a reliable testimony to the peaceful departure of Luther in a firm faith in his Redeemer soon became apparent when his enemies spread false reports concerning his death.[55]

The poignant grief produced by Luther's death found expression in many of Jonas' letters in the months that followed.[56] Because he had been with Luther during his last days, he was frequently asked to give an account to friends and rulers concerning the Reformer's end.[57] In mourning the death of Luther, Jonas did not forget the family Luther left behind, but offered to care for them. Gratefully, Hans Luther, the eldest son of the Reformer, acknowledged this affectionate concern on the part of Jonas at the time of their sorrow.[58] Strangely, too, with the death of Luther the comparatively tranquil period of Jonas' life came to an end. The future was going to unfold itself to him in years filled with lonely wanderings and manifold griefs, and in retrospect he could have joined the writer of Ecclesiastes in saying: "I have no pleasure in them."[59]

FOOTNOTES FOR CHAPTER 8

1. Franke, *op. cit.*, p. 147.
2. Kawerau, *op. cit.*, Vol. II, p. 76.
3. *Ibid.*, p. 57.
4. Franke, *op. cit.*, p. 147.
5. Dreyhaupt, *op. cit.*, Vol. I, pp. 982-986.
6. Pressel, *op. cit.*, pp. 85-86.
7. Kawerau, *op. cit.*, Vol. II, pp. 76-77.
8. *Ibid.*, p. 64.
9. *Ibid.*, pp. 78-79.
10. Enders, *op. cit.*, Vol. XIV, p. 308.
11. Franke, *op. cit.*, pp. 151-152.
12. Pressel, *op. cit.*, p. 86.
13. Enders, *op. cit.*, Vol. XV, pp. 173-175.
14. G. Kawerau, "Der Streit über die *Reliquiae Sacramenti* in Eisleben, 1543," *Zeitschrift für Kirchengeschichte.* Edited by Theodor Brieger and Bernard Bass. Vol. XXXIII (1912), pp. 298-300.
15. *Ibid.*, p. 302.
16. Enders, *op. cit.*, Vol. XV, pp. 182-183.
17. Kawerau, *op. cit.*, Vol. II, pp. 114-115, 117.
18. Kawerau, *op. cit.*, Vol. II, pp. 124-125.
19. *Ibid.*, pp. 121-125.
20. *Ibid.*, pp. 126-127.

21. *Ibid.*, p. 134.
22. Enders, *op. cit.*, Vol. XVI, pp. 106-107.
23. Kawerau, *op. cit.*, Vol. II, pp. 135-136.
24. *Ibid.*, pp. 136-137.
25. Dreyhaupt, *op. cit.*, Vol. I, pp. 987-988.
    Franke, *op. cit.*, pp. 154-155.
26. Kawerau, *op. cit.*, Vol. II, p. 168.
27. Kawerau, *op. cit.*, Vol. II, pp. 158-160.
28. Margaret A. Currie, *op. cit.*, p. 454.
29. *Ibid.*, pp. 453-454; cf. Enders, *op. cit.*, Vol. XVI, pp. 223-225.
30. Kawerau, *op. cit.*, Vol. II, pp. 161-165.
31. *Corpus Reformatorum*, Vol. V, p. 785.
32. Pressel, *op. cit.*, p. 90.
33. Koestlin, *op. cit.*, Vol. II, p. 620.
34. Enders, *op. cit.*, Vol. XVI, p. 335.
35. Koestlin, *op. cit.*, Vol. II, p. 625.
36. Hasse, *op. cit.*, p. 198.
37. Margaret A. Currie, *op. cit.*, p. 469.
38. "Dat vitrum vitro Ionae vitrum ipse Lutherus Ut vitro fragili similem se noscat uterque." *Tischreden*, Weimar Edition, Vol. VI, p. 299; cf. Koestlin, *op cit.*, Vol. II, pp. 628-629.
39. Koestlin, *op. cit.*, Vol. II, p. 628; Hasse, *op. cit.*, p. 199.
40. Walch, Editor, *Luthers Sämmtliche Schriften*, Vol. XXI b, p. 3382.
41. Koestlin, *op. cit.*, Vol. II, p. 631.
42. Margaret A. Currie, *op. cit.*, pp. 474-475.
43. Walch, *op. cit.*, Vol. XXIb, pp. 3206-3210.
44. Kawerau, *op. cit.*, Vol. II, p. xlvii.
    Luthers Werke, Weimar Edition, Vol. LIV, pp. 478-496.
45. Walch, *op. cit.*, Vol. XXI b, p. 3385.
46. *Ibid.*
47. *Ibid.*, p. 3386.
48. *Ibid.*
49. *Ibid.*, p. 3387.
50. Kawerau, *op. cit.*, Vol. II, pp. 181-184.
51. Walch, *op. cit.*, Vol. XXIb, p. 3389.
52. *Two Funeral Sermons on the Death of Dr. Martin Luther.* Delivered at Eisleben February 19, and 20, 1546, by Dr. Justus Jonas and Pastor Michael Coelius. Translated by E. Greenwald, p. 26.
53. *Ibid.*, pp. 26-27.
54. Walch, *op. cit.*, Vol. XXIb, pp. 3381-3392.
55. Kawerau, *op. cit.*, Vol. II, pp. 185-186
56. *Ibid.*, pp. 182-190.
57. *Ibid.*, pp. 189-190, 195.
58. *Ibid.*, p. 185.
59. Ecclesiastes 12:1b.

Chapter 9

The Schmalcald War

At the Diet of Speyer in 1542 the Protestant estates reached an agreement with Charles V according to which they granted the Emperor military aid in his war against the Turk, and he in turn promised a prolongation of a peaceful relationship between Romanists and Protestants for the next five years. This gave the Protestants the opportunity of winning considerable ground in Germany for the Reformation. At a subsequent Diet at Speyer in 1544 the Emperor was able to renew this agreement. In addition, the Protestants granted him help against the King of France. The pledges made at the Regensburg Conference were to be upheld and all seemed to augur well for the Protestant cause.

In September, 1544, the Peace of Crepy brought the Emperor's war with France to a close, and this treaty was the harbinger of ominous clouds on the political horizon which finally vented their fury on the Protestants in the Schmalcald War.[1] Jonas had received news of the Emperor's peace pact with France.[2] The sudden turn in the political situation did not cause any forebodings as yet, especially because the Emperor had so far successfully concealed his actual design, the extermination of the Wittenberg "heresy" by force of arms.[3] He continued holding the religious conferences with the Protestants in order to make it appear as if he had no intention of using force in settling the issue.

156

Luther even informed Jonas of the Pope's protest against the independent actions of the Emperor who was continuing the conferences
with the Protestants and calling for a General Council.[4] At the Diet
of Worms in March, 1545, the compromise formulae which had been
worked out by Butzer and Melanchthon were not, however, presented
to the Emperor by the legate from Saxony. The Protestants had lost
faith in a compromise. Moreover, the ensuing General Council which
Pope Paul III, at the Emperor's insistence, had been persuaded to call
at Trent, filled the Protestants with misgivings, and at the Diet they
announced their intention not to attend its sessions.[5]

On September 24, 1545, Cardinal Albrecht, one of the chief foes of
evangelical reform in Germany, died in his residence at Aschaffenburg.
The senate of Halle, apprehensive lest the people might construe his
death as propitious for a full-scale offensive against the last remnants
of Catholicism in the city, bade the evangelical ministers issue a warning to the citizens that no one was to commit any acts of violence
against the monasteries. The senate believed that since the Cardinal
was dead, it could do away with the remaining Catholic monasteries
in a peaceful, unobtrusive way.[6] The appointment of a successor to
Cardinal Albrecht of Mainz was delayed for some time. Toward the
end of October, 1545, Jonas heard a rumor that John Albert, the former
prefect of the city and coadjutor of the Cardinal, had succeeded him as
Archbishop of Magdeburg and Halberstadt.[7] This rumor was subsequently confirmed. Archbishop John Albert, known as "the lame
bishop" because of an injured hip that caused him to limp, was as
determined an enemy of evangelical truth as his predecessor had been.
The city of Halle refused to swear fealty to the new Archbishop unless
a redress of its grievances was granted and it would be allowed
religious freedom.[8] This situation gave rise to a prolonged dispute
between the two opposing parties. Events intervened which postponed
an immediate decision.

In January of 1546 the Emperor renewed the religious conference at
Regensburg. Melanchthon, who was supposed to appear there, could
not attend because of ill health. Martin Butzer, Schnepf, Brenz, and
George Major were the Protestants who were present to negotiate

with the Catholics. Butzer especially believed that a compromise for the entire German church could be worked out. In fact, however, the Emperor had called the colloquy only to mark time until he could, at an opportune moment, force the Protestants to submission by armed might.[9] Luther's death occurred in February of the same year, and so it was not until April, 1546, that the controversial issue concerning Halle's rights and privileges under Archbishop John Albert was finally decided.

Probably early in April "an Opinion to the venerable senate as to what is to be treated at the Wittenberg Convention with the new Archbishop, Markgrave John Albert, particularly with regard to the abolition of the monasteries" was submitted to the senate by Jonas, Benedict Schumann, and Matthias Wanckel.[10] In this Opinion the senate was reminded that the monasteries were a belligerent element in the city, and that the monks who inhabited them were the most bitter and hardened foes of evangelical doctrine. These monks were continually molesting the people and were responsible for a great deal of propaganda by which they lured Christians away from their evangelical beliefs. Besides, in matters relating to matrimony the position of Halle's Protestant ministers was made difficult because the episcopal jurisdiction prevented them from making any binding decisions. The Opinion therefore urged that a consistory, taking the place of the episcopal authority, should be set up so that order and justice might be secured in this important sphere. Unless something could be done to effect a change, the Opinion stated that its signers would have to take a more aggressive stand against the monks of the city and would even go so far as to seek the advice of the Elector of Saxony.[11]

In the same month Jonas was able to have the Wittenberg theologians submit an Opinion which made specific recommendations to the senate at Halle as to how it was to carry out a thorough reform in the city. "And because it pertained to God's glory and the peace of the city," was the advice of the Opinion, "it would be well that one would admonish the Bishop to order matters so that the monks and nuns would have to keep silent and no incidents might occur."[12] The Elector of Saxony, by reason of the Burgraviate which he exercised over

Halle, was called upon as arbitrator. The final settlement was made in the Wittenberg Compromise of April 20, 1546, according to which the city received religious liberty, the power to appoint its own ministers, and other rights and privileges pertaining to the church's property and the legal scope of its jurisdiction. Matthias Metz, the inveterate opponent of Jonas and of all evangelical reform, was compelled to leave Halle and went to Erfurt.

A growing mood of apprehension was making itself felt among the leaders of the evangelical churches. Melanchthon, as early as May, 1546, took a grave view of the times. The Council of Trent (1545-63) had condemned the evangelical doctrine, and the religious conference at Regensburg had been a failure. Still Melanchthon assured Jonas in a letter that God was to be thanked for the revelation of the light of the Gospel and the gathering of his church. Melanchthon begged Jonas not to mourn unduly over the death of Luther but to take courage in spite of disheartening events. And Jonas did continue his work at Halle in a hopeful and energetic manner. He reported to Melanchthon that each Sunday as many as ten or eleven thousand persons attended the services which were held simultaneously in the three evangelical churches.[13] Jonas also maintained his interest in the affairs of his friends and the church at large. When John Spangenberg reported to Jonas that he had left Nordhausen and gone to Eisleben, Jonas congratulated his friend very cordially upon his induction into his new position. In the same letter he reported on the Emperor's preparations for war and the support which German bishops and the Pope were giving him.[14]

Exile and Return

By mid-summer of 1546 the Schmalcald War broke out. Charles V had not only secured an alliance with Pope Paul III but had been able to come to a secret understanding with Duke Maurice of Saxony who, though a member of the Schmalcald League, was won over to the Emperor's side by being promised an Electorate in the event of a victory by the Emperor. After placing John Frederick and Philip of Hesse under imperial ban because of disloyalty to the empire, the Emperor began the war.

Jonas naturally sided with the Schmalcald League and interpreted the war as a religious one. Early in August he wrote to Elector John Frederick and stated his views on a campaign that had been planned against the Emperor. Hopeful that the war would result in a disaster for the Emperor and the Pope, he closed with a prayerful wish that Christ might strengthen and preserve the Elector and his praiseworthy, Christian soldiers.[15]

At first the outlook for a Protestant victory was favorable, but the invasion of Electoral Saxony by King Ferdinand of Austria, brother of Charles V, and Duke Maurice altered the situation. Jonas' son, Justus, had to leave Wittenberg and flee to Halle because of the advancing hostile armies. The hope for an early peace proved false. Jonas and the ministers in Halle continued to exhort their people to pray that the Protestant princes might gain a decisive victory and so punish the "great perfidy of Charles V, the Spanish Diocletian." In the public prayer in the churches of Halle the name of the Emperor was omitted and placed beside that of Pontius Pilate in the Apostles' Creed.[16]

On Monday, November 22, Halle itself was beleaguered by the troops of Duke Maurice, and after the senate willingly surrendered the city to the Ducal army, it was ordered to appear before the Duke, the legates of the Emperor, the Archbishop John Albert, and his councilors on Wednesday, November 24. When the senate appeared before these authorities, its members and the entire population of Halle were accused of disobedience to their rightful ruler, the Archbishop. The senate was given the strictest injunction to expel from the city the superintendent of its churches, Jonas, and the syndic, Kilian Goldstein. The wrath of the Emperor and the Duke was directed especially against Jonas because he had compared Charles V with Diocletian and Pontius Pilate. The senate disavowed the charge of disobedience on the part of the city and put forward a most importunate petition that Jonas might remain, for he, the members of the senate argued, had taught and preached the truth of the Scriptures and had been very helpful in the evangelical reform carried out by the Duke's father, Duke Henry of Saxony. This request was emphatically denied. Instead Jonas had to bear the insult of having an officer of the Bohemian mercenaries and other soldiers lodged in his house, while in mockery a reproduction of a gallows was put over his door. Early on Thursday the senate appeared before Duke Maurice to renew its requests on behalf of Jonas and Goldstein, but to no avail. The two men were given ten days in which to prepare for their departure. The city was allowed to retain the evangelical form of service, but was compelled to agree to cease its attacks on the Emperor and the Archbishop, and to renew its loyalty and obedience to them.[17]

Jonas went to Mansfeld. He felt that he had been exiled for no just cause, and in a lengthy letter to Prince George of Anhalt he reviewed his meritorious services on behalf of evangelical Christianity in Halle. "In supporting and adorning the state and church at Halle, Dr. Kilian, the syndic, and I expended all faithful diligence and, as it were, paternal labors." Banishment for such conduct seemed to him most unreasonable.[18] Fortunately the sympathetic comfort of friends was not lacking. Even King Christian III, upon hearing of Jonas' expulsion from Halle, addressed a letter of comfort and encouragement to the latter. Their faith, he wrote, was directed toward God and the basis of all hope.[19]

During this stay in Mansfeld the superintendency of the church at Hildesheim was offered to Jonas by Medler; but the fortunes of war made an early return to Halle possible. The Elector John Frederick had occupied Halle with his troops on January 1, 1547, and, guaranteeing to the city all privileges, liberties, and rights, permitted the return of Jonas and Goldstein. On January 9 both men returned to Halle. Only two days later Archbishop John Albert fled his castle in order to seek safety in Würzburg.[20]

During the brief rule of the Saxon Elector over Halle the last vestiges of the papal religion were removed from the city under Jonas' supervision. Jonas wisely secured an injunction from the Elector to this effect before undertaking the task. The monks and nuns were driven out of the city. In the rural areas surrounding Halle the Romanist clergy were deposed and pious and learned ministers of evangelical persuasion were put in their places. These thoroughgoing measures, which abolished all papal influence, achieved that goal which Jonas had sought to attain during the six years he was at Halle.[21]

Victory for the Emperor

But all too soon the scales of war were to be decidedly balanced in favor of the Emperor, who inflicted a crushing defeat on the Elector John Frederick near Mühlberg on April 24, 1547, and took his opponent captive. After this victory Charles V entered Wittenberg and from there proceeded to Halle with a large and powerful army. Jonas and Goldstein were forced to seek safety in flight a second time because, in virtue of Duke Maurice's representations before the Emperor, they had fallen into imperial disfavor and would no doubt have suffered injury if apprehended.[22] The senate had urged Jonas to leave the city quickly and to wait until the wrath of the Emperor against him had subsided somewhat. Jonas' flight with his family was made in great haste. In the space of an hour the household goods were placed on two wagons and Jonas, his wife, who was expecting a child, and their six children left Halle.[23] "On account of the magnitude and diversity of the danger it should have been necessary for us to make detours and to continue our trip during the night and on forest paths, but the unwarlike nature of my wife and children could not endure nocturnal traveling or winding about in forests," reported Jonas to Duke Albrecht of Prussia, as he recalled this flight two years later. At first the exiles went to the Counts of Mansfeld who received them with genuine friendliness and hospitality. From Mansfeld Jonas journeyed with his family to Nordhausen. Since it was not safe for him to enter the city publicly, he hid for the space of a whole month in an isolated summer-house belonging to the burgomaster of Nordhausen, Andrew Wende.

Melanchthon, who had likewise fled to Nordhausen during the perilous situation in Wittenberg, was able to aid Jonas in securing a call to Hildesheim as superintendent of the church in that city. On June 1, 1547, Melanchthon wrote to Lorenz Moller, rector of St. Andrew's School in Hildesheim, that Jonas was willing to go there to take charge of the churches in the city, if the senate would send him a call.[24]

Before final arrangements for the call to Hildesheim were completed, Jonas wrote a letter full of tender sympathy to the Saxon Elector John Frederick, a captive of the Emperor. Relating that Melanchthon's exile in the same city was a source of mutual comfort to both of them, he assured the Elector that they, along with all God-fearing Christians, were moved to sincere compassion over the misfortune which had overtaken the Prince. The tragic conditions plunged Jonas into a mood of sadness so that he was almost unable to write. Still he felt constrained to address this letter to the Elector in order to commend Melanchthon and himself as "poor, old people" and "his preachers and servants" to his Electoral Grace.[25]

At Hildesheim

Very soon after this letter had been written, Jonas received the call to Hildesheim and went there, leaving his family behind in Nordhausen. In Hildesheim he became the minister of St. Andrew's Church and superintendent of all the churches. The evangelical church at Hildesheim had been founded by Bugenhagen in 1542.[26] A certain Jodocus Isermann was the regular superintendent of the Hildesheim churches, but since he wielded no decisive influence in the city, he could not introduce the desirable order and discipline. Isermann had concurred in the decision to call Jonas so that the latter might improve the organization of the churches in the city and bring about order and stability.

Jonas attacked the problem of creating an orderly form of worship and church government and restoring concord and peace among the citizens with characteristic vigor. He preached assiduously in St. Andrew's Church, of which he was the minister, and also in the Church of the Holy Cross. In the Church of the Holy Cross he delivered a series of discourses on the letters of the Apostle Paul to the Ephesians and the Galatians, several selected Psalms, and the Prophet Jeremiah.[27]

Before long he appears to have attained his goal of achieving unity and order.

In view of the temporary nature of his position and the confused conditions that followed in the wake of the Schmalcald War, Jonas was not as well cared for in Hildesheim as he might have been. The annual income of 100 guldens that had been sent to him regularly from Wittenberg prior to the war, was no longer received. His remuneration in Hildesheim was probably quite modest, for he was grateful when a neighboring pastor, Antonius Corvinus, forwarded a shipment of grain to him. The letters of faithful friends, like Nicholas Medler and the above-mentioned Antonius Corvinus, became beacons of hope and encouragement amid the gloom of frequent sickness and loneliness. Corvinus promised to maintain an unbroken tie of friendship and came to visit Jonas on several occasions. Nicholas Medler also corresponded frequently with Jonas and informed him of conditions in the churches, sending a gift of some kind, and seeking to strengthen their common faith.[28]

After a period of five months Jonas was eager to leave Hildesheim. In late October he wrote to John Lange in Erfurt, complaining that the manner of living in Hildesheim was aggravating his sickness. He saw that the calamities prophesied by Luther were coming true. Jonas hoped that the wrath of the Elector Maurice could be assuaged so that he would soon be able to return to Halle. He was thinking of going to Erfurt temporarily and inquired of Lange whether he could find secure shelter there. In November conditions were virtually intolerable, for his wife and one daughter became dangerously ill, while Jonas was still suffering from his old illness, kidney-stone. "I am compelled because of my health to return home," he wrote to Prince George of Anhalt. He implored his friend to obtain for him a safe-conduct from the Elector Maurice so that he could leave Hildesheim. He felt free to do so at any time because he had promised to serve as superintendent and minister at Hildesheim only temporarily. Then, too, he considered Halle his proper field of work to which he was bound by a call of a permanent nature. To Halle he was therefore ready to return at a moment's notice.[29]

In this predicament he sent a similar request to Melanchthon, who was again in Wittenberg. Melanchthon's reply was not encouraging, for he advised Jonas that Prince George was inclined to help him, but that the opportunity to do so had not presented itself. Melanchthon and the widowed Duchess Elisabeth of Goettingen and Kalenberg prevailed upon the Elector Joachim II, who enjoyed the close friendship of the Elector Maurice, to intercede for Jonas.[30] By December the prospects for a return to Halle became brighter. The city's senate was now negotiating with the Emperor for permission to have Jonas and Kilian Goldstein return to their former posts. Ever impatient and anxious to leave Hildesheim, Jonas again planned to move to Erfurt for several months so that he might be able to hurry the negotiations that were in progress. On January 6, 1548, Melanchthon was granted an interview with the Elector Maurice. Addressing his appeal to the ruler on behalf of Jonas and some other prisoners, Melanchthon asked him magnanimously to overlook "the foolish talk" of Jonas, and, according to the example of King David who, when returning to his country, promised to spare his foes, show a similar mercy in this instance. Melanchthon therefore begged that the Elector should no longer look with disfavor upon "the old, weak man, Dr. Jonas" but grant him permission to return to Halle.[31]

The Return to Halle

In February Jonas left Hildesheim with his family and went to Nordhausen. His own ill health as well as that of his wife made their departure mandatory. His work in Hildesheim had met with general approval and the position he had held was left open to him and he was given the privilege of returning if he so desired. "The good and pious lovers of the Gospel have let me go very unwillingly," he reported to Nicholas von Amsdorf.[32] In Nordhausen Jonas continued to negotiate with the senate of Halle concerning his return to the city. As an expression of his sincere friendship with Jonas, John Spangenberg of Eisleben declared himself ready to go to Halle to present Jonas' wishes before the senate. Within two days Spangenberg reported to Jonas that he "had moved every stone" to end his friend's exile, and that, though there was a sincere desire on the part of Halle's citizens to have him return, the senate advised that he wait for a more opportune time. With characteristic impulsiveness Jonas did not await the official invitation of the senate to come back to Halle, but, as soon as he had obtained a letter from the Elector Maurice granting him safe-conduct in Saxon territories, he departed from Nordhausen and arrived in Halle on April 5, 1548, after an exile of approximately one year.[33]

It is not unlikely that a brief composition entitled: "Prayer and Thanksgiving" was written by Jonas when he returned to Halle after his first exile.[34]

Disfavor and Disappointment

When Jonas, with a letter of safe-conduct from the Elector Maurice, returned to Halle on April 5, 1548, he little dreamed that the senate would not permit him to resume the whole round of his activities as superintendent and minister. There was considerable joy manifested by evangelical Christians over Jonas' return;[35] but the changed political situation had altered the attitude of the senate in the city. Moreover, Sebastian Boetius, a young and learned pastor, had satisfactorily taken Jonas' place during the latter's absence. So when Jonas appeared before the senate and presented his letter of safe-conduct, its members did not show any eagerness to reinstate him as superintendent. They thought it advisable for him to wait with the resumption of all of his duties until conditions became more favorable. The curtailment of Jonas' activities in Halle was made in one obvious area, that of public preaching. Evidently the senate, not wishing to incur the displeasure of the Elector or fall into imperial disfavor, thought that such a precautionary measure would prove wisest.

In the face of this dilemma, Jonas did not passively and patiently await a favorable turn in the political situation. He appealed to the same friend who had aided him in obtaining the letter of safe-conduct —Prince George of Anhalt—to secure from the Elector Maurice per-

mission for him to preach. Consequently, Jonas did not wish to accept
a call to the church of Denmark which had come to him through the
mediation of a friend; he had obligated himself to serve the church
in Halle for life. Meanwhile he had learned that the Elector Maurice
was returning after Pentecost from a convention and would perhaps
come to Merseburg, where Prince George was coadjutor. Jonas promptly wrote to the Prince, requesting that he intercede before the Elector
so that he might again be allowed to preach in Halle.[36]

Although Jonas was denied the privilege of preaching, he was permitted to dwell in his home and seems to have discharged the remaining duties connected with the superintendency. He lectured in Latin
twice a week to a sizable number of learned persons and found some
satisfaction in this public function. In Halle he was again in possession of his library which he had so keenly missed during his exile.
"From the books of the revered Luther (which I read daily) the
very truth of God thunders and trumpets forth with boldness," he
wrote to Andrew Poach, a deacon in the church at Halle for several
years.[37]

Jonas afterwards learned the real reason why he had been banished
from his own pulpit for months and then finally for a year and more.
Two members of the senate, who were in Augsburg at the imperial
Diet during the summer of 1548, had heard many complaints and accusations about Jonas from certain influential men at court. The monks
of Halle, the irreconcilable foes of Jonas, had successfully made his
name odious in imperial circles. As a result the citizens of Halle were
disposed not to permit Jonas to preach "lest this city through this vehement accusation incur still greater indignation of the ruler."[38]

The victory of the Emperor over the Protestants at Schmalcald
meant that he would attempt to make Catholicism dominant in Germany. But since Pope Paul III withdrew his support after the war,
Charles V was left to his own devices in this endeavor. The Augsburg
Interim, upholding the Romanist doctrines of transubstantiation, the
seven Sacraments, adoration of the Blessed Virgin, and the sacrifice
of the mass and declaring the Pope to be head of the church, made
only very insignificant concessions to the Protestants. The Interim per-

mitted the cup to be given to the laity in the Lord's Supper and allowed priestly marriage until a meeting of a General Council would make further pronouncements. At the Diet of Augsburg this Interim was handed to the estates on May 15, 1548, and on June 30, it became imperial law. Maurice of Saxony was compelled by the Protestant estates in his territories to introduce the Leipzig Interim which made far-reaching concessions to the Protestants but nevertheless compromised the evangelical teachings. The doctrine of justification by faith was retained, and the mass was abolished; but the jurisdiction of Catholic bishops was acknowledged and Romanist ceremonies were upheld.

Disagreement with Melanchthon

Complaints about the Interim arose in all parts of Germany. In South Germany the evangelical churches suffered greatly and countless evangelical ministers became exiles because the Emperor was able to enforce the Interim and reestablish the Catholic religion there. In North Germany its enforcement was not possible on account of the passive resistance of the evangelical population and the heroic stand of men like Matthias Flacius and Nicholas von Amsdorf.

Jonas received frequent reports from Melanchthon and other Protestant leaders on the comparative success or failure of the Augsburg and Leipzig Interims, while he was waiting to see to what extent it was to be forced upon the church at Halle. Antonius Otho, a Lutheran minister in Nordhausen, reported indignantly to Jonas on the failure of some Protestants to oppose the Interim more uncompromisingly. In Nordhausen, he stated, they were not prevented from preaching the evangelical faith, even though expressed criticism of the Interim was frowned upon by the authorities.[39] From Nuremberg, Veit Dietrich wrote that the Interim was responsible for much confusion; but it was being opposed by the senate and could not be forced upon the evangelical churches.[40]

The church at Halle was faced by a twofold threat, the Interim and the return of the Archbishop John Albert. On July 12, 1548, at the Diet of Augsburg the Emperor reinstated John Albert as Archbishop of Magdeburg and Halberstadt. With manifest satisfaction the Archbishop addressed a letter to the nobility of his Magdeburg Chapter, announcing his reinstallation as Archbishop at Halle on August 26, and inviting them to be present. The provincial Diet, presided over by the Archbishop, was supposed to take place on the following day, August 27.[41] This announcement of John Albert's return and the ensuing Diet provoked considerable concern among the evangelical population of Halle. On August 24 the Archbishop entered Halle, bringing with him a number of monks who immediately entered the empty Dominican and Barefoot Cloisters and restored the Catholic worship in the Castle Church and Cloister churches.[42] At the provincial Diet the Archbishop tried to put the Interim into effect, but the attempt proved futile.[43] In a letter addressed to Jonas, Melanchthon voiced his cordial approval of the declaration of the Halle clergy concerning the Interim and promised to pay Jonas a visit in the near future.[44] Happily the church at Halle continued to defy the Interim, as Jonas' letters from this period conclusively state. Unable to preach publicly, Jonas used his influence in other ways to deprive the Interim of its effectiveness. He heartily commended the brave resistance of the cities of Hamburg, Lübeck, and Lüneburg. In May, 1549, Jonas could report: "In the church at Halle even under the jurisdiction of the Archbishop the pure doctrine, worship of God—all things are as formerly." One half-year later the situation was still the very same, and it remained thus throughout the following year.

The Interim was producing an open cleavage within the evangelical Lutheran Church. Associated by the ties of a close friendship with Melanchthon, Jonas was loath to attack the mediating and compromising tactics of Melanchthon and the Wittenberg University in matters pertaining to the Interim. He had called upon Antonius Otho in Nordhausen not to join others in condemning Melanchthon's position on the Interim. Melanchthon might be willing to make concessions in unessential points of doctrine, but there would come a time when he would say to those who tried to unite Wittenberg with Rome: "Woe unto you, scribes and Pharisees." Otho was at first satisfied with these reassuring statements by Jonas, but soon after Otho raised a cry of protest and made bitter accusations against Melanchthon and his party, claiming that the Wittenbergers were resorting to a falsification of Luther's writings.[45] Desiring to uphold the Lutheran position and also to retain Melanchthon's friendship, Jonas sought to bring about an understanding and reconciliation between the strict Lutheran party led by Amsdorf and Matthias Flacius, and the Melanchthonian group. The sensitive Melanchthon was apparently offended by this attempt on the part of Jonas, for a noticeable break in their regular correspondence with each other occurs.[46] As time went on Jonas was, by virtue of his firm evangelical convictions, attracted more and more to men who showed an uncompromising hostility toward the Interim and an unwavering loyalty to the Lutheran position. His correspondence with men of this stamp and his own views show clearly where his sympathies lay.

Final Leavetaking

The years 1549 and 1550 brought their full share of disappointments and sorrows to Jonas. Again and again he expressed his dissatisfaction that the senate did not allow him to preach. The Wittenberg Compromise had secured for Halle the privilege of appointing its own ministers, and yet the senate was not prepared to reinstate Jonas in his office. "Of such a nature is the distress of these times, illustrious Prince," Jonas complained to Duke Albrecht of Prussia, in a letter of May 1549, "that ministers of people everywhere are tested more severely, the more conscientious they have been in office. At least I who, seven years ago, at the time of the Cardinal endured many dangers and amid most difficult controversies with utmost diligence first sowed the seeds of the Gospel, like an exile in the midst of my church, have not preached for a whole year."[47] Only a month later Jonas was appeased by the promise of the senate that he would soon be able to exercise his office as superintendent and minister unhampered by present restrictions.[48] Meanwhile Jonas did everything possible to bring about the long-desired privilege of preaching in Halle by asking influential persons to secure permission for him to preach. Toward the end of the year the senate renewed its pledge of seeking to grant Jonas his wish. While his patience was put to a severe test by a procrastinating senate, he showed no signs of bitterness or ill-will toward his fellow-ministers in Halle. In fact, during this long period of waiting Jonas lived in commendable harmony with them. He praised the youthful Sebastian Boetius as "a learned, honest young man," who preached well, and manifested a charitable and selfless concern for the future ministry of the church by expressing the hope that God might grant able, God-fearing young men who would spread the pure teaching of the Gospel among posterity.[49]

All efforts of Jonas to achieve permission to preach in Halle were, in spite of the frequent promises made by the senate, doomed to failure. Besides, he was unsuccessful in securing the 100 guldens per year which the Elector had promised him when he had demitted his provostship in Wittenberg.[50] Even Prince George of Anhalt, whom Jonas asked for help in both of these matters and whom he visited sometime in 1549,[51] was, through his efforts of mediation, unable to alter the dismal situation.

A letter from Duke John Ernest of Coburg as early as December, 1549, reveals that Jonas had, through a friend, offered his services to him.[52] The Duke's determination to resist the Interim in order to defend the truth of the Gospel made a deep impression on Jonas. On May 17, 1550, the Archbishop John Albert died and Jonas' hopes were raised once more, for he thought that now at last he would be reinstated as preacher in Halle. In June, 1550, the report was conveyed to Jonas that Erfurt was planning to call either him or George Major as minister. Later in the same month Jonas addressed a letter to Jerome Weller, clearly showing that Jonas' hope of obtaining preaching privileges had completely faded during the protracted negotiations with the senate and other authorities. Even while he contemplated traveling to Coburg for a visit, he was in a mood of despondency and dissatisfaction. His good friend John Spangenberg had died on June 13, he related. "Thus we old men withdraw from the stage of this life. The younger ones can hardly await our death. In advance they seize from us who yet live both place and honor and whatever is ours."[53] All this reminded Jonas impressively that the time of his own death was close at hand.

By the end of June and in July friends were advising Jonas to leave the ungrateful city of Halle, which was according him such unworthy treatment. Perhaps it was Jerome Weller's sympathetic and ingenuous letter of July 20 which gave the final impetus to the decision of Jonas to leave Halle. "Not without great grief and indignation did I read in your letters," wrote Weller, "that you as a great light in the church of Christ are still banished from your pulpit, even in the midst of your church." The learned sermons of an aged man like Jonas should be heard especially now, contended Weller. Jonas' Lutheran spirit, which was so tragically absent among many disciples of Luther, was needed to confirm the faith of others, even as Jonas' example in patient endurance would serve to strengthen the belief of all God-fearing Christians.[54] Shortly after this letter had been written, Jonas withdrew temporarily from the city which, in no small measure, owed him a debt of gratitude for the Gospel which it had received through him and which was now being proclaimed by others.

FOOTNOTES FOR CHAPTER 9

1. Moeller, *op. cit.*, pp. 133, 136.
2. Kawerau, *op. cit.*, Vol. II, p. 131.
3. Appel, *Kurzgefasste Kirchengeschichte*, p. 204.
4. Enders, *op. cit.*, Vol. XVI, pp. 181-182.
5. Moeller, *op. cit.*, p. 137.
6. Franke, op. cit., p. 158.
7. Kawerau, *op. cit.*, Vol. II, p. 167.
8. *Ibid.*, Vol. II, p. 173.
9. Koestlin, *op. cit.*, Vol. II, p. 625.
   Corpus Reformatorum, Vol. VI, pp. 34-37.
10. Kawerau, *op. cit.*, Vol. II, p. 191.
11. Dreyhaupt, *op. cit.*, Vol. I, pp. 210-216.
12. Kawerau, *op. cit.*, Vol. II, p. 194.
13. *Ibid.*, p. 193.
14. *Ibid.*, p. 203.
15. C. A. H. Burkhardt, "Neue Mittheilungen zur Korrespondenz der Reformation," *Zeitschrift für kirchliche Wissenschaften*, X Jahrgang 1889. Edited by C. E. Luthardt, pp. 430-431.
16. Kawerau, *op. cit.*, Vol. II, p. 210.
17. *Ibid.*, pp. 213-218.
18. *Ibid.*, pp. 379-380.
19. *Ibid.*, p. 222.
20. Franke, *op. cit.*, p. 186.
21. Kawerau, *op. cit.*, Vol. II, pp. 224-225.

22. *Ibid.*, pp. 227-228.
Jerome Weller has left an account which tells of a captain who had been quartered in Jonas' house and to whom the Emperor had given the command to kill Jonas. After Jonas had accorded the captain the best of treatment, the latter confessed openly: "Good doctor, I do not wish to conceal it from you that I have an order from the imperial majesty to slay you; but I see that you are such an honest, pious, and brave man that I can do you no harm." On the basis of the known facts it is impossible to determine just when this incident in Jonas' life occurred. Kawerau, *op. cit.*, Vol. II, p. L.
23. Jonas, two years later, claimed to have fled Halle with seven children. He evidently included the child born during this second exile. Previous to this his second wife had given birth to one child, a boy named Philip. Kawerau, *op. cit.*, Vol. II, p. 280.
24. *Corpus Reformatorum*, Vol. VI, p. 554.
25. This letter was written on June 9, 1547. Burkhardt, "Neue Mittheilungen zur Korrespondenz der Reformation," *Zeitschrift für kirchliche Wissenschaften*, X Jahrgang 1889. Edited by C. E. Luthardt, pp. 432-433.
26. W. Ruccius, *John Bugenhagen Pomeranus*, pp. 106-107.
27. Franke, *op. cit.*, p. 262.
28. Kawerau, *op. cit.*, Vol. II, pp. 230, 232, 233-235, 235-236, 244-245.
29. *Ibid.*, pp. 237, 239.
30. *Ibid.*, pp. 239, 240, 242-243, 245.
31. *Ibid.*, pp. 241, 247-248.
32. *Ibid.*, pp. 250-251.
This letter of Jonas to Amsdorf written from Nordhausen disproves an assertion made and repeated in many biographies of Jonas, that he left Hildesheim suddenly when he was informed about the Augsburg Interim of 1548 according to which all Catholic doctrines, the form of worship and organization were to be retained. Only priestly marriages and the Sacrament "under both kinds" were to be permitted (Appel, *op. cit.*, p. 205). An account taken from a chronicle of the city has it that when Jonas was reading the eleventh lesson of the Epistle to the Galatians, his servant came and whispered something to him about the Interim. Thereupon Jonas arose, saying: "Gentlemen, I commend you to God and the church," and left the city, after having been well cared for by the community for three quarters of a year (Pressel, *op. cit.*, p. 97).
33. Kawerau, *op. cit.*, Vol. II, pp. 252-254.
34. *Ibid.*, pp. xlvi-xlvii.
35. *Ibid.*, p. 255.
36. *Ibid.*, pp. 258-260.
37. *Ibid.*, p. 272.
38. *Ibid.*, p. 281.
39. *Ibid.*, pp. 261-262, 265.
40. *Ibid.*, pp. 268-270.
41. *Ibid.*, pp. 266-267.
42. *Ibid.*, pp. 284-285.
43. Pressel, *op. cit.*, p. 98.
44. *Corpus Reformatorum*, Vol. VII, p. 170.
45. Kawerau, *op. cit.*, Vol. II, pp. 288-289.
46. *Ibid.*, pp. 302, 319.
47. *Ibid.*, p. 281.
48. *Ibid.*, p. 284.
49. *Ibid.*, p. 296.
50. *Ibid.*, pp. 306-307.
51. *Corpus Reformatorum*, Vol. VII, p. 541.
52. Kawerau, *op. cit.*, Vol. II, pp. 294-295.
53. *Ibid.*, pp. 301-302.
54. *Ibid.*, pp. 303-306.

Chapter 10

And Strong Men
Are Bent

Jonas, as has been noted, had received a letter from Duke John Ernest of Coburg, the brother of the imprisoned Elector John Frederick, in December, 1549.[1] The Duke was a committed evangelical Christian, and so it was natural that there was a mutual interest. Jonas must have left Halle in late July or August of 1550 in order to visit this admirable, courageous ruler, for on September 5 of that year Matthias Wanckel, minister of St. Maurice's Church in Halle, reported to Flacius of Magdeburg that Jonas had written to him from Coburg.[2] It seems that he left his family in Halle while he paid this extended visit to the Duke. The personal discussions between him and the Duke John Ernest no doubt revolved in part about Jonas' position at Halle. As a result, Jonas was appointed superintendent of the church in Coburg and chaplain to the Duke. The acceptance of the call to Coburg meant that a final and complete severance of his connections with the church at Halle took place.[3] Apparently, Jonas and his family arrived in Coburg early in 1551, for on July 14 of that year George Major addressed a letter to Jonas as superintendent of the church at Coburg.[4]

As superintendent at Coburg, Jonas no longer mentioned the church at Halle or his relations with it. His complete silence concerning that church, which had been so dear to him, is perhaps an indication of the painful humiliation which he had experienced during the last years of restricted activity there. Since he was now in a strange place and was advancing in years, he felt the need of renewing old friendships. He wrote to the Abbot Frederick of Nuremberg several times during the first months of his stay in Coburg. "At this advanced age," he informed the Abbot, "I delight in nothing more than to converse with learned, pious and old friends through letters. I myself am an old and gray man, I have few who are of equal age. My second wife, a lady of most outstanding and incredible piety, lived with me five years and even into the sixth year. Lest the Pope might be too favorably inclined toward me, after twenty-seven years of married priesthood, I felt constrained to become married a third time." Jonas, imploring his old friend to let no opportunity of writing to him go by, closed by asking the Abbot to remember him to his friends.[5]

Melanchthon, whose position in the Interim had brought about an alienation in his friendship with Jonas, again resumed his correspondence with the Coburg superintendent after an interval of about three years. Reminding Jonas of their old friendship, he expressed his regret that the theological convention in Saxon lands, suggested by Jonas as a means of settling the dispute with Osiander, did not meet with the approval of the princely courts. He informed Jonas that he had read the latter's Opinion concerning Osiander's teaching on justification and that he desired certain modifications in it. The possibility of the visit of which Melanchthon wrote was received by Jonas with joyful anticipation.[6] He replied to Melanchthon's letter in a spirit of renewed hope, even though he admitted that he was "an old man" and decreasing in vigor. The joy which animated Jonas over the resumption of the correspondence with Melanchthon was unconcealed. He called Melanchthon "my revered and most beloved father and friend." "I shall talk to you personally," he wrote to Melanchthon, "concerning my foolishness and my truly foolish wanderings that I, without consulting you or Prince George of Anhalt, departed from Halle to come here for a time." The reassurance of Melanchthon's friendship, he claimed, had awakened him, "a gloomy old man, as if from a deep slumber."[7] In March, 1552, Jonas once more wrote to Melanchthon in a most cordial manner and recommended a young student for a scholarship.[8]

In 1552 Maurice of Saxony, dissatisfied with the Emperor's treatment of his father-in-law, Philip of Hesse, was able to bring about the defeat of Charles V, with the help of King Henry II of France. In the Passau Treaty of August 2, 1552, an armistice for Protestants and Catholics was achieved, and both the aged Elector John Frederick and Philip of Hesse were released from their long captivity.[9] Jonas was gladdened by the liberation of the onetime Saxon Elector, under whose rule he had labored so willingly. Perhaps he fondly hoped that now a brighter future lay in store for the evangelical Lutheran Church and for himself.[10]

Final Years

Toward the end of the year 1552 the city of Regensburg petitioned Duke John Ernest of Coburg to permit Jonas to come there and restore order in the evangelical church. For in Regensburg the Augsburg Interim had caused confusion and unrest. Permission for a leave was granted Jonas and so, later in November or early in December, he arrived and preached his first sermon in Our Dear Lady's Church in Regensburg.[11] In spite of occasional sickness he achieved notable results in a comparatively short period of time. Stability and order in the evangelical church were soon brought about. In February, 1553, Jonas reported to his old Nuremberg friend, the Abbot Frederick: "Our efforts in the church at Regensburg are, with the help of God, proceeding favorably, and we have a moderate devotion on the part of the majority of the distinguished and common people; may God grant a further increase and bless his elect and holy church."[12]

As was the case in Halle, Jonas was not spared a conflict with the Romanists in Regensburg. The continual progress of the evangelical cause under Jonas' leadership proved annoying to the Catholics in the city. On June 3, 1553, Jonas ordained two ministers for the evangelical church there. The Catholic chronicler, in recording the event, did not conceal his obvious vexation over the popularity of the affair and maliciously noted that Jonas would not rest until he had ousted all ministers and was himself bishop.[13]

In spite of this evident progress Jonas had neither the inclination nor the intention of remaining at Regensburg. Also when Duke John Ernest of Coburg died in February, 1553, he did not desire to return to Coburg. In April 1553 he wrote to Duke John Frederick the Medium, the son of the old Elector John Frederick. He presented the Duke with a small book, informed him of the recent death of Duke John Ernest, and, as an old man of sixty who had faithfully served the Saxon Elector for a period of thirty-two years, asked that the Duke bestow his favor and protection upon him and his seven children.[14] Supported by the Duke and his brothers, Jonas was considering the possibility of a return to Halle. Never wearying of his efforts to secure the annual income promised him when he surrendered the provostship in Wittenberg, he once more implored Melanchthon to intercede on his behalf in this matter at the Wittenberg University.[15]

On August 10, 1553, Jonas and his family left Regensburg and made their way back to Saxony.[16] At first Jonas went to Jena where, for a brief period of time, he assisted in some organizational work connected with the newly founded University of Jena. After the Electorate had been taken away from their father, the sons of John Frederick undertook the founding of this new university in order to make it a new center of evangelical influence in their territories. On August 23 Jonas left Jena. John Stigel wrote a poem on the occasion of his departure and in it mentioned that Jonas' destination was Eisfeld. Duke John Frederick, the oldest son of the Elector, had appointed Jonas as inspector of the evangelical churches in Franconia and as chief minister and superintendent of the church in Eisfeld.[17] Jonas arrived in Eisfeld on August 25 and on the following Sunday, August 27, preached his first sermon.[18] The unusual length of this sermon (two hours) was especially noticed because Jonas, like Luther, was in the habit of preaching brief sermons.

In Eisfeld Jonas dedicated himself, with all the energy he could muster, to the improvement of the sadly neglected churches and schools in the territory. He set up a consistory composed of three theologians, three jurists and three men from the nobility.[19] On March 3, 1554, the aged Elector John Frederick died. As a token of esteem for the man, under whose rule he had served the church for many years, Jonas sent to the Elector's three sons a copy of the sermon he had preached at Regensburg on Easter, 1553. The preface to the sermon showed a keen realization by Jonas that he was nearing the end of his life; and a longing for peace permeated the expression of his faith. The apparent brevity of the remainder of his days on earth now made the appeal of eternity powerful and sustaining.[20]

In 1555 Jonas fell seriously ill of asthma. For some time already, two commissioners, appointed by the senate, had been performing the active duties of Jonas' work. Once more, Jonas, conscious of the seriousness of his illness, assayed to secure the annual payment of 100 guldens which he had not received since 1547. He appealed to the three sons of the late Elector John Frederick, to intercede on his behalf before the Elector August. As a grateful acknowledgment of Jonas' services, John Frederick the Medium and John Frederick the Younger presented Jonas' plea, only to receive a negative reply.[21]

On September 25, 1555, the Religious Peace of Augsburg came into existence. It permitted the territorial rulers to determine the religious confession of their domains—either evangelical or Romanist—and gave those of a differing faith the right to emigrate without loss of honor or property. Though offering peace to the strife-weary churches, neither party was completely satisfied.

While this Peace of Augsburg was being ratified, Jonas' life was fast slipping away. Some old accounts tell of an intense spiritual struggle that took place as his end approached. Temptations, similar to those that had beset Luther in 1527 and which Jonas had described, cast shadows of darkness across his mind. Doubts concerning his salvation assailed him and his soul was troubled by fear over his approaching end.[22] After all efforts of his fellow-ministers failed to bring him the Christian comfort and hope he himself had proclaimed, the reading of a selection from John 14 by his servant dispelled all gloom and filled his soul with faith and hope. All contemporary records here concur: With a cheerful spirit and "in the pious and sincere confession of the Son of God, Jesus Christ," he repeatedly uttered Christ's saying: "In my Father's house are many mansions," and at length commended

himself to Christ with these words: "Lord Jesus Christ, into thy hands
I commit my poor soul. Thou hast redeemed me." On October 9, 1555,
at about nine o'clock in the evening, Jonas, his body supported by the
arms of his wife and his soul grasping firmly the word of faith he had
preached, in peaceful composure died, certain of resurrection and
everlasting life.[23]

A memorial of a unique kind was erected in honor of Jonas' peaceful departure in a hymn by Cyriacus Schnauss of Coburg entitled: "The
Word of the Lord Our God," in which the opening words of the
stanzas form the sentence: "Doctor Justus Jonas' blessed departure."[24]

The memory of Jonas as one of the faithful sons of the Reformation
age and its evangelical principles and beliefs was fittingly kept alive
in Eisfeld. Over the entrance of the Church of God's Acre a marble
relief portrayed Jonas and his predecessor, Nicholas Kindt, the first
evangelical pastor and superintendent of Eisfeld, kneeling before the
crucified Christ.[25] Behind the altar in the same church the coat of
arms of Justus Jonas was engraved on a stone. A Latin inscription
paid tribute to his peaceful departure in the faith and his loyal service
in spreading the Gospel of the Son of God.[26] In the raised gallery of
the church a wooden plaque with a Latin epitaph, written by John
Stigel, extolled his notable achievements in the many places where he
had served the Reformation cause with unflagging zeal and exemplary
faithfulness.

The University of Wittenberg, mindful of his membership on its
faculty, entered an obituary notice in its official records.[27] His good
friend Melanchthon seems to have passed over his death in complete
silence.[28] Whatever the cause of this omission in Melanchthon's correspondence may have been, the whole evangelical church of Germany
knew that it had lost one of its noble servants.

FOOTNOTES FOR CHAPTER 10

1. Kawerau, *op. cit.*, Vol. II, pp. 294-295.
2. *Ibid.*, p. 383.
3. A hiatus in Jonas' correspondence between July 27, 1550, and July 14, 1551, has led to many different assumptions by various biographers concerning his whereabouts during this time. The letter of Wanckel to Flacius alluded to is proof that Jonas was in Coburg as early as September 1550. But the explicit statement in the chronicles of the city of Coburg: "In the year 1551 the new court preacher, Dr. Justus Jonas, was made a present of 5 guldens and 3 pounds of coin at his entry" (Knapp, *Narratio de Justo Jona*, note 78, p. 46), seems to be conclusive evidence that he did not move to Coburg with his family and begin his official duties there until 1551.
4. *Corpus Reformatorum*, Vol. VII, p. 809.
5. Kawerau, *op. cit.*, Vol. II, pp. 307-309.
6. *Corpus Reformatorum*, Vol. VII, pp. 927-928.
7. Pressel, *op. cit.*, p. 138.
8. Kawerau, *op. cit.*, Vol. II, pp. 320-321.
9. Moeller, *op. cit.*, pp. 145-146.
10. Kawerau, *op. cit.*, Vol. II, p. 321.
11. *Ibid.*, p. liv.
12. *Ibid.*, p. 322.
13. *Ibid.*, p. liv.
14. Burkhardt, "Neue Mittheilungen zur Korrespondenz der Reformation," *Zeitschrift für kirchliche Wissenschaften*, X Jahrgang 1889. Edited by C. E. Luthardt, p. 434.
15. The letter to Melanchthon is printed in Pressel, *op. cit.*, pp. 139-140.
16. Kawerau, *op. cit.*, Vol. II, p. liv.
17. Franke, *op. cit.*, pp. 268-269. Hasse, *op. cit.*, p. 216.
18. Knapp, *Narratio de Justo Jona*, p. 48.
19. Pressel, *op. cit.*, p. 141.
20. Kawerau, *op. cit.*, Vol. II, pp. 325-327.
21. *Ibid.*, pp. 331-337.
22. Knapp, *op. cit.*, p. 49. This report of his last struggle has been used by Romanists in order to prove that the evangelical faith leads to an "unhappy and desperate end." Doellinger, *Reformation*, Vol. II, p. 117. His peaceful death is a direct refutation of this assertion made by ultramontane Catholics.
23. Kawerau, *op. cit.*, Vol. II, pp. lv-lvi.
24. P. Wackernagel, *op. cit.*, Vol. III, p. 45.
25. Kawerau, *op. cit.*, Vol. II, p. lvi.
26. Hasse, *op. cit.*, p. 218.
27. Kawerau, *op. cit.*, Vol. II, p. lvii.
28. *Ibid.* It is related that Melanchthon, en route to Coburg with Camerarius, dreamed that Jonas had died, and when this dream was confirmed by the actual news, he is said to have wept for grief. Laurentius Reinhard, *Commentatio Historico—Theologica de Vita et Obitu Justi Jonae*, leaf 43.

Chapter 11

A Servant of Christ[1]

In the context of the Reformation movement in Germany, Justus Jonas stands out as one of its foremost interpreters and leaders. Understanding the deep spiritual significance of this historic event, he dedicated himself completely to its vindication and triumph. In his quest for morality and true religion Jonas was at first attracted by Humanism, which attempted to reform the church by a return to the primary sources of the Christian religion, the New Testament documents, and by making the moral standard of the apostolic era the norm for Christian living. Erasmus was chiefly responsible for Jonas' transfer from the study of law to that of theology, and Jonas, as a disciple of Erasmus, threw himself into the Humanist program of reform with enthusiastic abandon. But were a rigorous criticism of current evils in the church and the exhortation to follow the ethics of the Sermon on the Mount able to effect the moral renovation which seemed so desirable? Was the easy optimism justifiable which held that the spiritual rulers, including the Pope, could be persuaded to give up their rapacity and corrupt practices, that the monks would become less worldly if criticized, and that the gross superstition of the people would be dispelled by disseminating knowledge? The Humanists were persuaded that the path they were following would lead to the desired goal, the reform of morals in Christendom.

While Jonas was in Erfurt explaining the New Testament in a Humanist spirit to students at the university, he heard of another reform movement, which had begun in Wittenberg. His moral earnestness compelled him to examine it, and before long he was convinced that the man who led it, Luther, was doing what Erasmus sought to do. The Wittenberg monk had gone beyond an attack on the moral decay of the church—he had pierced to the very heart of its grave corruption. In his own spiritual distress, Luther was led by God's Spirit to understand the New Testament meaning of faith. The heart's trust in Jesus Christ as the Savior from sin was at once the supreme requirement and the most glorious gift offered to man by God. No mediation of the church's priesthood was necessary to attain to such a faith; only a living trust in God's words and promises was needed in order that a person might for the sake of the suffering, death, and resurrection of Christ, the Son of God, be pronounced righteous. "Therefore we conclude that a man is justified by faith without the works of the law."[2] These authentic accents of the apostolic message, reverberating from Wittenberg, convinced Jonas that the inner dynamic of the Christian religion had been apprehended anew. The solution to the deepest spiritual problem of human nature, the absolute assurance of the forgiveness of a person's enormous load of sin and the consequent renewal of his life, had thus been recovered. It was the basic answer to a need felt throughout the length and breadth of Christendom, a need which had been recognized time and again prior to the Reformation itself.

The conciliar movement under the leadership of Pierre d'Ailli and Jean de Gerson in France had tried to remedy the worst abuses of the papacy; Wyclif and Huss had called attention to the obvious departure of the Medieval Church from the New Testament ideals and had attempted to reform it. The medieval mystics, Eckhardt, Tauler, Suso, John of Ruysbroeck, and Gerhard Groote, had placed renewed emphasis upon the idea of fellowship with God without priestly mediation. Humanists like Desiderius Erasmus and John Colet, with their interest in learning and their return to the Greek sources of the New Testament, had endeavored by moral suasion to make the ecclesiastical life of their day conform to the ideals of primitive Christianity. However, the religious experience of a direct fellowship with God, resulting from a right understanding of the Pauline quotation: "He who through faith is righteous shall live,"[3] became the motivating force of a true reformation. In God's providence his sovereign Word in Jesus Christ was heard and believed in Wittenberg, from where it was spreading over all Germany and Europe, demanding genuine repentance and offering the costliest treasure of life, divine sonship, to all who believed.

The Man and the Reformer

When Jonas came to Wittenberg as provost of All Saints' Chapter, he did not foresee where the Reformation, which was still in its initial stages, would lead; but the profound conviction that it was God's truth which was there proclaimed, made him ready to venture all for the sake of the Gospel. He had seen Luther in Worms defying Pope and Emperor on the basis of his convictions. Jonas was ready to follow in the Reformer's train. It was no accident that Jonas, like Melanchthon, Bugenhagen, Cruciger, Spalatin, and others, as a man of outstanding intellectual ability, was won for the Reformation; for the heritage of a Humanist training, combining a thorough acquaintance of the New Testament in the original Greek language with a zeal for moral renovation, was inclined to make a man like Jonas eager to embrace the truth of God's Word. Prejudice and misunderstanding often precluded the acceptance of the Reformation principles on the part of some Humanists, especially the older men. Still the Reformation in Germany, without a doubt, attracted and retained as its leaders and interpreters many of the most gifted scholars in the church.

Precisely because Jonas grasped the meaning of the Gospel for his own life and the lives of men in general, he was able to proclaim the Reformation message with tremendous force and marvelous success. As a preacher his native oratorical gifts were clearly an advantage. With characteristic humility Luther called attention to Jonas' oratorical ability in a letter. "I do not wish, without reason, to try to emulate you, dear Jonas, in letter-writing; first, because you far surpass me in genius and eloquence, undoubtedly hereditary gifts, and secondly, you have more to write about. . . ."[4] Luther also mentioned the excellent memory for words which Jonas possessed.[5] His persuasive speech led Luther to make the assertion in the presence of his friend that if Jonas so desired, he could, within the space of a year, convince a person of anything.[6] On various occasions Luther lauded the preeminent gifts of Jonas as a preacher.[7] Once when Luther was prevented from preaching in Wittenberg, he recommended Jonas as his substitute so that the latter might overthrow the arguments of the papists.[8] The excellence of his oratory was marred by a fault on which Luther commented: "A preacher who has a hundred virtues, throws them all into the shade by one fault. The world is so wicked. Dr. Jonas has all virtues of a good preacher: except that one cannot excuse the good man for clearing his throat so often."[9]

Melanchthon's estimate of the preaching of Luther, Bugenhagen, Jonas, and himself has been preserved for us in a sermon by John Mathesius. Melanchthon is reported to have said: "Dr. Pomeranus is a grammarian who places the emphasis upon the words of the text. I am a dialectician and am concerned how the text fits together and what may be said and concluded therefrom in a Christian way and with good reason. Dr. Jonas is an orator who can enunciate, explain, and phrase the words of the text marvelously and plainly. Dr. Martin excels in all things. . . ."[10] Contemporaries of Jonas with one accord bear witness to his undisputed eloquence as a preacher of the Word, even celebrating this talent in poetry.[11] Without reserve, Jonas dedicated the oratorical gifts he possessed to the service of the Gospel, thus becoming a powerful preacher of the Word who, before great and small, learned and unlearned, testified to evangelical truth.

As a theologian and teacher Jonas stood in high repute. His insight into the basic truths of Scripture was combined with clarity of expression so that he was well able to communicate theological knowledge to his students. Luther advised that anyone who desired to study should have Jonas and Melanchthon as teachers.[12] The astonishing popularity which his sermons on the Catechism enjoyed in Halle is an indication that he was also a competent instructor of the Christian laity.

His productivity as a writer was necessarily limited because of his pressing obligations in the practical affairs of the church at large. His *Annotations of the Acts of the Apostles* and his popular explanation of *The Seventh Chapter of Daniel Regarding the Turk's Blasphemy against God* are but modest contributions to the exegetical studies of the Reformation period. Though these writings cannot lay claim to any outstanding merit in the field of theology, they served their purpose during that age. Jonas did not engage in a mere repetition of what Luther and others said and wrote. As a disciple of Luther, he made the basic insight of the Reformer his very own and reproduced the resulting ideas in his writings in an excellent literary form. His brochures on the teachings of the evangelical church proved to be very popular because he ranked next to Luther in the ability to use his mother tongue, while his Latin writings were surpassed in elegance of style and felicitous phrasing only by Melanchthon.[13] The hymns which Jonas wrote were a forceful expression of his living trust in God during times of distress and danger. His hymn, "If God the Lord's not on our side," is included in the collection of hymns that make up the German hymnal of the church at Halle.[14] His other hymns seem to have enjoyed usage for only a limited time.

In his literary endeavors Jonas rendered a most significant service to Protestantism as a whole by his selfless labor of translating the writings of his contemporaries, especially those of Luther and Melanchthon. Occasionally Melanchthon gave his German writings to Jonas so that the latter might put them into a more polished and attractive form. Praising Jonas' linguistic ability, Melanchthon believed that God had endowed Jonas with this talent in order that he might use it as a weapon in defending the Reformation.[15] Both Luther and Melanchthon demonstrated confidence in Jonas' aptitude as a translator by giving him permission to reproduce the sense of their words in a free way. When Luther asked Jonas to translate his commentary on the prophet Jonah "especially for the glory of the faith," he reminded Jonas that he should put into his "elegant and brilliant style" what the Reformer had written in "barbaric and unrefined language." Luther was confident that through Jonas' "genius and eloquence" his exposition of the prophet would not only be improved "with more fitting words," but its contents would also become "more powerful and vivid to the readers."[16] Jonas, "exceedingly burdened with the less strenuous labor of this kind of public proclamation," as he once expressed himself,[17] believed that he was engaging in a task that served the propagation of the Gospel nationally and internationally. His translation of one of Luther's most important writings, *Concerning the Bondage of the Will,* was done so well that it has remained a standard German translation of the Latin original.[18] All in all, Jonas translated from Latin into German and conversely from German into Latin a total of thirty-five literary works, most of which were authored by Luther and Melanchthon.[19] In his work as preacher, teacher, author, and translator he mightily supported the movement begun in Wittenberg by a faithful use of his talents, thus joining others with wholehearted devotion in extending the influence of the Gospel by means of the spoken and written word.

The Man and His Church

At the very outset the principles of the evangelical church were vigorously challenged by the church of Rome. In the open conflict between the two churches Jonas proved to be an eager and able defender of the church to which he belonged. Fearlessly he championed the truth of the Gospel, defending it against perversion and slander. In his polemic against the Romanist theologians, he sought with grim determination to drive his opponent into an indefensible position from which there was no retreat. As a result of his legal training he often proceeded as would a prosecuting attorney who was bent on winning his case. Jonas, like his contemporaries, frequently resorted to rough and uncouth invective so that a controversy sometimes degenerated into vituperation. However, in spite of these shortcomings he proved to be a deft defender of what he believed to be the truth of the revealed Word of God.

When the Reformation was confronted by the problem of the relationship between church and state, its leaders insisted that there ought to be a careful distinction between the two realms. Jonas subscribed to this principle. His primary concern was that the Word of God should not be bound but that it might have free course. A Christian, he held, was obligated to obey the governing authorities in civil affairs. But no ruler, prince, or political power had any right to interfere with the divine mandate of preaching the Word of God and ordering one's life according to it. If the state or ruling authority transgressed its divinely appointed limits and tried to command man's conscience, the believer had the clear duty of refusing to obey and of being willing to suffer the consequences for such disobedience. At the same time Jonas believed that it was the responsibility of God-fearing rulers to make possible the proclamation of the Gospel in their realms without let or hindrance. Consequently, in his relationship with potentates and princes he impressed upon them their sacred obligation toward the church. The welfare and future destiny of a land were, in his opinion, conditioned in a most significant way by the attitude of both the ruler and his subjects toward the Gospel.

The abandonment of sacerdotal celibacy in the evangelical church brought about an altered situation for its clergy. The evangelical ministers, who were married and had families to support, were obliged to make satisfactory provision for them. Jonas, in the interest of personal chastity, married when the Reformation was still in its early stages and established a happy Christian home. In his desire to provide for his growing family, he displayed undue anxiety about the means of livelihood. In fact, his constant quest for personal financial benefits, motivated by his concern for adequate material security, constitutes a definitely negative trait in his character.

It is related that in the course of a walk, Luther, Jonas, and Veit Dietrich met a poor man to whom Luther promptly dispensed alms. Jonas, following Luther's example, also gave a gift to the needy person. Then he remarked: "Who knows whether God will return it?" Luther turned to his friend, laughing, and said: "As if God had not given it to you in the first place; one must give freely, sincerely, out of pure love and willingly."[20] In another instance the conversation in Luther's presence revolved about the wealth of merchants and how Cruciger's father had, by the blessing of God, become rich. Jonas, on hearing this, is reported to have said: "God be praised that a pious theologian also becomes rich once."[21]

Though somewhat impatient and impetuous by nature, Jonas was possessed of a cheerful disposition. For that reason he was often called upon to bring solace to Luther when the latter was in a melancholy mood. Combining a sense of humor with a serious view of life's duties and responsibilities, he once wrote to his friend John Lange: "Here I am overwhelmed with ecclesiastical labors, but Christ, enduing me with all power, is strengthening me in the midst of conflicts and dangers. Amsdorf has been made a true bishop of Naumburg. There remains yet that Lange becomes one at Erfurt and I in Halle, or even now a suffragan at Erfurt according to the will of God. Pardon the jest...."[22]

In the midst of his strenuous work, Jonas endured frequent periods of illness, especially from a recurring kidney-stone. Of this ailment Luther said that it was a medicine that made Jonas exercise the Christian virtues of patience and hope.[23] Jonas was at times also afflicted with temptations of a spiritual nature. Concerning these he once wrote to Frederick Myconius, whom he asked to intercede on his behalf in prayer.[24] His numerous activities and his diverse achievements seem even more remarkable when one considers the handicaps under which he labored.

Jonas' faithful friendship with Luther, Prince George of Anhalt, Lange, Melanchthon, and other men of his day belongs to one of the most attractive qualities of his personality. Throughout the changes of time and circumstances he maintained the ties of friendship through correspondence and personal intercourse. His admiration for Luther was profound, so that he always sought to keep the relationship between the Wittenberg Reformer and himself free from suspicion and misunderstanding. A short anecdote from the pen of Cyriacus Spangenberg beautifully illustrates Jonas' high regard for Luther. After an association of over twenty years with Luther, Jonas happened to be in Nordhausen among a group of persons who were discussing the relative merits of ministers. After mentioning the names of various men, Luther was designated as one of the ablest of all preachers. At this Jonas remarked: "My dear brethren, when speaking of preachers we should not include or count Dr. Martin Luther among ourselves; for he was an entirely different man; that man could do what he wanted to do."[25] Spalatin, Jerome Weller, Nicholas Medler, and Caspar Cruciger also belonged to that intimate circle of friends whose interest in the common cause of the Reformation knit them together in an unbroken chain of friendship with Jonas.

Jonas' efforts to effect reconciliation and harmony within the Protestant fold deserve special mention, even if his labors in this area were not always successful. He desired an all-inclusive unity of Protestantism, especially in Germany, and he sought to prepare the way for an agreement with English Protestantism. He never permitted a disagreement or controversy among colleagues and co-workers in the church to continue unchecked. His fierce opposition to Rome was born of the firm conviction that the Pope was opposed to the evangelical principles of God's Word. Therefore he could see no basis for a reconciliation with the Roman Church. Herein he was completely at one with the view of Luther. Because of Rome's intransigent policy he felt justified in maintaining this position throughout his life.

His contribution toward the success of the Reformation in Germany was considerable. In the work of the church visitations he demonstrated decisively that the basic task of the evangelical Lutheran Church of Germany was a concern for the souls of men. His clear insight into the meaning of the Gospel message made him realize and emphasize the fact that the primary purpose of the ministry consisted in bringing the saving Word of God to men. To this end his organizational ability was a valuable asset. The many church orders which he drafted provided the necessary pattern for the ordered expression of the life of faith within the evangelical churches. His suggestions and preliminary work in organizing consistories also proved to be of far-reaching importance in the continued progress of the Church of the Reformation because his knowledge of church and civil law as well as his practical ability enabled him to avoid many difficulties and unnecessary legal entanglements.

As a leader of the Reformation in Halle his many-sided abilities came to their most consummate expression. There he preached the glorious Gospel of Jesus Christ before thousands of persons with amazingly popular appeal and success; there he taught the evangelical truth with sincere simplicity to all kinds and conditions of men; there he intrepidly faced the threats and dangers of his responsible calling; there he defended the precious truths for which he was prepared to die and attacked all falsehood and misrepresentations; there he experienced the truth that the church on earth is the church militant and gladly expended his strength in valiant battle against its foes; there he came to know from experience that the church is "hidden beneath the cross." When he left Halle reluctantly and sadly, he also left behind a church that was instructed in the faith, organized in its ministry and work, and well prepared to bequeath to the succeeding generations the Word of God which it had received. The church at Halle was the most impressive monument of his ministry, an epistle written in the hearts of its citizenry, to be known and read by all men.

With What Great Gifts

Jonas' forceful leadership, his theological ability, his organizational talent, and his literary work secured for him a place next to Luther and Melanchthon among the Wittenberg theologians. The Reformation in Halle might well have failed, had it not been for his fearless and energetic direction, and no one among Luther's collaborators, except Melanchthon, contributed more effectively toward the progress of the reform movement in so many different areas of church life than the loyal Reformer of Halle.

Eleven years after Jonas' death his friend, Jerome Weller, addressed a letter to the senate of Halle. In reverent and affectionate words he reminded the evangelical Christians in that city of the selfless labors and eminent gifts with which Justus Jonas had served their church. Referring to their acceptance of the restored teaching of the Gospel, Weller warmly praised the Christians there for the support and honor they had accorded Justus Jonas "as a prophet of the Lord." Then he went on to tell of the life-long and intimate friendship between Jonas and Luther. When Luther was in a dejected mood, Jonas was often invited to share a meal in the Reformer's home in order that he might revive his languishing spirit. Continuing his description of Justus Jonas' character and achievements, Weller wrote:

> . . . With what great gifts he was truly endowed his admirable writings show. He possessed a remarkable knowledge of the Latin, Greek and German languages, a mediocre knowledge of Hebrew. His eloquence was truly so outstanding that he could be compared with the greatest orators. For great were the brilliance and wealth of his words in his speech. He was able to enlarge upon whatever he wished in a marvellous manner by frightening the profane and secure with divine threats and by lifting up and strengthening the truly afflicted with the sweetest comfort. In addition, he possessed admirable skill in translating Luther's Latin and German writings. In this respect he had no equal, and he rendered a distinguished and useful service to the church, very plainly meriting praise from all posterity. His nature was truly heroic. For the forcefulness of his genius was seasoned by an extraordinarily pleasant disposition and by good breeding. In conflict with his adversaries he was as courageous as a lion, toward the meek and afflicted as gentle as a lamb. Such is the manner of heroic men.
>
> Indeed, what an immense benefit he conferred upon the church of Christ is evident. For he planted and firmly established the three renowned churches, at Naumburg, at Halle and at Regensburg, so that he can rightfully be numbered among those most distinguished teachers who, going through the valley of tears, make many fountains there, whence they carry off many brilliant victories (Psalm 84:7). But how many labors, how many difficulties, conflicts and dangers he endured in this warfare can readily be estimated. He also bore in his own body the marks of Jesus Christ. For he was not only afflicted with cruel sicknesses, but even oftener his heart was wounded by the fiery darts of the devil, and, like Luther, he spent many sleepless nights. For it is the custom of the devil to buffet (to use the Pauline figure) all pious teachers who earnestly strive to make known the glory of God and to preach Christ sincerely; and such satanic buffetings cause them much severer pain than any outward afflictions. . . . Rightly, therefore, Jonas also could make use of this saying of Paul: "in distress, in afflictions, in hardships, in labours, in vigils etc." These indeed are the noble ornaments of a pious teacher by which he is to be distinguished from false teachers.[26]

After this summary of the person and work of Jonas, Weller concluded the letter by expressing his own gratitude to his friend who had bestowed the doctor's degree upon him. Simultaneously he congratulated the people of Halle upon their good fortune of having had such an illustrious and gifted preacher and teacher in their midst. The sincere tribute paid by this contemporary and friend of Justus Jonas to the tireless and selfless labors of the Halle Reformer and to the indisputable magnitude of his achievements on behalf of evangelical Christianity may well serve as a closing testimony that his record has been indelibly inscribed upon the pages of Reformation history.

FOOTNOTES FOR CHAPTER 11

1. The phrase is taken from Jonas' motto from Scripture, Galatians 1:10b RSV.
2. Romans 3:28.
3. Romans 1:17 RSV.
4. Enders, *op. cit.*, Vol. XI, p. 344.
5. *Tischreden*, Weimar Edition, Vol. V, p. 9.
6. *Ibid.*, Vol. IV, p. 564.
7. *Ibid.*, p. 646.
8. *Ibid.*, p. 329.
9. Walch, Editor, *Luthers Sämmtliche Schriften*, Vol. XXII, p. 641.
10. Johann Mathesius, *Luthers Leben in Predigten, Ausgewählte Werke*, Vol. III, p. 423.
11. Kawerau, *op. cit.*, Vol. II, p. 343, Vol. I, p. 264. Knapp, *op. cit.*, p. 3 and p. 5.
12. *Tischreden*, Weimar Edition, Vol. III, p. 112.
13. H. A. Erhard, *op. cit.*, Vol. 22, p. 407.
14. Martin Schellbach, *op. cit.*, p. 44.
15. *Corpus Reformatorum*, Vol. III, p. 308.
16. Kawerau, *op. cit.*, Vol. I, p. 435.
17. *Ibid.*, p. 291.
18. The German has of course been modernized. The latest edition came out in 1924 under the title: M. Luther, *Vom unfreien Willen*. Nach der Übersetzung von Justus Jonas herausgegeben und mit einem Nachwort versehen von Friederich Gogarten. München, 1924.
19. For a complete list of translations and titles see Kawerau, *op. cit.*, Vol. II, pp. xxiii-xxxi.
20. *Tischreden, Weimar Edition*, Vol. IV, p. 140.
21. *Ibid.*, p. 174.
22. Kawerau, *op. cit.*, Vol. II, p. 63.
23. *Tischreden*, Weimar Edition, Vol. IV, pp. 61-62.
24. Kawerau, *op. cit.*, Vol. I, p. 94 and p. 406.
25. *Ibid.*, Vol. II, p. xlix.
26. *Ibid.*, pp. 343-344.

Chronology

1493	June 5 (6?)	Birth of Justus Jonas at Nordhausen
1506	Spring	Enters University of Erfurt
1507		Bachelor of Arts
1510		Master of Arts
1511	Summer semester	Matriculation at Wittenberg
1515		Bachelor of Civil and Canon Law
	Spring	Returns to Erfurt
1516		Begins to preach
1517		Goes to Nordhausen to practice law
1518		Returns to Erfurt
	August	Doctor of Civil and Canon Law
		Canon at St. Severi Church
		Lectures at university
1519	Spring	Visits Erasmus at Antwerp
	May 2	Elected rector of Erfurt University
		First contact with Luther
1520	August 28	Lectures on 1 and 2 Corinthians published
	October	Sides with Luther against Eck
1521	April	Joins Luther on Journey to Worms
	April 16	Enters Worms with Luther's entourage
	April 24	Takes part in hearing at Worms
	May	Goes to Wittenberg
	June 6	Installed as provost of All Saints' Chapter
	July	Moves to Wittenberg and joins theological faculty

	September 24	Licentiate of Theology
	October 14	Doctor of Theology
1522	February 9	Marriage to Catherine Falk
	March 6	Luther's return to Wittenberg
1523		Jonas' first polemical writing
1524		Publishes *Annotations on the Acts*
1525	June 13	Present at Luther's marriage
1526		Rector of University of Wittenberg
1527	August	Goes to Nordhausen during plague
1528	January	Return to Wittenberg
	October 22	Begins church visitation in Electoral Saxony
1529	October 2-4	Participates in Marburg Colloquy
		Publishes *The Seventh Chapter of Daniel*
1530	January	Church visitation in Belzig
	April 3	Goes to attend Diet of Augsburg
	June 25	Witnesses reading of Augsburg Confession
	October	Rector of University of Wittenberg
1532	November	Beginning of friendship with Prince George of Anhalt
1533		Dean of theological faculty at Wittenberg
1534	Summer	At court of Prince George of Anhalt
1535	Summer	Plague at Wittenberg and stay at Schlieben
	December	Returns to Wittenberg
1536	April	Takes part in negotiations between English delegation of Henry VIII and Wittenberg theologians
	May 22-29	Wittenberg Concord with South Germans
	October	Rector of University of Wittenberg
1538		Drafts Church Order for principality of Anhalt
1539	July 21	Takes part in church visitation of Ducal Saxony

1540	March	Bigamy of Philip of Hesse
		Schmalcald Convention
1541	April 14	Arrives at Halle
	September	Jonas' family moves to Halle
1542	December 22	Death of Jonas' wife
1543		Drafts Church Order for Halle
	June	Second marriage
1544	December 11	Called as chief minister in Halle
1545	May	Visits Wittenberg
	August 2	At ordination service of Prince George of
		Anhalt
1546	January 24	Luther's arrival at Halle en route to Eisleben
	January 28	Accompanies Luther to Eisleben
	February 18	Witnesses Luther's death
	Mid-summer	Outbreak of Schmalcald War
	November	Jonas' flight to Mansfeld
1547	January	Return to Halle
	April 24	Defeat of Schmalcald League by Emperor
		Second flight from Halle
	June	Call to church at Hildesheim
1548	February	Leaves Hildesheim for Nordhausen
	April 5	Returns to Halle
1549	July 8	Death of Jonas' second wife
1550	May 4	Jonas' third marriage
	July	Leaves Halle
1551		Superintendent of church at Coburg
1552	August 2	Treaty of Passau
	November	Begins ministry at Regensburg
1553	August 10	Departure from Regensburg
	August 25	Superintendent and chief minister of the
		church at Eisfeld
1555	September 25	Religious Peace of Augsburg
	October 9	Jonas' death at Eisfeld

Bibliography

PRIMARY SOURCES

Works of Justus Jonas

"Acta et Res Gestae, D. Martini Lutheri in Comitijs Principu Vvormaciae, Anno MDXXI," in *Deutsche Reichstagsakten unter Kaiser Karl V, Deutsche Reichstagsakten Jüngere Reihe*. Edited by A. Wrede. Vol. II, pp. 541-569. Gotha: F. A. Perthes, 1896.

Adversus Iohannem Fabrum Constantien. Vicarium scortationis patronum, pro coniugio sacerdotali, Iusti Ionae defensio. (66 pages.) Vvittembergae: N. Schirleutz, 1523.

Annotationes Iusti Ionae, in Acta Apostolorum. Wittembergae: MDXXIIII. Bound in *Reformationsschriften*, Vol. IX, (1527-1546).

"An Unprinted Letter by Justus Jonas," in "Notes from English Libraries" reprinted by Preserved Smith, *Zeitschrift für Kirchengeschichte*. Edited by T. Brieger and Bernhard Bess. Vol. XXXII, pp. 111-114. Gotha, 1911.

"Bedenken, ob die Kloester zu Halle abzuschaffen oder nicht," in J. C. Dreyhaupt's *Pagys Neletici et Nodici oder diplomatisch-historische Beschreibung des Saal-Creyses*. Vol. I, pp. 982-986. Halle: in Verlag des Waysenhauses, 1772.

Church Orders reprinted in *Die Evangelischen Kirchenordnungen des XVI Jahrhunderts*. Edited by E. Sehling. 2 vols. Leipzig, 1902, 1904.
1) "Hallische Kirchenordnung" in Vol. II, pp. 434-436.
2) "Meissener Kirchenordnung" in Vol. I, pp. 264-281.
3) "Zerbster Kirchenordnung" in Vol. II, pp. 544-547.
4) "Der Theologen Bedenken von wegen der Consistorien" in Vol. I, pp. 200-209.

Das siebend Capitel Danielis von des Tuercken Gottesleserung vnd schrecklicher morderey mit vnterricht. (32 leaves.) Wittemberg: Hans Lufft, 1530.

"De gradibus in Theologia," *Corpus Reformatorum*. Edited by C. G. Bretschneider. Vol. XI, pp. 227-231. Halle, 1843.

"De studiis Theologicis," in Philip Melanchthon's *Selectarum Declamationum*. Vol. I, pp. 15-30. Wittenberg, 1546.

Der Briefwechsel des Justus Jonas. Edited by G. Kawerau. 2 vols. Halle: Druck und Verlag von Otto Hendel, 1884, 1885.

"Ein ungedruckter Brief des Justus Jonas aus dem Jahre 1537" reprinted by Paul Vetter in *Archiv für Reformationsgeschichte*. Edited by D. W. Friedensburg. Vol. VII, Jahrgang 1909-1910, pp. 121-134. Leipzig: M. Hensius Nachfolger, 1910.

"Eine fast troestliche Predigt und Auslegung der Historien von den wunderbaren XL Tagen in *Actis Apostol. Cap. I . . . .,*" in *Die bedeutendsten Kanzelredner der lutherischen Kirche des Reformationszeitalters*. Edited by W. Beste. pp. 149-162. Leipzig: Mayer, 1856.

Enchiridion, oder eyn Handbuchlein eynem yetzlichen Christen fast nutzlich bei sich zu haben zur stetter vbung vnnd trachtung geistlicher gesange vnd Psalmen Rechtschaffen vnnd kunstlich vertheutscht. Probably edited by Justus Jonas and John Lange. Erfurt, 1524. Reprint in Erfurt, 1848.

"Intimatio Erphurdiana pro Martino Luther," in P. Kalkoff's *Humanismus und Reformation in Erfurt (1500-1530)*. pp. 92-94. Halle (Saale): Buchhandlung des Waisenhauses, 1926.

"Jonas, Ein Bedenken wegen künftiger Handlung und Gespraech in der Religion, 1530," *Corpus Reformatorum*. Edited by C. G. Bretschneider. Vol. II, pp. 305-306. Halle, 1835.

"J. Jonae iudicium de conditionibus pacis faciendae, 1530," *Corpus Reformatorum*. Edited by C. G. Bretschneider. Vol. II, pp. 368-371. Halle, 1835.

Justus Jonas' Hymns reprinted in *Das deutsche Kirchenlied von der ältesten Zeit bis zu Anfang des XVII Jahrhunderts*. Edited by P. Wackernagel. Vol. III, pp. 42-45. Leipzig: B. G. Teubner, 1870.
1) "Wo Gott der Herr nicht bey uns helt," based on Psalm 124.

2) "Der Herr erhör euch in der noth," based on Psalm 20.
3) "Herr Jhesu Christ, dein Erb wir sind," based on Psalm 79.
4) "Herr Jhesu Christ, o warer Gott," based on Psalms 22 and 71.
Vom christlichen abschied aus diesem tödtlichen Leben, des Ehrwirdigen Herrn D. Mart. Lutheri, bericht, durch D. Justum Jonam, M. Mich. Celium vnd andern die dabei gewesen, kurtz zusamengezogen. Wittemberg: durch Georgen Rhaw, 1546.
"Vorschläge zur Verbesserung des Gottesdienstes," reprinted in *Kleine Nachlese, einiger, grössten Theils noch ungedruckter und sonderlich zur Erläuterung der Reformations-Geschichte nützlicher Urkunden.* Edited by Erhard Kapp. Vol. II, pp. 589-593. Leipzig, 1727.
Zwo Tröstliche Predigt über der Leich Dr. Martini Luther, zu Eisleben den 19. u. 20. Febr. 1546 gethan durch D. Justum Jonam und Mich. Coelium. Wittemberg, 1546. (Translated into English by E. Greenwald, 1883).

OTHER PRIMARY SOURCES

Allen, P. S. and Allen, H. M., Editors, *Opus Epistolarvm des. Erasmi Roterodami.* Tom. IV, 1519-1521. Oxonii: In Typofrapheo Clarendoniano, MCMXXII.
Berbig, Georg, Editor, *Acta Comiciorum Augustae ex litteria Philippi, Jonae et aliorum ad M. L., Quellen und Darstellungen aus der Geschichte des Reformationsjahrhunderts.* Vol. II. Halle (Saale): Nietzschmann Ploetz'sche Verlag, 1907.
Bretschneider, C. G., Editor, *Corpus Reformatorum.* Vols. I-XI. Halle, 1834-1843.
Buchwald, Georg, "Georg Helts Wittenberger Predigttagebuch," *Archiv für Reformationsgeschichte.* Edited by D. W. Friedensburg. XVII Jahrgang 1920, pp. 241-276. Leipzig: Verlag von M. Hensius Nachfolger, 1920.
Burkhardt, C. A. H., Editor, "Neue Mittheilungen zur Korrespondenz der Reformation," *Zeitschrift für kirchliche Wissenschaft und kirchliches Leben.* Edited by C. E. Luthardt. X Jahrgang 1889, pp. 430-434. Leipzig: Doerffling u. Franke, 1889.
Clemen, O., "Georg Witzel und Justus Jonas," *Archiv für Reformationsgeschichte Texte und Untersuchungen.* Edited by D. W. Friedensburg. XVII Jahrgang 1920, pp. 132-152. Leipzig: Verlag von M. Hensius Nachfolger, 1920.
Curric, Margaret, A., Editor, *The Letters of Martin Luther.* London: Macmillan and Co., Limited, 1908.
Enders, E. L. Editor, *Dr. Martin Luthers Briefwechsel.* 18 vols. Vol. I, Frankfurt am Main, 1884; Vols. II-XI, Calw and Stuttgart, 1887-1907; Vols. XII-XVIII, Leipzig, 1910-1923.
Foerstemann, K. E., Editor, *Album Academiae Vitebergensis 1502-1540.* Ex Autographo. Vol. I. Leipzig, 1841.
Kawerau, G., "Der Streit über die 'Reliquiae Sacramenti' in Eisleben 1543," *Zeitschrift für Kirchengeschichte.* Edited by T. Brieger and Bernhard Bess. Vol. XXXIII, pp. 286-308. Gotha, 1912.
Luther, M., "Begleitbrief zu der Schrift des Jonas *Adversus Johannem Fabrum* 1523," *Luthers Werke,* Weimar Edition, Vol. XII, pp. 81-87. Weimar, 1891.
Luther, M., *D. Martin Luthers Werke, kritische Gesamtausgabe.* Edited by J. K. F. Knaake, et al. 58 vols. Weimar, 1883 ff.
Luther, M., *D. Martin Luthers Briefwechsel, D. Martin Luthers Werke, kritische Gesamtausgabe.* Edited by Konrad Burdach et al. 11 vols. Weimar, 1930 ff.
Luther, M., *Tischreden, D. Martin Luthers Werke, kritische Gesamtausgabe.* Edited by Karl Drescher. 6 vols. Weimar, 1912-1921.
Mathesius, J., *Luthers Leben in Predigten, Ausgewählte Werke.* Edited by G. Loesche. Vol. III. Prag: J. G. Calvesche k. u. k. Hof-u.-universitäts-Buchhandlung, 1906.
Richter, A. L., Editor, *Die evangelischen Kirchenordnungen des sechzehnten Jahrhunderts.* Vol. I. Weimar, 1846.
Sehling, E., Editor, *Die Evangelischen Kirchenordnungen des XVI Jahrhunderts.* Vols. I, II. Leipzig, 1902-1904.

Smith, P., Editor, *Luther's Correspondence and Other Contemporary Letters*. 2 vols. Vol. I, (1507-1521); Vol. II, (1521-1530), in collaboration with C. M. Jacobs. Philadelphia, Pa.: The Lutheran Publication Society, 1913, 1918.

Walch, J. G., Editor, *Dr. Martin Luthers Sämmtliche Schriften*. Vols. XXIa, XXIb, XXII. St. Louis, Mo.: Concordia Publishing House, 1887-1904.

de Wette, W. M. L., Editor, *Dr. Martin Luthers Briefe, Sendschreiben und Bedenken*. 5 vols. Berlin: bey G. Reimer, 1825-1828.

Works of Martin Luther, Philadelphia Edition. 6 vols. Philadelphia, Pa.: 1915.

Wrede, A., Editor, *Deutsche Reichstagsakten unter Kaiser Karl V, Deutsche Reichstagsakten Jüngere Reihe*. Vol. II. Gotha: F. A. Perthes, 1896.

SECONDARY SOURCES

Appel, H., *Kurzgefasste Kirchengeschichte für Studierende*. 3rd. edition. Leipzig, Erlangen: A. Deichert'sche Verlagsbuchhandlung Werner Scholl, 1925.

Barge, H., *Andreas Bodenstein von Karlstadt*. Vol. I. Leipzig: Friedrich Brandstetter, 1905.

Boehmer, H., *Road to Reformation*. Translated from German by J. W. Doberstein and T. G. Tappert. Philadelphia, Pa.: Muhlenberg Press, 1946.

Burkhardt, C. A. H., *Geschichte der sächsischen Kirchen- und Schulvisitationen von 1524 bis 1545*. Leipzig: Fr. Wilh. Grunow, 1879.

Delius, Walter, *Justus Jonas*. Gütersloh: C. Bertelsmann Verlag, 1952.

Delius, Walter, *Justus Jonas, 1493-1555*. Berlin: Evangelische Verlagsanstalt, 1952.

Doellinger, J. J. I. von, *Die Reformation, ihre innere Entwicklung und ihre Wirkungen im Umfange des Lutherischen Bekenntnisses*. Vol. II. Regensburg: G. Joseph Manz, 1848.

Dreyhaupt, J. C., *Pagvs Neletici et Nodzici oder diplomatisch-historische Beschreibung des Saal-Creyses*. 2 vols. Revised by J. F. Stiebritz. Halle: in Verlag des Waysenhauses, 1772, 1773.

Foerstemann, E. G., *Kleine Schriften zur Geschichte der Stadt Nordhausen*. Nordhausen, 1855.

Foerstemann, E. G., *Urkundliche Geschichte der Stadt Nordhausen bis zum Jahre 1250*. Nordhausen, 1840.

Franke, K. C. L., *Geschichte der Hallischen Reformation*. Halle: C. A. Schwetschke und Sohn, 1841.

Hasse, H. G., *Justus Jonas Leben*, in *Johann Bugenhagens Leben* von Moritz Meurer, *Justus Jonas Leben* von Hermann Gustav Hasse, *Caspar Crucigers Leben* von Oswald Gottlob Schmidt, pp. 117-223. Leipzig, Dresden: Verlag von Justus Naumann, 1862.

Hort, F., "Zur Komposition und Geschichte der Agende Herzog Heinrichs," *Zeitschrift für kirchliche Wissenschaft und kirchliches Leben*. Edited by C. E. Luthardt. VII Jahrgang 1886, pp. 483-498. Leipzig: Doerffling u. Franke, 1886.

Kalkoff, Paul, *Der Wormser Reichstag von 1521*. Muenchen und Berlin: R. Oldenbourg, 1922.

Kalkoff, Paul, *Humanismus und Reformation in Erfurt (1500-1530)*. Halle (Saale): Buchhandlung des Waisenhauses, 1926.

Kampschulte, F. W., *Die Universität Erfurt in ihrem Verhältnisse zu dem Humanismus und der Reformation*. 2 vols. Trier: Verlag der Fr. Lintz'schen Buchhandlung, 1858, 1860.

Kawerau, G., *Johann Agricola von Eisleben, Ein Beitrag zur Reformationsgeschichte*. Berlin: Wilhelm Hertz, 1881.

Kindervater, M. J. H., *Nordhusa Illustris oder Historische Beschreibung Gelehrter Leute*. Wolfenbuettel: Gotfried Fraytag, 1715.

Koester, F., "Beiträge zur Reformationsgeschichte Naumburgs von 1525 bis 1545," *Zeitschrift für Kirchengeschichte*. Edited by T. Brieger and Bernhard Bess. Vol. XXII, pp. 278-330. Gotha, 1901.

BIBLIOGRAPHY

199

Koestlin, J., *Martin Luther, Sein Leben und seine Schriften*. 2 vols. Berlin: Verlag von Wiegandt und Schotte, 1889.

Knapp, G. C., *Narratio de Justo Jona*. Halis Saxonum, 1817.

Krause, C., *Helius Eobanus Hessus, sein Leben und seine Werke*. 2 vols. Gotha: Friedrich Andreas Perthes, 1879.

Lindsay, T. M., *A History of the Reformation*. Vol. I. Edinburgh: T. & T. Clark, 1907.

McCrie, C. G., *Beza's "Icones," Contemporary Portraits of Reformers of Religion and Letters*. Being Facsimile Reproductions of the Portraits in Beza's "Icones" (1580) and in Goulard's Edition (1581). London: The Religious Tract Society, 1906.

Mackinnon, J., *Luther and the Reformation*. 4 vols. London: Longmans, Green and Co., 1925-1930.

Moeller, W., *Lehrbuch der Kirchengeschichte*. Vol. III. Revised by G. Kawerau. Freiburg I. B. und Leipzig: J. C. B. Mohr, 1894.

Pressel, T., *Justus Jonas, in Leben und Ausgewählte Schriften der Väter und Begründer der lutherischen Kirche*. Inaugurated by K. I. Nitzsch, pp. 1-144. Elberfeld: Verlag von R. L. Friderichs, 1862.

Reinhard, Laurentius, *Commentatio Historico-Theologica de Vita et Obitu Justi Jonae*. Vinariae: Johann Leonhard Mumbachius, 1731.

Reu, J. M., *Quellen zur Geschichte des Katechismus-Unterrichts, in Quellen zur Geschichte des kirchlichen Unterrichts in der evangelischen Kirche Deutschlands zwischen 1530 und 1600*. Vol. 2, part 1. Guetersloh: C. Bertelsmann, 1911.

Ritschl, A., "Georg Witzels Abkehr vom Luthertum," *Zeitschrift für Kirchengeschichte*. Edited by T. Brieger. Vol. II, pp. 386-417. Gotha, 1887-1888.

Ruccius, W. M., *John Bugenhagen Pomeranus*. Philadelphia, Pa.: United Lutheran Publication House, 1925.

Schellbach, Martin, *Justus Jonas*. Essen: Lichtweg Verlag, 1941.

Schindel, J. J., "Justus Jonas," *Leaders of the Lutheran Reformation*. Edited by A. T. W. Steinhaeuser. Philadelphia, Pa.: General Council Publication Board, 1917.

Schwiebert, E. G., *Luther and His Times*. St. Louis, Mo.: Concordia Publishing House, 1950.

Seifert, F., "Die Durchführung der Reformation in Leipzig 1539-1545," *Beiträge zur Sächsischen Kirchengeschichte*. Edited by F. Dibelius and G. Lechler, pp. 125-168. Leipzig: Johann Ambrosius Barth, 1882.

Tschackert, P., "Justus Jonas Bericht aus dem Jahr 1538 über Martin Luthers Eintritt in das Kloster (1505)," *Theologische Studien und Kritiken*. Edited by J. Koestlin and E. Kautzsch. Jahrgang 1897, pp. 577-580. Gotha, 1897.

ENCYCLOPEDIAS

Erhard, H. A., "Justus Jonas der Ältere," *Allgemeine Encyklopädie der Wissenschaften und Künste*. Edited by J. S. Ersch and J. G. Gruber. Vol. 22, 2nd. section, pp. 393-408. Leipzig: F. A. Brockhaus, 1842.

Frank, G., "Justus Jonas," *Allgemeine Deutsche Biographie*. Vol. XIII, pp. 492-494. Leipzig: Duncker und Humblot, 1881.

Fritz, "Justus Jonas," *Kirchenlexikon der Encyklopädie der katholischen Theologie und ihrer Hilfswissenschaften*. Edited by J. Hergenroether and F. Kaulen. Vol. VI, 2nd. edition, pp. 1810-1812. Freiburg: Herder'sche Verlagshandlung, 1889.

Fuchs, G. F., "Justus Jonas," *Calwer Kirchenlexicon*. Edited by P. Zeller. Vol. I, pp. 858-859. Calw und Stuttgart, 1891.

"Justus Jonas," *Kirchliches Handlexicon*. Edited by C. Meusel, C. Haack and B. Lehmann, Vol. III, pp. 609-611. Leipzig: Justus Naumann, 1891.

Kawerau, G., "Justus Jonas," *The New Schaff-Herzog Encyclopedia of Religious Knowledge*. Edited by S. M. Jackson. Vol. VI, pp. 224-225. New York, London: Funk and Wagnalls Co., 1910.

Kawerau, G., "Justus Jonas," *Realencyklopädie für protestantische Theologie und Kirche.* Edited by Herzog and A. Hauck. Vol. IX, 3rd. edition, pp. 341-346. Leipzig: Hinrichs'sche Buchhandlung, 1901.

Koehler, W., "Justus Jonas," *Die Religion in Geschichte und Gegenwart.* Edited by H. Gunkel and L. Zscharnack. Vol. III, 2nd. edition, p. 370. Tuebingen: J. C. B. Mohr, 1929.

"Nordhausen," *Encyclopedia Britannica.* Vol. 7, 14th. edition, pp. 487-488. London, New York, 1929.

"Nordhausen," *The New International Encyclopaedia.* Vol. 17, 2nd. edition, p. 200. New York, 1916.

Schmidt, O., "Justus Jonas," *Realencyklopädie für protestantische Theologie und Kirche.* Edited by J. J. Herzog and D. G. L. Plitt. Vol. VII, 2nd. edition, pp. 87-91. Leipzig: Hinrichs'sche Buchhandlung, 1880.

Schneider, K. F. T., "Justus Jonas," *Encyklopädie für protestantische Theologie.* Vol. 7, 1st. edition, pp. 1-3. Stuttgart und Hamburg, 1857.

Schottenloher, K. L., "Justus Jonas," *Bibliographie zur Deutschen Geschichte im Zeitalter der Glaubensspaltung 1517-1585.* Vol. I, pp. 391-392. Leipzig: Karl W. Hiersemann, 1933.

Wolf, G., "Justus Jonas," *Quellenkunde der deutschen Reformationsgeschichte.* Vol. II, part II, pp. 73-75. Gotha: F. A. Perthes, 1922.

Index

201

Chrysostom, 56
Church orders, 78, 79, 85, 86, 88
Coburg, 24, 62, 81, 90, 103, 171, 174, 175, 177, 179
Coburg, Fortress, 61
Cochlaeus, Johann, 32, 66, 100-102, 105
Coelius, Michael, 77, 150, 151, 153
Colditz, 75
Colet, John, 182
Cologne, 15, 69
Colossians, Epistle to, 116
Companus, 96
"Concerning Faith, Concerning the Church, Concerning Human Traditions," 48
Concerning the Bondage of the Will, 37, 113, 186
"Concerning the Study of Theology," 51-53
Conferences with English delegation, 68
Consistories, 80, 81
Constance, 92
Cordatus, Conrad, 50
Cordus, Euricus, 23
Corinthians, Epistles to, 6, 23, 24, 94
Corpus Christi, 62
Corvinus, Antonius, 100, 164
Council of Trent, 145, 147, 149, 157, 159
Cranmer, Thomas, 116
Crato, Adam, 21, 27
Creitzen, Melchior von, 82, 83
Crépy, Peace of (1544), 156
Cromwell, Thomas, 68
Cruciger, Caspar, 46, 47, 50, 57, 65, 68, 69-70, 71-72, 76, 81, 82, 117, 134, 140, 183, 187, 189
Cuspinian, John, 30

D

"Declaration on Behalf of Martin Luther," 24-26
Demosthenes, 95, 114
Demuth, Nicholas, 122
Denmark, 78, 89, 115, 167
Dessau, 78, 87
Deventer, 12
Diatribe on Free Will, 38
Dietrich, Veit, 168, 187
Diocletian, 160
Doleatoris, 33
Dominicans, 137, 140
Dominican Cloisters, 169
Draconites, John, 3, 18, 23, 27, 34
Drechsel, Thomas, 43
Dresden, 83, 84

E

Eberbach, Henry, 3, 14, 27
Ecclesiastes, 114, 154
Eck, John, 1, 22-24, 26, 63, 66, 72, 105
Ecken, John von der, 30, 31
Eckhardt, 182
Einsiedel, Henry, 43, 47
Eisenach, 11, 33
Eisfeld, 177, 179
Eisleben, 46, 101, 141, 142, 148, 149, 150, 151, 152, 153, 159, 165
Enchiridion or Handbook for Every Christian, 110
England, 67, 68, 88
English delegation, 68
Ephesians, Epistle to, 163
Erasmus, Desiderius, 1, 2, 4, 5, 6, 12, 18-19, 21, 22, 23, 26, 27, 33, 34, 35, 36-39, 64, 113, 181, 182
Erfurt, 5, 8, 11, 13, 14, 15, 17, 18, 19, 21, 22, 23, 24, 26, 27, 28, 29, 33, 34, 36, 40, 41, 46, 47, 61, 95, 97, 113, 159, 164, 165, 171, 182, 188
Erfurt, University of, 1, 2, 3, 4, 10, 11, 12, 15, 16, 23, 96
Ernest, Duke of Saxony, 114
Eucharist, 57. See also Mass
Europe, 1, 67, 69, 183
Eutzsch, 143

F

Faber, John, 66, 92-95
Falk, Catherine, 43
Farneso, Alexander de, 70
Ferdinand, King of Austria, 160
Ferer, Nicholas, 13
Flacius, Matthias, 168, 170, 174
Forchheim, 67
Forchheim, George Helt of, 27, 87, 128
Fox, Edward, 68
France, 156, 182
Francis I, King of France, 60, 67
Franciscan Cloister, 2
Franciscans, 137
Franconia, 177
Frank, Sebastian, 70
Frankfurt, 2, 82
Frankfurt Armistice (1539), 69
Frederick, Abbot of Nuremberg, 67, 175, 176
Frederick the Wise, Elector of Saxony, 1, 2, 11, 17, 18, 23, 27, 28, 33, 37, 40, 41, 42, 44, 45, 92, 107

study of law, Humanist and professor at Erfurt, 12-14, 16-19, 21-22
student at Wittenberg, 15
early friendship with John Lange, 18, 19, 21-22
shift from jurisprudence to theology, 23
sides with Luther against Eck and papal Bull, 24-27
recommended to post in Wittenberg, 27, 28
with Luther at Worms, 28-32
"Acts and Exploits of Doctor Martin Luther," 32-33
return to Erfurt, 33-35
call to Wittenberg as provost of All Saints and professor of theology, 39-41
Carlstadt and radical reform at Wittenberg, 41-43
reform under Luther's leadership, 44-45
activities as lecturer, dean and rector at Wittenberg University, 46, 48-49, 50, 51-53
as mediator in church affairs in Wittenberg area, 47, 50, 50-51
drafts Church Order for Zerbst, 51
dispute with sacramentarians, 55-56
attends Marburg Colloquy, 57-59
participation in Wittenberg Concord, 59-60
at Torgau, 60-61
Diet of Augsburg and Augsburg Confession, 61-67
failure of alliances with France and England, 67-69
Schmalcald Convention and religious conferences, 69-72
church visitations in Saxony, 74-76
at Naumburg Church, 77-78
Church Order for Anhalt, 78-79
proposes consistories, 79-81
at Leipzig, 81-82
visitation in and Church Order for Meissen, 82-85
Church Order for Halle, 85-86
correspondence and friendship with rulers, 89-90
polemics against John Faber, 92-95
controversy with Witzel, 95-102
against Osiander on doctrine or justification, 103-106
Annotations on the Acts of the Apostles, 106-108
treatise on faith for Halle Christians, 108-110
hymns by Jonas, 110-113

translations by Jonas, 113-117
evangelical reform in Halle, 126-133, 134-135
report on Regensburg Conference, 134
reform opposed in Halle, 137, 138
superintendent at Halle, 139-141
Wolferinus at Eisleben, 141-142
sermons on Catechism, 142-143
surrender of Wittenberg provostship and stay in Halle 144-148
visits from Luther at Halle, 148-150
at Eisleben with Luther and Luther's death, 150-154
funeral sermon for Luther, 152-153
further progress in reform at Halle, 157-158
Schmalcald War, Jonas' exile, return and flight from Halle, 159-162
Call to Hildesheim, 163-165
return to Halle, 166-167
Augsburg and Leipzig Interims, 167-168
Melanchthon's concessions, 168-170
final departure from Halle, 170-172
superintendent at Coburg, 174-175
superintendent at Regensburg, 176-177
superintendent at Eisfeld, 177
illness and death at Eisfeld, 178, 179
estimate of Jonas, 181-192
Jonas, Justus, Jr., 89, 112, 115, 160
Joseph, 94
Jovius, Paul, 114
Justification by faith, 28, 50, 68, 83, 96, 102, 103-106, 168, 175, 182

K

Kindt, Nicholas, 179
Kitzscher, 15
Koch, Jodocus, 10. *See* Jonas, Justus
Koch, Jonas, 9
Koenigstein, 58
Krause, John, 124

L

Lange, John, 3, 18, 19, 21, 22, 24, 26, 27, 28, 38, 41, 46, 61, 72, 111, 164, 188
Lee, Edward, 19, 27
Leipzig, 1, 23, 24, 81, 82, 83, 84, 97, 101, 126
Leipzig Disputation, 21
Leipzig Interim, 168
Leipzig, University of, 87
Leisnig, 75
Leo X, Pope, 120
Letters of Obscure Men, 16